ADVANCED LEADER COACHING

Accelerating Personal, Interpersonal and Business Growth

CHRIS EDGER AND NOLLAIG HEFFERNAN

IMPRINT

First published in 2020 by Libri Publishing

Copyright © Libri Publishing

The right of Chris Edger and Nollaig Heffernan to be identified as the editors of this work has been asserted in accordance with the Copyright, Designs and Patents Act, 1988.

ISBN 978-1-911450-63-4

A CIP catalogue record for this book is available from The British Library

Design and cover by Carnegie Publishing

Images by Helen Taylor

Printed by Severn

Libri Publishing
Brunel House
Volunteer Way
Faringdon
Oxfordshire
SN7 7YR

Tel: +44 (0)845 873 3837

www.libripublishing.co.uk

ABOUT THE AUTHORS

Professor Chris Edger PhD, MBA, MSc (econ), FCIPD, FHEA

Chris is a university leadership academic and the owner of the Multi-Unit Leader Company, a consultancy specialising in Advanced Leader Coaching. Previously, in a commercial career spanning over twenty years, Chris held executive director positions leading Operations, Commercial, Sales and HR functions in UK and internationally owned blue-chip leisure organisations. At the turn of the century he was a member of an executive board that conducted two M&A transactions (for £2.3bn and $1.7bn respectively) and in 2010, as a GHRD, he and his team won the Personnel Today HR Impact Award. Since then, in his professorial and consultancy roles over the past decade, he has built a strong leadership, coaching and mentoring reputation, presiding over leadership programmes for hundreds of leaders from some of the UK's fastest-growing retail and leisure companies, many of whom have transitioned into executive director roles. A prolific shortlisted author on branded and franchised multi-site leadership and coaching (with books available in 943 university libraries worldwide as at May 2020) he is also the inventor of a number of leadership and coaching models and analytics, including the Inspirational Leadership Model, SHOP Leader Qualities Model, Big Six Tasks Model, BUILD-RAISE solutions-based coaching model and a number of leader analytics (ODQ9, AMQ9, BDM9 and FAM9). A graduate of the London School of Economics with a PhD from the Warwick Business School (analysing executive leadership behaviour during critical events), Chris also has a Level 7 Advanced Award in Coaching and Mentoring (with distinction).

Nollaig Heffernan PhD, CPsychol, AFBPsyS

Nollaig is an independent management consultant working with businesses from sole traders to multinationals specialising in Leadership and Management, Organisational Psychology, Workplace Performance and Stress Management. She is a recognised executive coach, leadership mentor, business consultant and specialist lecturer (primarily executive education) and has worked extensively world-wide. Also an award-winning conference speaker, she is frequently invited to contribute to panel discussions and to contribute articles to mainstream media. Her interests include the neuroscientific make-up of high-performing individuals, the cross-discipline transfer of effective coping strategies, resilient leadership and enhancing wellbeing in the workplace. After completing her MSc in Work and Organisational Psychology, Nollaig completed her PhD specialising in leadership and its psychological measurement. Her research led to the development of the commercially available leadership styles questionnaire ILM72. Nollaig is passionate about sport, and her practical and theoretical use of psychology in sport led to chartership (BPS) and registration (HCPC) as a sport and exercise psychologist. In this role, she has worked with a wide range of sports with athletes from beginner to elite, but as a successful rowing coach with wins at national and international level (Ireland and England), rowing has been her main sport of interest. Nollaig now incorporates sport psychology strategies when working with business clients to enhance performance, develop teams and manage talent. Nollaig is a member of the Centre for Neuroscience, UK and is on the International Editorial Advisory Board for the *International Journal of Stress Prevention and Wellbeing* and the *European Journal of Applied Positive Psychology*. She is also a contributing author to several business books including the Association for Coaching's *Psychometrics in Coaching* and *Leadership Coaching* (Kogan Page). As a believer in the value of continuous personal and professional development, Nollaig holds a green belt in Lean Six Sigma and a certificate in project management, and has more recently started to play the piano.

Chris would like to dedicate this book to all of the business leaders
he has coached over the last decade

Nollaig would like to dedicate this book to her father

TABLE OF CONTENTS

Introduction   **10**

1 Advancing Leader Personal Growth   **17**
1.1 Coaching Leaders to RAISE SELF-AWARENESS   18
1.2 Coaching Leaders to BUILD MENTAL TOUGHNESS   33
1.3 Coaching Leaders to INCREASE CAPACITY   47
1.4 Coaching Leaders to ADJUST STYLE   60
1.5 Coaching Leaders to TRANSITION ROLES/CAREERS   88

2 Advancing Leader Interpersonal Growth   **112**
2.1 Coaching Leaders to MOTIVATE EMPLOYEES   113
2.2 Coaching Leaders to IGNITE CUSTOMERS   124
2.3 Coaching Leaders to DEVELOP TEAMS   141
2.4 Coaching Leaders to ALIGN STAKEHOLDERS   153

3 Advancing Leader Business Growth   **165**
3.1 Coaching Leaders to CLARIFY STRATEGY   166
3.2 Coaching Leaders to GRIP OPERATIONS   177
3.3 Coaching Leaders to SPARK A CHANGE CULTURE   192
3.4 Coaching Leaders to DRIVE INNOVATION   209

4 Courageous Coaching   **226**
4.1 The Courageous Leader Coaching Concept   226
4.2 The Importance of Courageous Leader Coaching   228
4.3 Key Leader Coach Qualities   230
4.4 The BUILD-RAISE Coaching Process   232

Build	**R**apport	233
Uncover	**A**im	235
Identify	**I**nterference	236
Locate	**S**olutions	239
Determine	**E**xecution	242

4.5 Reframing and Magic Questions   244
4.6 Leader Coaching Case Study (Using Reframing and Magic Questions)   246

5 Further Insights and Final Words   **253**

Sources and Further Reading   **267**

LIST OF FIGURES

Figures 1 & 2 — Advanced Leader Coaching Model   11, 16

Figure 3 — Life Wheel   17

Figure 4 — A Model of Stress   34

Figure 5 — Four 'C's Mental Toughness Components   45

Figure 6 — MTQ 48 Normal Distribution Curve   45

Figure 7 — MTQ 48 Plus Components   46

Figure 8 — The CPD Cycle   59

Figure 9 — The Integrated Leadership Styles Model   61

Figure 10 — The ILM Leadership Style Scales   83

Figure 11 — ILM Normal Distribution Curve   84

Figure 12 — The Big Six Tasks and Six 'R's of Interference   93

Figure 13 — The Affirmations Model   108

Figure 14 — Interpersonal Skills Model   112

Figure 15 — Two Factor Motivation Model   117

Figure 16 — Reward and Recognition Model   120

Figure 17 — Value Proposition Model   131

Figure 18 — Service Culture Wheel   133

Figure 19 — Team Development Lifecycle Model   143

Figure 20 — Belbin Team Roles   152

Figure 21 — Enabling Networks Model   157

Figure 22 — Five Bases of Power Model   159

Figure 23 — Influencing Without Authority Model   161

Figure 24 — Strategic Growth Focus Model   165

Figure 25 — Strategic Process Model   169

Figure 26 — Strategic Pyramid Model 172

Figure 27 — De Bono's Six Thinking Hats 175

Figure 28 — Operational Excellence Model 180

Figure 29 — Internal Value Chain Model 181

Figure 30 — KPI Cascade Model 183

Figure 31 — Values Transfer Model 185

Figure 32 — The GAPPAR Model 187

Figures 33a, b & c — Ishikawa Diagram 189, 190

Figure 34 — Change Difficulty Pyramid 194

Figure 35 — Eight Phases of Change Model 195

Figure 36 — Force-Field Analysis of Change Model 196

Figure 37 — Square of Communication Model 199

Figure 38 — Culture Web 203

Figure 39 — Grief Cycle Model 205

Figure 40 — Change Curve Model 206

Figure 41 — D.A.B.D.A. Grief Stages 206

Figure 42 — Formal Innovation Process Model 216

Figure 43 — Knowledge Barriers/Solutions Model 217

Figure 44 — Upwards Impact and Influencing Model 219

Figure 45 — Creativity Grid 221

Figure 46 — The Egg Timer Model 222

Figure 47 — Courageous Leader Coaching Concept 227

Figure 48 — BUILD-RAISE Coaching Model 232

Figure 49 — Johari Window of the 'Self' 237

Figure 50 — Performance-Potential Model 260

ABBREVIATIONS

4Cs	Control, Challenge, Commitment, Confidence
6Rs	Relationships, Resistance, Resources, Recognition, Respect, Resolve
ALCM	Advanced Leader Coaching Model
ANT	Actor Network Theory
AQR	Active Quality Research
BUILD-*RAISE*	Build *Rapport*, Uncover *Aims*, Identify *Interference*, Locate *Solutions*, Determine *Execution*
CEO	Chief Executive Officer
CLC	Courageous Leader Coaching
COO	Chief Operating Officer
CPD	Continuous Professional Development
CSR	Corporate Social Responsibility
DABDA	Denial, Anger, Bargaining, Depression, Acceptance
EFQM	European Framework for Quality Management
ELQ	Effective Leader Questionnaire
EQ	Emotional Quotient (Intelligence)
fMRI	Functional Magnetic Resonance Imaging
GAPPAR	Gather, Analyse, Prioritise, Plan, Act, Review
HRM	Human Resource Management
ILM	Integrated Leader Measure
IQ	Intelligence Quotient
JV	Joint Venture
KPI	Key Performance Indicator
LQ	Learning Quotient (Intelligence)
LUT	Licensed User Training
MBTI	Myers–Briggs Type Indicator
MNC	Multi-National Corporation
MSc	Master of Science
MTQ48	Mental Toughness Questionnaire (48 Questions)
OEM	Operational Excellence Model
PDCA	Plan, Do, Control, Act
PESTLIED	Political, Economic, Societal, Technological, Legal, International, Environmental, Demographic (forces)
POV	Point of View
RRM	Reward and Recognition Model
SBU	Strategic Business Unit
SCAMPER	Substitute, Combine, Adjust, Modify, Put to other uses, Eliminate, Reverse

SHOP	Spiritual, Holistic, Optimistic, Proactive
SLT	Situational Leadership Theory
SMARTER	Specific, Measurable, Assignable, Relevant, Timely, Evaluated, Reviewed
SME	Small or Medium Enterprise
SMV	Service Management View
SPF	Service Personality Framework
SPM	Strategic Process Model
SWOT	Strengths, Weaknesses, Opportunities, Threats
TFMM	Two Factor Motivation Model
TGROW	Topic, Goal, Reality, Options, Will
TQM	Total Quality Management
TRIZ	Theory of Inventive Problem Solving
TTC	Targeted Transitional Coaching

INTRODUCTION

Inspirational business leaders can achieve the most improbable feats. They can create great businesses from scratch or salvage lost causes, *galvanising* those around them by their sheer force of personality, focus and drive. Leaders make a difference – not just at the apex of organisations, but at all levels. But today many organisations face a leadership deficit. Why? A couple of decades of hyper-digitalisation has reduced the need or opportunity for face-to-face interaction in the workplace. Also, a new generation of managers coming into the workplace – having developed their interactive skills digitally rather than socially – display seriously underpowered leadership capabilities. Finally, many businesses – in spite of what they say ('people are our greatest asset' etc.) – continue to propagate transactional, output-led behaviours due to their obsession with 'hitting the numbers', paying lip service to the consequences this might have upon employee health and wellbeing. Investing in leadership, to ameliorate some of these forces, has never been more important.

In order to arrest or reverse a decline in leadership capability in the workplace, many companies have designed development programmes aimed at increasing leader capability. Indeed, for the past decade, we have taught on a ground-breaking MSc leadership programme – which we both conceived and delivered to nearly 1,000 corporate managers – for this very purpose. We have also written or contributed to thirteen books that have focused upon capturing outstanding leadership and coaching in UK and international branded and franchised service contexts. But this, we felt, was not enough. There was something missing. In our experience, the most dramatic progress one can make with business leaders occurs not in the classroom, but on a one-to-one basis. Deep, experiential, challenging leader coaching, conducted by seasoned practitioners, that promotes serious critical reflection and significant attitudinal/behavioural change is more effective than 'chalk and talk'.

So, immersive one-to-one leadership coaching is important; but how is it done? Whilst there are thousands of books on leadership and coaching, few academic reference books – with the exception of Passmore's outstanding *Leadership Coaching* (2015) – tie the two domains together. Indeed, most books in this area are more slanted, for commercial reasons, towards notions of executive coaching, enabling their authors to pursue lucrative consultative careers coaching C-suite occupants! Coupled with this absence of instruction on Advanced Leader Coaching, there is no integrated, guiding framework that Leader Coaches can use *specifically* to raise the capabilities and impact of business leaders. This book is a response to this gap.

Written for all Leader Coaches (whether organisationally or consultancy based) this book provides a practical guide for Advanced Leader Coaching by:

– Outlining an integrated Advanced Leader Coaching Model (ALCM), which provides a holistic framework for Leader Coaches to accelerate business leader *personal, interpersonal and business growth*, and

– Detailing a proven coaching methodology, using our own Courageous Leader Coaching technique, supported by our BUILD-RAISE coaching model.

Replete with *models, questions, case studies and novel techniques* that are easy to digest and utilise, this book is designed to make the task of Leader Coaches easier and their growth impact upon coachees far greater. In short, this book on Advanced Leader Coaching will help Leader Coaches get results quickly.

One outstanding feature of the book requires further explanation, namely, our integrated Advanced Leader Coaching Model (ALCM). We designed this model because once a Leader Coach has understood both the fundamentals of leadership and coaching, they require a comprehensive route map showing how to go about one-to-one leadership coaching interventions.

Figure 1: Advanced Leader Coaching Model

The book will go into an explanation of each facet of the model (with the concepts, models, questions, tools and techniques that Leader Coaches require to accelerate growth) but it would be useful for the reader to understand its core principles and underlying internal logic. The model is:

- **Integrated** – the ALCM combines the three main factors of leader success: *personal, interpersonal and business growth*, which are underpinned by advanced *behavioural (EQ), cognitive (IQ)* and *technical (LQ)* intelligence (so-called emotional, intellectual and learning quotients)

- **Interdependent** – far from conceiving these three factors as being mutually exclusive, the ALCM shows them as mutually dependent; personal growth is thus linked to interpersonal growth, which in turn is linked to business growth

- **Harmonious** – relatedly, the model argues that business leaders will only reach a state of harmonious high performance if they THINK and FEEL positively (personal growth), enabling them to BEHAVE inspirationally (interpersonal growth), resulting in OUTPERFORMANCE (business growth)

- **In depth** – also, each factor is supplemented by sub-components each of which are vital to accelerate growth in the 2020s:
  - o Personal: self-awareness, mental toughness, capacity, style and transitioning
  - o Interpersonal: customers, teams, stakeholders and employees
  - o Business: strategy, operations, change and innovation

- **Experiential, promoting critical thinking** – finally, we provide Leader Coaches with a vast array of models, questions and exercises that they can use with their coachees to provide a richer experiential learning process, which raises their levels of critical reflection and evaluation; this is essential if they are going to make meaningful, sustainable progress.

We believe that this model enables the Leader Coach to take a more rounded approach to their coaching, providing a framework that, we would argue, has greater saliency than many others that exist in the generic coaching market. Having applied it ourselves, we know that it leads to faster and more satisfactory outcomes for leaders, their teams and organisations.

One question the reader might have in relation to our ALCM is why have we focused upon thirteen *specific* sub-components within our model? How were they chosen and what is their significance? The five subcomponents underpinning **personal growth** (*self-awareness*, *mental toughness*, *capacity*, *style* and *transitioning*) have been targeted because they represent – according to our practical experience and empirical analysis – the significant 'human' dimensions of leadership. Coaches need to start with 'person' (their attitudes and feelings) before they address 'interpersonal' and 'business' behaviours and actions. The eight subcomponents underpinning **interpersonal growth** (*employees*, *customers*, *teams* and *stakeholders*) and **business growth** (*strategy*, *operations*, *change* and *innovation*) have been selected because they manifestly drive superior performance within organisations. In fact, these essential ingredients of business leadership practice have been validated by a major global leadership study undertaken by Korn Ferry (2020). Having surveyed 1,427 major global corporations about which leadership competencies would be critical over the next decade, they were able to isolate some key behavioural factors (i.e. *self-awareness*, *motivational style* and *resilience*) and technical factors (i.e. *operational* project management, *customer* experiential design and digital *innovation*) as being the most significant requirements for the 2020s. There is major convergence between their findings and our model. To this extent our ALCM and its subcomponents will enable Leader Coaches to ensure their coachees 'futureproof' their leadership approach over the next decade.

One thing that readers might be surprised to find absent is a reference to a financial focus or results orientation. Why? We take it as a given that leaders undergoing intensive coaching have these underlying core motivations. Coaching them is impossible. Often financial information is bound by a high level of confidentiality, preventing coachees from disclosing sensitive information and restricting the coach's access into this facet of their coachee's area of responsibility. However, most business leaders are either predisposed to win and aspire to 'blow the lights out' or they are comfortable enough just to do the bare minimum. The coachees that Leader Coaches are tasked with firing up and instilling with greater *confidence* should already be imbued with the basic motivation to crush costs, optimise sales, maximise profit and – in order to 'crisis proof' their business – build capital reserves. Otherwise, why have they opted for a commercial life?

So we wish you well as you use this book to accelerate your coachees' leadership growth. Dipping in and out of it will, at the very least, refresh your knowledge and expertise in this critical area. Because in the end, all sustainable businesses can only thrive through strong, purposeful leadership. As a Leader Coach, you have a vital role in nurturing and strengthening this vital component of organisational performance! Read on.

ADVANCED LEADER COACHING

As stated, there are thousands of books that highlight and advocate exemplary leadership behaviours. There are few books that elucidate effective one-to-one leader-coaching techniques that are focused upon building business leader capability and impact. This book – and particularly its next three chapters – aims to fill this gap by outlining a structured form of advanced leader-coaching practice.

Over the past decade we have taught and coached hundreds of business leaders who have displayed congruous needs and issues. Very often, business leaders come to us with organisational or operational issues when, really, the roots of their problems lie within themselves. In turn, their *personal* issues, which make them think and feel negatively, impact their attitudes and behaviours, adversely affecting their *interpersonal* relationships with their peers, stakeholders and teams. The net result? Almost always *business* underperformance, which exacerbates their sense of negativity and poor wellbeing. But how can you help jolt business leaders out of this cycle?

How do you coach leaders? A critical starting point is to understand how business leaders *learn, change and grow*. Classic texts on learning give us the following clues as to how they think, and what their learning preferences and levels of intellectual behaviour are:

- *Structures of Thinking* – according to Dilts' Logical Levels Model (Young, 2004), corporate managers are 'bounded' by a *six level structure of thinking* which – in part or whole – explains how individuals are held back from thinking, changing and growing within organisations. The six levels are: their *environment, behaviour, capabilities, beliefs, identity* and *purpose*. Therefore, developmental interventions need to take a flexible, multi-dimensional approach to help managers **make sense** of internal and external factors so that they can, firstly, 'think and cope' and, secondly, 'grow'.
- *Learning Preferences* – but what learning preferences do managers have? Over the past fifty years, learning-preference *psychological theory* has progressed from a *behavioural* paradigm (a belief that

stimuli such as incentives motivate managers – Skinner, 1965), to a *cognitive* paradigm (learning is more effective when knowledge transfer promotes critical thinking – Piaget, 1970), onto a *constructivist* paradigm (learners fundamentally learn through the process of doing) to – the dominant view at present – the *experiential* paradigm, namely: learning is only properly embedded once the learner feels a connection through rich experiential processes (Kolb, 1984; Illeris, 2008). This experiential perspective endorses Dale (1969) who argued that learners 'retain knowledge' best through *discussion (50%), doing (74%)* and *teaching others (90%)*. This *experiential* paradigm accords with our own teaching and learning philosophy with regards to developing corporate managers. Quite simply, managers learn more when they *personally* interact with the subject matter at hand through **analysing, considering and applying concepts and models within their own world** and/or conducting rigorous case study diagnosis. They *do not* learn in inert 'chalk and talk' teaching and learning contexts.

- *Level of Intellectual Behaviour* – extending Bloom's famous learning taxonomy, Anderson and Krathwohl (2001) posit *six levels of intellectual behaviour* that are important in managerial learning: *remembering* (recalling information), *understanding* (explaining concepts), *applying* (using information in a new way), *analysing* (distinguish between different data), *evaluating* (justifying a stand or position) and *creating* (a new product or point of view). Most managers have been taught essential technical facts that are critical to their specific job roles through remembering, understanding and applying information. What they lack is the ability to **critically analyse, synthesise, evaluate and reflect** upon data and situations in order to move things forwards. Therefore any 'experiential' learning (see the point above) is at its most effective, promoting higher levels of critical thinking, when it forces learners to practically use **novel techniques and pictorial models** not only to consider '*what, when* and *where*' but also '*why* and *how*' they can 'grow' and improve their performance.

So, business leaders are more likely to *learn and grow* if they are encouraged to understand both *internal* (personal) and *external* contextual (organisational/environmental) factors and engage in *experiential learning* which raises their levels of *critical reflection*. As a result of these insights – and our own experience of coaching hundreds of corporate leaders – we designed the Advanced Leader Coaching Model (ALCM) which provides Leader Coaches with a robust framework (encapsulating 'internal and external' realities) that will assist high-performance coaching conversations.

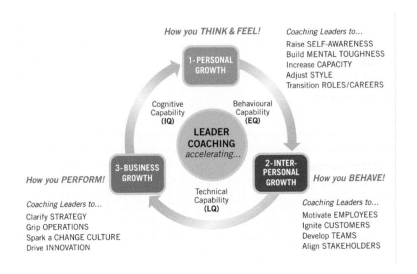

Figure 2: Advanced Leader Coaching Model

This model is different to all the other coaching frameworks on the market because it, first, deals *solely* with coaching improved leader capability, second, provides an integrated and holistic approach to leader coaching and, third, recognises the key *internal and external interdependencies* of personal, interpersonal and business effectiveness. The next three chapters will now unpack this model, examining each of the three main constructs and their various sub-components, furnishing Leader Coaches with the main concepts and **key concepts/models/techniques** that can be **experientially** deployed to accelerate business leader personal, interpersonal and business **critical thinking** and growth.

1 ADVANCING LEADER PERSONAL GROWTH

The start point in our Advanced Leader Coaching Model (ALCM) focuses upon accelerating *personal growth*. Why? The basis of all sustained business leader performance flows from how people feel and think. A generation of American 'pop' self-help psychologists has ploughed this furrow to great effect, selling the benefits of optimal positivity and success-based visualising as the primary requirements for inordinately successful lives and careers. Whilst we certainly wouldn't endorse or buy into the snake-oil practices of a lot of these pseudo-psychologists, we cannot deny that they are onto something, even if they shamelessly exploit the hopes and fears of thousands of clients/ disciples that are searching for meaning and purpose in their lives. Henry David Thoreau once wrote 'the mass of men lead lives of quiet desperation' and, certainly, the internal dark conversations that many people have are ripe for an industry of unqualified and ill-informed soothsayers to provide some temporary relief.

What the Leader Coach must do first is establish where their coachees' heads are with regards to their deepest hopes, anxieties and fears. A useful first step is to use the Life Wheel to establish a holistic view of a coachee's thoughts and feelings.

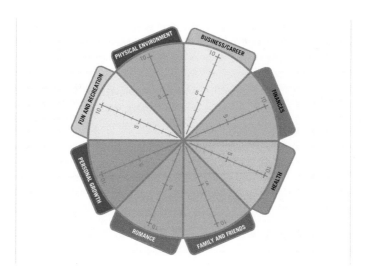

Figure 3: Life Wheel

We don't propose to give an in-depth explanation of how Leader Coaches should use this tool; suffice to say, they should use it to: first, establish which areas are the coachee's 'life priorities' and, second, calibrate (on a scale of one to ten) where their desired level of satisfaction is in relation to their actual level. A subsequent discussion on the whys and wherefores can then follow, from which the Leader Coach can build up a more complete picture of the coachee sitting before them.

But ultimately, the coachee – a business leader – has been coerced or volunteered for a coaching conversation that will improve their leadership impact and overall performance. The coachee might begin by stating that their overall goal is career progression and/or greater on-the-job success, but inevitably, all roads will lead back to a number of individually related issues that are impeding their progress. What are some typical impediments? A *deficit of behavioural (EQ) and cognitive (IQ) capability* manifested in a lack of *self-awareness*, febrile *mental toughness*, a perceived lack of time and *capacity*, an inappropriate leadership *style* and poor *transitional* readiness; all of which threaten to hamper personal growth. The Leader Coach can help accelerate the coachee's advancement by addressing one or all of these areas. How? The next five sections will explain.

1.1 COACHING LEADERS TO RAISE SELF-AWARENESS

Self-Awareness is the starting point for unlocking higher performance and personal growth amongst leaders. Why? You cannot lead yourself if you do not know yourself. But what is Self-Awareness? It is the deep understanding leaders have of their own behaviour, why they behave that way and the impact that behaviour has on both themselves and others. It includes but is not limited to an awareness of emotions, preferences, traits, values, energy levels, circadian rhythms (sleep–wake cycles), physical tolerances and stressors.

When Self-Awareness is fully embraced, it allows leaders to understand that they can be proactive agents in their own lives rather than passive victims as they take responsibility for their behaviour; or in other words, they realise they have influence over outcomes. This realisation about Self-Awareness is a powerful change catalyst because 'Self-awareness in itself is an invaluable tool for change, especially if the need to change is in line with the person's goals, sense of mission, or basic values – including their belief that self-improvement is good' (Goleman, 1996, p.67).

A lack of Self-Awareness leaves leaders feeling frustrated when things don't go their way and makes them more likely to lose focus, believing their input is irrelevant to the outcome. Renowned psychoanalyst Carl Jung captured this bystander complex succinctly: '[u]ntil you make the unconscious conscious, it will direct your life and you will call it fate'.

Leaders with strong Self-Awareness manage their emotions appropriately, take responsibility for their own actions and are approachable. Through understanding, valuing and respecting themselves, they demonstrably value and respect others; that is to say, they are empathetic. Self-aware leaders manage their shortcomings by working on their weaknesses directly or engaging others to use their skills in that area. They proactively seek and assimilate feedback on how to be better. They learn from their mistakes and see failure as a learning opportunity rather than a sign of weakness that needs to be punished. Most importantly, self-aware leaders have a robust feedback loop and always ask what it was about their leadership that might have caused the problem. Such honesty and integrity instils pride, loyalty and a work ethic in their workforce.

An extreme lack of Self-Awareness in the leadership role results in toxic management where the manager is blind to his/her own destructive behaviour and the impact it has on the workplace. Toxic management manifests as a blame culture, resource-draining hidden agendas, cliques, bullying, high staff turnover, absenteeism, high levels of stress-related illness, underperformance and, at its worst, where communication channels have become closely monitored, groupthink (mob-like behaviour) and dictatorship take hold.

Acquiring Self-Awareness can be an uncomfortable process. The discomfort arises from the need for assumptions to be challenged, life experiences to be probed and mindsets to be shifted. Furthermore, developing Self-Awareness runs a high risk of leaders confronting their own issues, some of which might be more accurately termed demons. The Leader Coach must be sensitive to the difficult nature of this process and warn the coachee of the discomfort of confronting truths about themselves, reassuring the coachee that while it may be easier to deny responsibility, it contravenes all notions of effective leadership. Effective leaders will suffer the discomfort for the greater good of the role.[1]

MAIN SELF-AWARENESS COMPONENTS

Goleman's (1996) seminal work on Emotional Intelligence includes Self-Awareness as part of his Emotional Competence Framework, under the 'Personal Competence' section. While there are other Self-Awareness frameworks (e.g. Neisser, 1997), Goleman's work on Emotional Intelligence is prolifically referenced and will be used here. According to Goleman, Self-Awareness is 'knowing one's internal states, preferences, resources, and intuitions' (1996, p.26) and consists of three factors: *Emotional Awareness*, *Accurate Self-Assessment* and *Self-Confidence*.

Emotional Awareness

Effective leadership requires an individual to have 'swan-like' qualities, being gracefully poised above water (outward appearances) even when paddling furiously below the water's surface (inner turmoil). Leaders who achieve this are described as calm, steady and reassuring by those around them. The swan analogy is used to demonstrate the importance of leaders managing emotions in order to instil confidence in their followers. As role models, how leaders react sets the tone for the business. If the leader panics the followers will too, perceiving it as the correct situational response. Leaders require a large degree of Emotional Awareness to understand their emotions and the impact of these on others.

---

1   Leader Coaches should expressly state during the coaching 'contracting stage' what they will and will not engage with. The reflective nature of coaching to raise Self-Awareness may cause the coachee to bring up experiences, thoughts and feelings that the coach is not equipped to deal with (for example, personal history of a sensitive nature or extreme emotional states). Should this occur, the coach should graciously terminate the line of discussion/questioning and sensitively explain that what the coachee is expressing is beyond the Leader Coach's remit (which is strictly work-related). To cover all angles however a Leader Coach should be aware of the organisation's procedures in relation to the psychological care of its employees and highlight the options available.

Individuals who lack Emotional Awareness are unaware that they are allowing their emotions to control their lives and make for extremely difficult people to work with. A lack of Emotional Awareness may be perceived as inconsistent moods (being 'moody'), inappropriate emotional responses (e.g. going into a rage over something small, defaulting to a defensive response, showing no feelings in an extreme event, etc.) or indecision. None of these responses are acceptable in a leadership position.

A simple understanding of the psychological working of the brain is a useful starting point for gaining Emotional Awareness. Over the last three decades, our understanding of the human brain has dramatically increased thanks to functional scanning (fMRI scanning). The fMRI scanning equipment produces images of blood flow in the brain when working on specific tasks. Further contributions have come from the substantial cumulative findings of psychologists such as Daniel Kahneman and Amos Tversky. Kahneman received a Nobel Memorial Prize in Economics Sciences in 2002 for his evidenced explanation that human decision making is largely intuitive and emotional rather than rational, demonstrating the futility of using rational economic models to make market predictions.

Kahneman (2012) explains that this intuitive decision-making mechanism is due to the primitive wiring of the human brain, specifically the limbic region, which instantly assesses a situation, thought, plan, person and so forth, giving feedback in the form of an emotional response that has a physical interpretation or a feeling, often described as a gut reaction. Goleman claims that this judgement response happens within the first 30 seconds of exposure to whatever needs to be assessed – in other words, in considerably less time than an in-depth rational analysis can be carried out. Psychology describes this as a System 1 response.

A System 2 response is a slower, more rational process and comes from the more recently developed and more advanced area of the brain, the frontal region, also known as the executive control centre/system. In his book *The Chimp Paradox* and the associated self-management programme, Peters (2012) describes these concepts more tangibly by describing System 1 as our 'Chimp' and System 2 as our 'Human'.

Of importance to the leader from this understanding of the human brain is that System 1 (or the Chimp) can 'hijack' (as Peters puts it) our thoughts and behaviour if we allow it to. This hijacking has happened when we respond emotionally rather than rationally, to our detriment. In an extreme 'hijacking', an individual's emotions take longer-term control and overwhelm him/her; or at least that's how he or she interprets it. This passive interpretation of having no control over one's emotions leads to the individual feeling self-pity, feeling victimised and out of control.

However, Kahneman and Peters' work also demonstrates that, while System 1 can hijack us, being self-aware and in tune with our thoughts process can help regain and maintain Emotional Control. 'One of the secrets of success and happiness is to learn to live with your Chimp and not get bitten or attacked by it. To do this, you need to understand how your Chimp behaves, and why it thinks and acts in the way that it does. You also need to understand your Human and not muddle up your Human with your Chimp.' (Peters, 2012, p.12) Knowing how both your Chimp (System 1) and Human (System 2) impact you is the essence of Emotional Awareness. Indeed, Goleman's study of over 200 highly effective entrepreneurs and business leaders found that part of these individuals' success was the ability to use both System 1 and System 2 thinking effectively in the decision-making process and in life in general.

Developing Emotional Awareness allows leaders to progress to controlling their emotions. Emotional Control is discussed in further sections (1.2 'Build Mental Toughness' and 1.3 'Increase Capacity').

The Leader Coach can help coachees gain greater Emotional Awareness by facilitating them to:

o   Reflect on how they typically react to bad/stressful news

  •   *Think of an incredibly stressful situation: how did you react (e.g. sarcasm, aggression, humour, withdrawal, etc.)? Are you aware of warning signs that you are about to react like this (e.g. sneering, clenching fists, talkativeness, distancing yourself, etc.)?*

o   Listen to their inner dialogue (what they say to themselves) when they are under pressure

  •   *Reflecting on pressured situations, what's going through your head? For example, are your thoughts supportive/compassionate or are they self-deprecating/destructive? Do you find this inner dialogue reassuring or does it escalate your stress levels? What might be a more constructive conversation to have with yourself? How could you prompt this more positive inner dialogue?*

o   Assimilate feedback from others to improve their roles as leaders.

- *Who do you receive feedback from (see 'Accurate Self-Assessment' below)? How to you delve further into feedback you don't agree with? How do you manage feedback you believe to be insincere?*

- *How do you mentally prepare for receiving feedback? How do you implement feedback suggestions? How do you assess the impact of the feedback you've incorporated?*

Simple approaches[2] such as keeping a reflective journal[3] in which the coachees regularly score their mood, encouraging coachees to learn the skills of Mindfulness (the ability to be in the present and interpret current feelings) or meditation, and encouraging coachees to regularly seek feedback on their workplace behaviour from team members are all useful ways the Leader Coach can improve a leader's Emotional Awareness and overall Self-Awareness.

Accurate Self-Assessment

Accurate Self-Assessment is about 'knowing one's inner resources, abilities and limits' (Goleman, 1996, p.61). It is incumbent upon leaders to constantly self-review and develop to be effective in their role. Learning new skills, looking for and assimilating feedback and pre-emptively receiving training for upcoming role requirements are hallmarks of highly effective leadership. Alternatively, the leader aligns with others who have the skills he/she is deficient in so that the management team has all angles covered.

- ### Knowing

   Acquisition of new skills firstly requires the knowledge that a skill is absent. According to the Conscious Competence Learning Model developed by Noel Burch for Gordon Training International in the 1970s, an individual starts off unaware of a gap, being in a state of Unconscious Incompetence. When the individual realises what he/she doesn't know something, the individual has moved to the

---

2   Where a coachee is unreceptive to a proven technique, an alternative method that generates an equivalent outcome should be sought.

3   For leaders who are uncomfortable keeping a reflective journal or writing, creating a simple spreadsheet with dates across the top and a top-down list of reflective items to be scored can be a very useful way to acquire the same information but in a more acceptable (in this case numerical) format. This is particularly welcomed by more data-driven individuals who readily see patterns in numbers but cringe at the thought of writing about themselves.

Conscious Incompetence stage. Although there are two more stages in the model, Conscious Competence (effortful knowing, i.e. knowing that takes conscious effort) and Unconscious Competence (effortless knowing, i.e. doing without thinking), it is this second stage of Conscious Incompetence that is of relevance to the Accurate Self-Assessment component of Self-Awareness. Through failure on a task, feedback from colleagues/peers/managers/friends, training needs analysis (assessment of the gap between existing and required skills) and so forth, the leader can gain an understanding of development requirements (i.e. the leader becomes conscious of his/her incompetence).

- ### *The Challenge of Feedback*

  Relying on feedback to gain awareness of deficits is more challenging the more removed and powerful a leader becomes. Feedback is susceptible to the corruption of positional or legitimate power (French and Raven, 1959), with subordinates becoming reluctant to express their opinion of the leader as they fear the consequences. This happens even with the most approachable of leaders as others wish to impress them or protect their positions. It takes a considerable amount of Self-Confidence to speak without fearing the consequence and lacks political astuteness (Goleman, 1996) not to appreciate there is some degree of risk in doing so. Even the most egalitarian of organisations will have rules on what is allowable (see 3.3 'Spark a Change Culture') and, despite working for the greater good, the whistle-blower is always punished (Kellerman, 2008). Where the leadership role has degenerated into toxic management, the lack of feedback can create an illusion for the manager of being flawless in the role; and when feedback *is* given, it may be ignored or rejected, often with negative consequences for its provider. Eventually, the lack of forthcoming feedback gives the manager a belief in their own invulnerability and the role of dictator is established.

  It is often easier, therefore, for an outsider or a less directly involved party to provide feedback to the leader. This is often the remit of the human resources department in large organisations but even then, as company employees, there is a political imbalance. Enter the Leader Coach. As a bystander to the daily running of the business and thus being without agenda, the Leader Coach will be perceived as less personal and less threatening, and consequently more honest. Through the facilitative process of coaching, the Leader Coach has the further benefit of 'holding up a mirror' to the coachee rather than directly challenging certain behaviours. The Leader Coach is also the best option for small and medium businesses where scale makes feedback even more politically charged.

- **Abilities**

An Accurate Self-Assessment of abilities with a willingness to account for shortcomings in skillsets is the hallmark of an effective leader. When individuals demonstrably overvalue their abilities, there is a risk that they are doing so with the intention of being self-serving, although typically it is because of a genuine inability to recognise that they are not as competent as they believe themselves to be. The former is extremely toxic as it is driven by ulterior motives while the latter is more frustrating than damaging for those left to negate the deleterious impact of this weak management. Unfortunately, in many companies it is the most bombastic employee who is promoted or gets the choicest projects. This is because in busy workplaces people confuse self-promotion (*talking a good game*) with capability (*results*). An individual's Self-Awareness regarding their abilities is further discussed as a component of Mental Toughness (see 1.2 'Build Mental Toughness').

- **Inner Resources**

When a business is growing, a limited number of people take on multiple roles each. This personal investment is critical to the establishment of a viable enterprise, but it is incredibly draining on inner resources and unsustainable. Ambitious individuals who have pushed themselves hard to climb the organisational ranks have also heavily invested their inner resources. Learning to place such a high value on self-reliance makes it difficult to relinquish control and delegate when the role expands or the business scales, especially if the leader is also the founder and owner of the company. For this reason, it is a common downfall of capable and established leaders to overestimate the amount of or undervalue the importance of their personal resources when it comes to their role; they have learned to exploit them. What's more, these leaders have been rewarded with positive results (i.e. wealth creation, promotion) for pushing themselves to the limit, which makes this a very difficult habit to break.

Where leaders fail to assess their personal capacity accurately, they are demonstrating a poor management choice by not looking after the critical asset in their circle of influence: themselves (see 1.3 'Increase Capacity'). This may look like continuously taking on stressful workloads, insufficient sleep, poor protection of down-time, unrealistic expectations, breakdown of personal relationships, ignoring heath issues and so forth. Levitin's (2014) writings on the organised mind and Walker's (2017) longitudinal research on the value of sleep clearly demonstrate the need for managing our personal resources to be effective.

When leaders do look after their inner resources, it has often come about from a health-related scare or disruption to a personal relationship; an extreme event was required to stimulate change. This is learning the hard way. Learning to delegate (relinquish a degree of control) is one of the most valuable skills a leader can acquire to protect their inner resources. The Leader Coach can challenge coachees to express their concerns about delegating, to formulate an acceptable schedule of delegation and support coachees as they strive to 'rewire' their thinking that working close to burn-out, despite yielding results, is not as productive as working smarter.

The Leader Coach can help coachees to strengthen the accuracy of their self-assessments by facilitating coachees to:

o   Challenge the difference between self-perceived ability and results

- *When you describe yourself as X (e.g. the best/the worst), can you give me examples to support that statement? How do the results support that statement? Where is the evidence that you are amazing/rubbish? What is the difference between where you are and where you need to be?*

o   Consider who they receive feedback from and if those sources are biased (e.g. only positives)

- *Who do you seek feedback from? What are your criteria for selecting feedback sources? Have you a diverse source of feedback or do you pick those you know are more likely to tell you what you want to hear? What are the limitations of receiving only positive or sycophantic feedback? Is it possible you only seek feedback from sources that are happy to talk you down or enjoy a personal assassination? Have you thought about the motives behind giving you consistently negative feedback? How do you subsequently treat those who you feel have been negative or offensive, even if accurate?*

o   Protect their limited inner resources.

- *What does your typical working day look like? Are those working hours sustainable? Rate your effectiveness across the day. How much of each day would you rate yourself as working optimally?*

- *Do you work after hours? Do you work at weekends? Are you able to switch off? How would you feel if you hadn't access to your phone and email? When you are away from the workplace are others constantly trying to contact you?*

- *How many hours do you sleep? How would you rate the quality of your sleep? What proportion of your day is spent relaxing/investing in yourself? Do you believe this is sufficient downtime to perform optimally?*

The following simple approaches are useful ways a Leader Coach can improve a leader's Accurate Self-Assessment and overall Self-Awareness: using a JOHARI Window (see Figure 49) to demonstrate the need to seek feedback from others to improve self; a SWOT analysis of the coachee's performance in their current role and/or their potential for a new role; and encouraging coachees to invest in their own wellbeing (see 1.3 'Increase Capacity').

Self-Confidence

Considered the twentieth century's greatest corporate leader, the first chapter in Jack Welch's autobiography (2001) is titled 'Building Self-Confidence'. In it he describes how his upbringing gave him the Self-Confidence to overcome having a stutter, the ability to succeed in several sports despite his poor physicality and a firm belief that he could be successful in whatever he put his mind to. Welch expresses anecdotally what Goleman (1996) describes as 'a strong sense of one's self-worth and capabilities' and terms 'Self-Confidence'.

Self-Confidence, or at least perceived Self-Confidence, in a leader is critical. Self-confident individuals do not seek external validation and are therefore willing to make unpopular decisions. This is crucial in a leadership role where, at any time, the leader may be disliked by one, some or all the stakeholders impacted by a decision. In addition, as a focal point in times of uncertainty, followers turn to the leader to be reassured and do not wish to be met by self-doubt, fear or hesitation.

Individuals who lack Self-Confidence in the workplace will misrepresent themselves to others. It is assumed that misrepresentations of self are self-affirming whereas, often, people are more self-deprecating and talk themselves down rather than talk themselves up. Individuals who talk themselves down may talk themselves out of applying for deserved promotions, out of projects they could even take the lead on or from experiences or training that they merit. Such individuals often regret their lack of progression in the company while simultaneously resenting those less capable of getting ahead. These individuals lack the Self-Awareness to see that it is their lack of Self-Confidence and crippling Imposter Syndrome (for a definition of this, see 1.5 'Transition Roles/ Careers') that is holding them back. Highly effective leaders often recognise and value such team members and push them towards what they perceive them to be capable of. Leaders may also engage the Leader Coach to help these individuals to develop their Self-Confidence to the point of realising their potential.

Self-Confidence should not be confused with the self-proclaiming or bombastic persona described above (see 'Accurate Self-Assessment'). That is not to say that leaders with Self-Confidence are bashful when it comes to expressing their capability to do the job; that would be disingenuous. They are however more likely to praise the combined team effort and point to objective results to demonstrate their point than brashly engage in a first-person promotional speech.

The Leader Coach can help coachees to explore their Self-Confidence by encouraging coachees to:

- o   Remind themselves of what they have achieved to date
    - *Tell me how you arrived in this position. What obstacles have you overcome to get here? What hoops did you have to jump through to get this job? Tell me about a time that you achieved more than you believed possible and felt proud of your achievements. Describe a time you received positive feedback from a person whose opinion you genuinely admired. When we go through all of your achievements, does it surprise you to see how many there are?*
- o   Visualise positive outcomes for scenarios they lack confidence in
    - *Talk me through the ideal scenario for this situation. If Y happened instead of X, what would you need to do now to achieve the same positive outcome you described in the ideal scenario? Let's change some more variables and work out how you can still achieve the same positive outcome.*
- o   Develop their Mental Toughness.
    - See 1.2 'Build Mental Toughness' for developmental questions.

Simple approaches such as using appreciative inquiry, encouraging an interest in Positive Psychology and completing a SWOT analysis to focus on strengths and opportunities are all useful ways the Leader Coach can improve a leader's Self-Confidence and overall Self-Awareness.

ACCELERATING SELF-AWARENESS WITH COACHEES

As discussed, self-aware individuals are knowledgeable about their strengths and weaknesses, and will know what to request when working with a Leader Coach. For coachees who are not self-aware, the thought of walking into a coaching session blind (not knowing what to expect) can feel uncomfortable and overwhelming. Some pre-session preparation such as the completion of well-chosen *psychometric tests* provides a starting point to commence an exploratory discussion by providing the Leader Coach with valuable information about the client's preferences, abilities and potential. This optimises the coaching session by allowing the Leader Coach to engage immediately with a less intimidated coachee thanks to the test results providing something to focus on, helping rapport to be established sooner. The introduction of psychometric tests to an established coaching relationship can add an extra dimension to the Self-Awareness exploratory process.

Types of Psychometric Test

There are two main types of psychometric test. The first are *aptitude* or *ability* tests. They measure an individual's cognitive ability (mental capacity) and include tests of verbal ability, numerical reasoning, spatial ability, mechanical reasoning, abstract reasoning, data checking and work sampling. These tests are usually timed, forcing the individual to perform under pressure. Aptitude tests are most typically used as part of the entrance exam process in the educational system and in the early stages of a large organisation's selection process, where it has been established that a certain amount of ability is required to perform in the role. Candidates who do not reach the accepted cut-off score do not proceed to the next stage of the process. While candidates might describe 'being coached' to perform on entrance exams or for job applications, this is the more directive type of coaching associated with sport, where explicit instruction is given.

The Leader Coach primarily engages in facilitative coaching (sometimes the Leader Coach may take a consultative approach if they have relevant expertise), making the second type of psychometric tests, *personality* tests, more relevant. Personality tests, including inventories and questionnaires, seek to assess personality traits (for example, the 'Big Five' personality traits of openness, conscientiousness, extraversion, agreeableness and neuroticism), states (such as Mental Toughness – see 1.2), types (for example, MBTI profiles) and other aspects such as leadership style (see 1.4) and so forth.

Choosing Psychometric Tests

Central to the effectiveness of using a psychometric tool in the coaching process is using the correct questionnaire (called a 'measure'). In psychometrics, correctness covers two concepts. Firstly, the questionnaire selected should be the correct type of questionnaire. There is no point in choosing a numerical reasoning test to consider a coachee's degree of conscientiousness or work ethic. It is important that the coachee sees the merit or relevance (*face validity*) of using the measure to engage fully in the process rather than feel frustrated that they are completing an irrelevant exercise.

Secondly, it should be *valid* or *statistically robust* in measuring what it is required to measure. *'Validity'* is the protected term used to describe the questionnaire's competency to measure what it claims to measure consistently across time (*reliability*). If questionnaires cannot be proved valid (having not been put through, or having failed, the validation process) there is no way to guarantee that they measure what they claim to measure or ever will. A questionnaire's validity is clearly stated in its user handbook and should preferably be a value greater than 0.4.

There is a myriad of questionnaires available, particularly online, many of which come under the heading of popular psychology, but until recently comparatively few have been valid as described above. Those that are valid are typically also *licensed*, meaning they require a qualification to administer the test in addition to the cost of each test. Licensed User Training has been very costly when looking at the more established commercialised products but with the proliferation of computers, the advent of social media, vastly improved statistics programmes and the mushrooming of the consultancy and coaching industry in recent years, the number of fairly priced, valid questionnaires now available makes the addition of psychometrics to the Leader Coach's toolkit more tenable.

Licensed User Training (LUT) covers what the questionnaire has been designed to measure, how to administer the questionnaire effectively, how to interpret the results correctly and suggested feedback for the coachee. LUT also provides an excellent CPD opportunity for the Leader Coach and many of the training courses supply certificates of completion with refresher workshops available to keep licensees abreast of the latest research.

Due to psychometric tests reflecting an individual's psychological make-up in some form, the results have profound ethical implications. To control for this, many personality test companies insist on a prior qualification in psychometric test use such as the British Psychological Society's Test User: Occupational Ability and Personality (levels A and B) to ensure a degree of competence from an ethical perspective. Such qualifications add depth to the Leader Coach's offering as well as giving confidence to the Leader Coach to deliver feedback professionally.

What are the Benefits of Psychometric Tests?

- *Raising Self-Awareness is a large and daunting task; psychometric tests provide a useful starting point*
- *Coachees can find discussing test report results feels less intrusive (e.g. like discussing a third party: 'The results show a preference for… Is this an accurate reflection?')*
- *The reports of psychometric tests targeted at the coaching industry provide development examples, aiding the Leader Coach in his/her recommendations*
- *The return on investment of a soft skill such as coaching can be difficult to measure; some psychometric test publishers generate a Distance Travelled Report that shows the change in results from pre-intervention test completion to post-intervention test completion, demonstrating the value of the Leader Coach*
- *Being licensed to use psychometric tests enhances the Leader Coach's toolkit and credibility particularly with larger organisations.*

Some Cautionary Notes on the Use of Psychometric Tests

- *Psychometric tests are aids to the coaching process, not substitutes for it*
- *Psychometric tests should only be used as part of an encompassing process to raise Self-Awareness (the results of self-report tests may be*

inaccurate due to inaccurate self-perception, so it is necessary to use other sources)

- *Psychometric tests are indicators not absolutes; the coachee should be made aware of this point and reminded of it frequently*

- *The use of psychometric tests comes with an ethical obligation for the Leader Coach to acknowledge his/her limitations when handling psychological matters.*

QUICK RECAP: LEADER COACHING TO RAISE SELF-AWARENESS

- **Why?** – 'You cannot lead yourself if you don't know yourself' – getting leaders to understand their personal strengths and weaknesses is a critical starting point for developmental purposes

- **Main Concepts?** – Emotional Awareness, Accurate Self-Assessment, feedback, abilities, inner resources, Self-Confidence, Imposter Syndrome

- **How?** Coaching conversations using:
  - JOHARI Window
  - Feedback
  - Appreciative Inquiry
  - Visualisation
  - Reflection
  - SWOT Analysis

- **Accelerate Self-Awareness Coaching? Use:**
  - **Psychometrics**
    - Self-reports such as *personality inventories* or *styles questionnaires*
    - Discuss, facilitate and support interventions
    - 'Distance travelled' reports demonstrate return on investment

1.2 COACHING LEADERS TO BUILD MENTAL TOUGHNESS

'Mental Toughness' is the term used in everyday parlance to capture an individual's ability to withstand excess pressure or stress and to recover quickly from setbacks. The need for leaders to be mentally tough is undeniable. While exponentially rewarding when going well, leadership is an exposed and pressured position with leaders vying constantly to keep business and stakeholder objectives aligned. Furthermore, leadership involves tough decision making, resulting in leaders finding themselves unpopular, disliked and at times feeling very isolated.

Given the contribution of effective leadership, investing in and developing a leader's Mental Toughness is an obvious and worthy strategy. Sadly, it tends to be an afterthought at best, usually after a stress-related illness, and, at worst, written off as psychobabble. Perhaps this is because resilience and stress as psychological concepts are perceived as soft or less tangible in the 'hard facts' world of business.

It may help businesses to realise that much of the stress and resilience research has been conducted in settings with zero-sum outcomes, more specifically in the military and in sport, where nothing is soft or intangible and the outcomes are clear cut. In comparison to these arenas, it is business that begins to look soft!

The body of research on stress, including studies from the military and sport, demonstrates that there are several factors or individual differences that influence how an individual will react to stressful situations. Some of these, such as age (including experience) and gender (gender-specific stresses), cannot be changed; other factors such as the individual's personality, physical fitness and social support network can be readily managed, while *an individual's Mental Toughness can be directly influenced by the coaching process.*

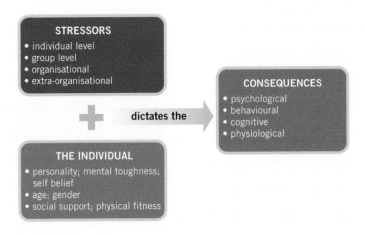

Figure 4: A Model of Stress

It is through an understanding of stress and Mental Toughness, specifically, that the Leader Coach can actively intervene to build an individual's resilience. Indeed, Mental Toughness has become an area of progressively insightful research over the last 20 years, contributing greatly to the disciplines of executive and leadership coaching.

UNDERSTANDING STRESS

Stress, as an emotional state, can at times feel like a catch-all phrase rendering us none the clearer as to what to do about it, with media hyperbole adding to the confusion.

A stress response at its most basic is an evolutionary early-warning system that something is not right in an individual's immediate environment, prompting action to be taken to eliminate or avoid that stressor. Central to this process is the body's release of hormones. When this survival mechanism evolved the threats were mainly physical, creating an opportunity for these hormones to dissipate and not reach toxic levels.

Although modern society's stresses are very different to those of our ancestors, our systems still respond in the same way; but instead of the often physical nature of our ancestors' stresses (animal attacks, tribal warfare, etc.), the stressors in our contemporary environment are more mentally challenging. These include poor workplace relations, deadlines, reporting, presenting, financial debt, commuting, long working hours, societal pressure and family expectations. For many people, these are aspects of their daily lives and there is little opportunity to unwind and assuage the detrimental impact of the stress hormones being released.

While stress in the form of pressure pushes us to greater performances by helping us focus, for example in the case of competitions, deadlines and exams, unmanaged excess stress has the potential to make people become psychologically (e.g. depression), behaviourally (e.g. withdrawn), cognitively (e.g. poor decision making) and physiologically (e.g. high blood pressure) compromised. Managing stress is therefore critical for any workplace, with special focus required on leaders who are invariably exposed to high degrees of stress.

Stress is further complicated by being both individual and transient. By 'individual' it is meant that everyone has their own interpretation of what is stressful, so there is no panacea for the modern-day stress epidemic. Being transient means that our interpretation of stress is dependent on the situation and our frame of mind at the time of experiencing the stress. It is due to this individual and transient nature of stress that the coaching process, as an intervention, has proven highly successful in the development of a leader's stress coping ability (resilience). This mostly happens when the Leader Coach focuses on developing the leader's Mental Toughness.[4]

MAIN MENTAL TOUGHNESS CONCEPTS

Although the term 'Mental Toughness' can be traced back to Loehr's (1982) work in Sport Psychology, it wasn't until Clough, Earle and Sewell's (2002) research that the term 'Mental Toughness' became operationalised (i.e. clearly defined and measurable to scientific standards). While other researchers have delved into this topic, the research and subsequent questionnaire developed

---

4   Due to the psychological consequences of excess stress, it is imperative that the Leader Coach understands his/her own limitations and seeks professional help for individuals gone past the threshold of the Leader Coach's capabilities.

by Clough, Earle and Sewell (the MTQ48) will be discussed here due to its widespread use in the coaching domain.

Clough, Earle and Sewell were interested in how the term 'Mental Toughness' was used by the sports media to describe the composure of an athlete under immense pressure in the 'arena' and considered whether such a skill could be measured. Drawing on research from the area of Health Psychology, Clough, Earle and Sewell built on Kobasa's (1979) work on hardiness or the hardy personality and Dyer and McGuinness's (1996) work on resilience. While Kobasa had concluded that the hardy personality consisted of the three aspects *Control*, *Challenge* and *Commitment*, Clough, Earle and Sewell went further and proposed the fourth component *Confidence* while defining Mental Toughness as the quality which helps determine how people deal with Challenge, stressors and pressure irrespective of prevailing circumstance.

It should also be noted that Mental Toughness, as measured by the MTQ48, is scored on a continuum rather than a bi-polar scale. As a result, the opposite is not being mentally weak but rather having low levels of Mental Toughness. While having average to high levels of Mental Toughness is considered crucial for leaders, Mental Toughness needs to be accompanied by a high level of Self-Awareness (see 1.1 'Raise Self-Awareness'). As will be seen below, individual's with high levels of Mental Toughness can be perceived as arrogant (*Confidence*), disruptive (*Challenge*), disengaged (*Control*) and embedded (*Commitment*). The mentally tough leader needs to be aware of his/her impact on others.

The Leader Coach can help the coachee with high Mental Toughness to not only maintain that level but to also manage the impression they make on the people around them and can help coachees with low levels of Mental Toughness to develop their Mental Toughness.

THE FOUR 'C'S OF MENTAL TOUGHNESS MODEL

The following is a fuller description of the Four 'C's of Mental Toughness Model (Clough, Earle and Sewell, 2002) with suggestions for the Leader Coach on how develop to each with the coachee.

- **CONTROL:** Due to the transient nature of stress there may be times in an individual's life when they feel out of Control due to uncontrollable circumstances such as a bereavement, family health issues, redundancy or market turbulence. For leadership effectiveness, however, the leader must at least be perceived by others to be in Control. Where the leader achieves this, others will feel reassured and more willing to follow.

Perceived Control arises from the leader's ability to manage their emotions in order to lead by example – to show composure in times of panic, to show sympathy in times of sadness, to show resolve in times of doubt, to show consistency in times of instability and so forth (see 1.1 'Raise Self-Awareness': 'Emotional Awareness'). It should be noted that individuals with high levels of Emotional Control may be viewed as cold or unapproachable, which is detrimental to productive leader–follower relationships. Leaders require Self-Awareness to manage how they are perceived. Daniel Goleman refers to this skill as Self-Regulation in his work on Emotional Intelligence.

While giving the *impression* (influencings others' perceptions) of being in Control is a powerful leadership skill, *being* in Control is considerably more important for leadership role sustainability. Contrary to popular belief, individuals with high levels of Control are not the 'control freaks' commonly referred to. In fact, they are quite the reverse, being willing to relinquish Control of tasks they need not be concerned with to others. They are leaders who engage their team members to take responsibility for their roles and give them the support and resources to do so. They do not micro-manage but rather pursue their own or the businesses objectives proactively and with agency. Bandura (1986) described an individual's belief that he/she has impact on or Control of a situation as Self-Efficacy. Leaders require ongoing high levels of Self-Efficacy to cope with the responsibility and pressure of being a leader.

Where an individual has low levels of Control there is often a narrowing of focus coinciding with a wish to have complete Control of the process, giving rise to micro-managing and receiving the title 'control freak'. This belief in a lack of Control can quickly descend to a *feeling* of being out of Control both emotionally (inappropriate emotional reactions) and practically (view themselves as victims). When leaders display these behaviours they quickly become viewed as weak or toxic managers losing the respect of and influence over their followers.

The Leader Coach can help coachees gain an understanding of the Control concept by facilitating coachees to reflect on:

o The factors that make them feel in/out of Control in a situation

- *When do you feel most in/out Control? What is the foundation of those feelings? What increases/decreases those feelings? On reflection, is there a pattern to these feelings that suggests specific triggers? How might you record your sense of Control so that you could potentially capture a pattern?*

o How they behave when they are in/out of Control

- *How do you behave? How might others perceive you? What is the impact on others? What is the risk of others misinterpreting your behaviour? How can you manage fallout afterwards?*

o What steps can be taken to maintain/regain a proactive feeling of Control.

- *Take the time to understand what factors cause you to feel out of Control. What would help you to recognise and pay attention to warning signs that you might be losing Control? Who could you co-opt to help in this identification of warning signs (see 1.3 'Increase Capacity': 'Social Support Network')? What simple steps can be taken to mitigate the impact of these signs?*

Simple approaches such as role-playing a coachee saying 'no' to their manager to encourage a more realistic workload, task prioritisation and stakeholder management (see 2.4 'Align Stakeholders') are all useful ways the Leader Coach can help improve a leader's Control and overall Mental Toughness.

- **CHALLENGE:** The Challenge element of Mental Toughness looks at how intimidated an individual is in the face of an obstacle, resistance or change. Given the demands of the leadership role, leaders need to cope well with or have a high tolerance for Challenge without creating challenges for their own sake.

Where an individual's tolerance for Challenge is low, change may be viewed as threatening and new experiences may be actively avoided. In the workplace this may look like non-participation in group decision making, inaction in the face of looming deadlines, stress-related absenteeism if the workload or routine is changed, and so on.

Individuals who cope well with Challenge have a more positive outlook and tend to view obstacles as challenges and development opportunities rather than blockages or threats. Such individuals will feel comfortable being stretched and relish learning about themselves when pushed beyond their comfort zone (Dweck, 2017). However, an unchecked high Challenge capacity may mean an individual gets bored quickly, becoming disruptive. Those with extreme tolerances for Challenge are often termed 'adrenalin junkies' and may even become workplace saboteurs to fuel their need for disruption.

It is essential to be aware that the constant demands of higher-level decision making, problem solving and managing others can deplete a leader's coping reserves very quickly, posing an ongoing threat to the leader's resilience. Yet again, Self-Awareness plays a pivotal role here as there is a fine line between peak performance and mistakenly taking on too much because of the false sense of stability experienced during peak performance (see 1.1 'Raise Self-Awareness': 'Inner Resources').

The Leader Coach can help coachees gain an understanding of the Challenge concept by facilitating coachees to:

o Differentiate between perceived and actual blockages

- *What are the factors that caused you to conclude there is a blockage? Have you tested these assumptions? Are there any immediate actions you could take to improve your readiness to tackle this? Who could you work with/ influence to overcome this blockage? What resources will you need?*

o Reframe problems as opportunities

- *What could be gained from taking this on? What are the learning opportunities? If you overcome this, how would you feel? What options have you? What's the worst that could happen?*

o Reflect on whether it is vanity or a rational decision to take on the next Challenge.

- *What is the driver behind pursuing this Challenge? Is this a choice (want) or something you must (need) do? What have you to gain? What have you to lose? What will be the impact on your other commitments? How might others perceive your pursuit of this?*

> • *Will this matter one week/one year/five years from now? If you commit, what would the repercussions of withdrawing be? If you pursue it and fail, are you willing to live with the consequences?*

Simple approaches such as SMARTER goal setting, the psychology root-cause analysis tool of Critical Incidents Technique (learning from challenging events to create a strategy for avoiding, pre-empting or dealing with similar events in future) and visualisation of important upcoming events are all useful ways the Leader Coach can improve a leader's Challenge tolerance and overall Mental Toughness.

• **COMMITMENT:** Commitment is the ability to see a task or endeavour through to its completion.

Individuals with low levels of Commitment get bored or distracted easily, struggle to complete tasks and easily give up. Interestingly, individuals with low levels of Commitment in one aspect of their life, such as the workplace, may not show such apathy in other areas of their life. In the workplace, however, it is necessary for leaders to have high levels of Commitment to remain appropriately and consistently focussed even if they are less interested or invested in the task.

Individuals with high levels of Commitment may be described as having a good work ethic with an ability to override the fickle nature of motivation. By delaying instant gratification, the leader does not get side-tracked by the myriad distractions that exist in even the most modest of operations (Mischel, 2014). However, individuals who have excessively high levels of Commitment may struggle with the fractured nature of the leadership role, where the leader may not see many processes through to their completion as they will be dealt with elsewhere. This is often a source of tension for promoted individuals who still want to be involved in their previous role's projects.

There is also the risk that the highly committed individual is committing to the wrong thing. High levels of Commitment should be regulated through a consistent and frequent process review to avoid the futility of committing to something that should not have been committed to at all. Highly committed individuals are at risk of perpetrating the Sunken Cost Fallacy (Dobelli, 2013) where they perceive it is easier to continue throwing good resources after bad rather than admit to the mistake. Should this happen, the individual is no longer a leader but rather a toxic manager.

The Leader Coach can help coachees gain an understanding of the Commitment concept by facilitating them to:

- o Gain greater understanding of the bigger picture to help them buy-in/commit

    - *Can you clearly articulate the company's vision? How does this task/team fit into that vision? How does it contribute? Who could clarify this for you? What is the risk for the business if this is not completed or not completed to the specified standards?*

- o Frequently review what they have committed to

    - *How often do you review the process? How often should you review the process? How often do you assess alignment of your Commitment with company/your personal strategy?*

    - *How certain are you of each task's/project's KPIs before commencing? Who can you discuss your concerns with if progression isn't as forecast? Have you an exit strategy for withdrawing from poorly conceived/redundant projects?*

- o Challenge their personal agenda when over committing/ holding off on committing.

    - *What's so enticing about it that you feel the need to invest your personal resources so heavily? What's in it for your team and the organisation? Who gains from this degree of input? List the other things you could be doing if you weren't doing this. Will the outcome truly justify the effort and the opportunity cost?*

    - *What's stopping you? Why are you afraid to commit to this? What are your reservations? What is the single biggest impediment to you committing? Can it be overcome? Is it worth overcoming? How might others perceive your lack of enthusiasm? What signals might you be sending to others? If you believe this is not worth committing to, how can you convince your manager(s) of this? What factors do you require to embark on this project confidently? How might you gain extra support and resources?*

Simple approaches such as asking coachees to list what they'd require to commit more to a project (a lack of appropriate resources can be an obstacle to committing) then presenting the list to their management, improving role clarity so the coachee is fully aware of the level of Commitment required of them and, for over-committed coachees, creating perspective by asking simple questions such as 'will this matter in a day/week/year?' are all useful ways the Leader Coach can help improve a leader's Commitment and overall Mental Toughness.

- **CONFIDENCE:** As humans, we are hardwired to follow the person we have most Confidence in to ensure our survival. Leaders must be perceived as confident for Confidence to be placed in them. Nowhere is this more obvious than in a business's strategy creation (see 3.1 'Clarify Strategy'), presentation and execution. A strategy without Confidence in the person executing it is short-lived.

Confidence as an integral aspect of Mental Toughness contributes to resilience by giving an individual self-belief in times of doubt or adversity. An inability to manage doubt or prolonged feelings of insecurity in a role can quickly undermine how efficacious a person feels, leading to anxiety, underperformance and inaction. High levels of Confidence on the other hand allow the individual to remain positive in the face of instability, criticism and challenges to their authority (see 1.3 'Increase Capacity': 'Positive Mindset'). These are commonplace threats to the leader's role, particularly in the early stages of a new leadership position or business uncertainty.

It should be noted, however, that high levels of Confidence in the absence of Self-Awareness can be damaging where an individual has misplaced Confidence in their own abilities. Such individuals believe they are the best and only person to do a task, making them unreceptive to critical feedback, incapable of self-development and limited in their career progression opportunities.

Having Confidence to allow others to do a task the leader could do better through experience/expertise is one of the most challenging steps on the journey from management to leadership. Leaders who lack the Confidence to invest in others and who believe the system can't operate successfully without them create a centralised dependence that quickly becomes viewed as toxic management rather than leadership. Counterintuitively, being critical to the system reduces the sustainability or resilience of the individual in that leadership role (see 1.3 'Increase Capacity': 'Striving for Obsoletion').

High levels of Confidence must be tempered with a strong degree of Self-Awareness and a willingness to hear the opinions of others. Where a leader has strong interpersonal skills, the opinion of others will be easier to accept and more readily sought. If the individual has low Confidence in their interpersonal skills, the opinions of others may be interpreted as criticism rather than constructive feedback and interpersonal interactions actively avoided.

The Leader Coach provides a credible sounding board for leaders to continuously assess their Confidence in the role; to intervene and enhance it when it has been weakened and to Challenge it when it has become self-embedded or arrogant. The Leader Coach can help coachees gain an understanding of the concept of Confidence by facilitating coachees to reflect on:

o   The situations in which they feel most confident and influential

- *When do you feel most confident? List the factors that contribute to this Confidence. Are these 1) contrived situations that you engineer to help you feel confident, 2) situations you gravitate towards because you know they'll fulfil your Confidence needs, or 3) happenstance that you turn to your advantage? How could you have more option 3 in your life i.e. the ability to feel confident regardless of circumstance?*

o   The factors that cause them to lose Confidence or lack Confidence

- *What single factor undermines your Confidence most (consider the most uncomfortable situation you could find yourself in)? Are you aware of more subtle factors that chip away your Confidence? Are there situations you actively avoid because you know they may threaten your Self-Confidence? What have/what could you learn about yourself from these uncomfortable experiences?*

o   What can be learned from the situations in which they feel confident to enhance their Confidence elsewhere.

- *How might you replicate the factors that make you feel most confident in situations where you lose or lack Confidence? How might you prepare in advance of entering a situation where you lose or lack Confidence to minimise the degree to which you lose further Confidence? What/ who might help you to feel more certain of yourself?*

Simple approaches such as writing an affirmation statement (see 1.5 'Transition Roles/Careers': 'The Affirmations Model') to be carried by the coachee (as a reminder of achievements to date and why he/ she deserves his/her position), an assertiveness training recommendation and positive thinking are all useful ways the Leader Coach can improve a leader's Confidence and overall Mental Toughness.

ACCELERATING MENTAL TOUGHNESS WITH COACHEES

As described in the previous section, Self-Awareness is the precursor to any change in behavioural capability and using a psychometric test is a useful place to start. Although already explained in detail (see 1.1 'Raise Self-Awareness') it is important to reiterate the importance of using a statistically valid questionnaire and being appropriately licensed to administer it. As feedback from psychometrics is personal to the coachee, the results need to be interpreted correctly and discussed with sensitivity and care, something which is emphasised on psychometric licensed user training. It is also worth remembering that psychometrics with subjective ratings are not absolute and should therefore not be used in isolation. The Leader Coach should use psychometrics as aids to the coaching process, not as substitutes.

Clough, Earle and Sewell's (2002) interest in the measurement of Mental Toughness resulted in the development of the 48 question (item) Mental Toughness Questionnaire, the MTQ48 (licensed by AQR International Ltd). Ongoing validation of the questionnaire has yielded a statistically robust, valid questionnaire which generates four report types (Candidate, Assessor, Development and Coaching Report) instantly on completion. These reports offer an overall Mental Toughness score and a score for each of the Four 'C's with Control and Confidence being further subdivided into two scales.

COMPONENT	SUBSCALE
	Emotional Control
CONTROL	*Life Control*
CHALLENGE	
COMMITMENT	
	Confidence in abilities
CONFIDENCE	*Interpersonal Confidence*

MTQ48

Figure 5: Four 'C's Mental Toughness Components

Each scale of the questionnaire produces a score on a scale of 1 to 10. This rating system is representative of the Normal Distribution Curve where 16% of all respondents will score below average, 16% will score above average and 68% will score in the average range.

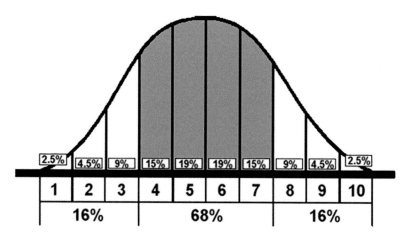

Figure 6: MTQ 48 Normal Distribution Curve

As part of the coaching process, the Leader Coach can explore (using the Coaching Report) what the score means by looking at other sources of feedback about the coachee and questioning the coachee about her opinion of why she received the score she did. Actions can then be agreed to (see the Four 'C's Model above). As the Four 'C's are robust individual constructs, although the overall Mental Toughness score might be average to high, the coachee may have scored particularly low in one area. This is where a questionnaire such as the MTQ48 can really add value to the coaching process by helping the Leader Coach home in on what really needs to be addressed. After enough time for Mental Toughness strategies to be implemented, the coachee can retake the questionnaire and a Distance Travelled Report can be generated for comparison purposes to see if the interventions have been effective. Of course, extreme events between the first and second completion of the questionnaire will show no-to-little forward movement, yet again demonstrating the importance of not overly relying on psychometrics.

Recently, the MTQ48 PLUS has been released onto the market (licensed by AQR International Ltd) subdividing the remaining Challenge and Commitment components into two scales, each through the addition of a further 20 items (questions) to the measure.

	COMPONENT	SUBSCALE
MTQ48 PLUS	CONTROL	*Emotional Control*
		Life Control
	CHALLENGE	*Risk Orientation*
		Learning Orientation
	COMMITMENT	*Achievement Orientation*
		Goal Orientation
	CONFIDENCE	*Confidence in Abilities*
		Interpersonal Confidence

Figure 7: MTQ 48 Plus Components

QUICK RECAP: LEADER COACHING TO BUILD MENTAL TOUGHNESS

- o **Why?** – Build resilience in the leadership role
- o **Main Concepts?** – Stress management, individual differences, Self-Awareness, situational factors, the Four 'C's (Control, Challenge, Commitment and Confidence)

- o **How?** Coaching conversations using:
  - Role Play
  - Task Prioritisation
  - Stakeholder Management
  - Goal Setting
  - Critical Incidents Technique
  - Visualisation
  - Reflection
  - Positive Affirmations
- o **Accelerate Mental Toughness Coaching? Use:**
  - **MTQ48 questionnaire (licensed to AQR International Ltd)**
    - Valid, statistically robust questionnaire
    - Measures Control (Life and Emotional), Challenge, Commitment and Confidence (in abilities and interpersonal)
    - Computer-generated reports provide coaching and development suggestions; ideal for advanced Mental Toughness conversations

1.3 COACHING LEADERS TO INCREASE CAPACITY

Capacity in any job role is about reaching potential or maximising the ability to be effective in that role. Effective leaders actively seek to maximise their contribution to the role and do so by increasing their personal Capacity to be instrumental.

Leaders who readily work on their Capacity stand out due to their ongoing willingness to stretch their existing capabilities and knowledge base. Effective leaders develop Capacity incrementally, however, understanding that overly challenging themselves may distract them from the business's strategy, as well as potentially depleting their inner resources.

The individual who misunderstands the importance of developing Capacity may aggressively pursue new skills to the detriment of the business's core objective, threatening their existing Capacity by overly pressuring their inner resources. The other possibility is the individual who, through self-embeddedness and inaccurate Self-Confidence, invests nothing in developing Capacity, believing himself/herself to already be operating maximally with further self-development unnecessary. This, of course, is toxic management and bears no resemblance to effective leadership.

MAIN CAPACITY CONCEPTS

Increasing Capacity commences with Self-Awareness including an Accurate Self-Assessment, an understanding of personal emotional responses and current levels of Mental Toughness (all previously discussed). With awareness established, the biggest challenge comes from selecting amongst the endless number of self-development tools available on the market courtesy of a multi-billion-dollar personal productivity industry.

Of the myriad ways to create Capacity, five will be discussed here for consideration by the Leader Coach with the sixth promoted as an accelerator to developing Capacity in the coachee. All six suggestions are sizeable independent topics and merit further in-depth exploration.

- **Self-Investment**

  Leadership literature expounds on the skillsets to be effective in a leadership role such as strategic, financial, process and people management capabilities but the actual person in the role as an asset is sadly missing. Even in the Transformational Leadership literature which is heroic or leader-centric, the fact that leaders are people is rarely alluded to.

  Covey's (1989) *The 7 Habits of Highly Effective People* provides a refreshing slant, through Habit Seven 'Sharpen the Saw', of the individual being of importance and thankfully leaders themselves and coaches have taken a greater interest in this concept than leadership research has. Viewing individuals, leaders, as the best instruments in their own environment, it makes sense to invest in them as an asset, not just a means to an end. 'We are the instruments of our own performance, and to be effective we need to recognise the importance of taking time to regularly sharpen the saw' (ibid., p.289).

  Covey lists the four areas of the individual to be sharpened as *physical*, *spiritual*, *mental* and *social/emotional*. *Physical* is about looking after the physical self through diet, exercise and general bodily functions such as sleep. Indeed, the conclusions from the considerable body of sleep research undertaken by Professor Matthew Walker and his colleagues are an indictment of our abuse of sleep, giving sobering examples of the deleterious impact Western society's modern average of 6.25 hours of sleep per night is having.

Looking after the *spiritual* area is about the individual returning to core values because 'he who has a "why" to live for can bear almost any "how"' (Friedrich Nietzsche). The Golden Circle proposed by Sinek (2011) clearly outlines the importance of *why*. Individuals who struggle to understand their purpose find it difficult to commit, get distracted easily and are overwhelmed by blockages.

The third area, *mental*, is discussed more fully below (see 'Accelerating Capacity with Coachees') while the *social/emotional* area is discussed in this section under 'Support Network'. While Covey assures us that working on any one of the four areas has a positive impact on the other three, this assurance comes with the caveat that overly focusing on one or some to the neglect of the others is counterproductive.

The Leader Coach can help coachees with Self-Investment by facilitating coachees to:

o Consider the importance of valuing themselves as the primary agents in their lives

  • *How much scheduled time off do you take each year? Do you allot any personal time yearly/monthly/weekly/ daily? What form does it take? If not, why not? What might be the advantages/disadvantages of doing so?*

  • *Do you apportion any of the training budget to your own development? Do you influence upwards to be invested in? How many CPD hours do you do a year? Have you significant relationships that will help with your development e.g. mentor, sponsor, etc.?*

o Schedule weekly physical exercise

  • *What are your exercise options? Which would be the easiest for you to commit to? Why? How can you incorporate these into your daily routine?*

  • *What inhibits you from exercising? How might you overcome these inhibitions?*

o Frequently review core values and filter their understanding of events through these values.

- *What do you stand for? What are you passionate about? What gets you out of bed every day? What gives you the greatest sense of contribution? If you could pursue any ambition, what would it be? Why?*

- *How aligned is your current role with what you believe? What could you do to create greater alignment with your values? How could you bring greater meaning to what you do? How often do you review where you are now and where you want to be? When you do review your status against your beliefs and values? What amendments do you make if they are misaligned?*

Simple approaches such as keeping a sleep and exercise diary, working on a personal Golden Circle and challenging assumptions about effectiveness are all useful ways the Leader Coach can facilitate a leader with Self-Investment and increase Capacity.

- **Effective Time Management**

Time Management as a learnable discipline is a multi-billion-dollar industry; after all, business is governed by the axiom 'time is money'. Time as a fixed asset, however, is used to varying degrees of effectiveness, and common to all stressed businesses and individuals is the perception of having insufficient time to get through their current impasse. Effective Time Management is therefore a key skill in increasing a leader's Capacity by minimising the consuming influence of stress.

Parkinson's Law (1958) informs us that 'work expands so as to fill the time available for its completion'. The implication of this maxim is that limiting the time available per task creates efficiency through focused application. This is a discounted rather than a cumulative view of task completion and is the established practice of highly effective leaders who understand that deadlines create focus. Working backwards (discounting) from the desired outcome is the premise of the second of Covey's seven habits of highly effective people, 'Begin with the End in Mind'.

Where leaders demonstrate Effective Time Management, they seek to work smarter not harder. They do not boast about how long they worked but rather pride themselves on what they got done, measuring productivity by jobs completed rather than how many items are on their task list. Most notable, however, is how effective leaders protect their personal time. This includes daily finishing times, work breaks and holidays. In addition, they schedule daily Self-Investment time, incorporate weekly downtime and take guilt-free annual leave. Consequently, the leader is consistently focused, productive, achievement-oriented and able to volunteer resentment-free extra time in extenuating circumstances. Through strict workload prioritisation and protection of their personal time, effective leaders are using Effective Time Management to increase their leadership Capacity daily.

Furthermore, as employing staff is fundamentally the purchasing of additional time, highly effective leaders aggressively account for that bought time by scheduling work, creating deadlines and assigning tasks to the most appropriate employees. This creates job clarity, intrinsic to which is the effective use of a person's time, thereby eliminating the leading cause of job dissatisfaction: lack of role clarity. This leadership of the human asset in turn increases the business's Capacity for sustainable growth.

Poor time management may manifest as time being wasted or as time being exploited. Where time is wasted, the individual is easily distracted, invests in the wrong thing (perfectionism falls under this) or lacks focus in application. When toxic management allows this behaviour to exist in the workplace, deadlines are missed, productivity is minimal, services/products are substandard, customer complaints are high and conscientious staff members leave. The option of increasing Capacity is unlikely to occur to anyone in this environment.

Where time is exploited, the individual is spread too thinly, is incessantly consumed with work-related issues and has limited to no downtime. When toxic management allows this behaviour to exist in the workplace, working long hours rather than productivity is rewarded, non-conformity to the long hours 'work ethic' is frowned upon, working smarter/more efficiently is seen as lazy and employees are persistently contacted outside of their working hours. Already at breaking point, Capacity is declining and will continue to do so until intervention or the system implodes.

The Leader Coach can help coachees with Effective Time Management by facilitating coachees to:

  o Map what they want to achieve

      • *What do you want to accomplish? What is your expected timeframe to do that? How does it breakdown? What resources do you need? What will prevent you? Are you being too ambitious/not ambitious enough? How often will you review your progress? How will you know you've succeeded?*

- *What are your main distractions? How do you recognise you are being distracted? What are the 'tells' that you are going to be distracted? How might those distractions impact your ability to achieve your goals? How can you avoid being drawn into those distractions?*

o Understand what activities they wish to protect

- *How do you prioritise activities? Which activity would you assign the greatest value to? Is this something you believe you need to achieve or would like to achieve? How do/would you protect that activity so that it is accomplished and not pushed aside (protected)? What factors might force you to reschedule your ambitions (e.g. family circumstances, promotion, etc.)?*

- *What activities are negotiable and could be dropped/ rescheduled in preference for your protected activities? What activities are you hanging onto (e.g. habit, nostalgia) that no longer serve their purpose? How might you use that liberated time to ensure completion of your protected activities?*

o Differentiate between 'busy-ness' (being busy) and productivity.

- *How do you 'triage' your task list? How frequently do you get through your daily task list? How often would you say you feel overwhelmed monthly/weekly/daily/ hourly? On a scale of 1 to 10, where would you rate yourself on productivity? Now on efficiency? How readily do you take on extra tasks not assigned to your role? How good are you at saying 'no'? Reflect on whether people give you extra work because you are the easy option but not always the right option.*

Simple approaches such as a discounted planner approach, task lists and Eisenhower Quadrants/Task Prioritisation model (see Covey, 1989) are all useful ways the Leader Coach can facilitate a leader's Effective Time Management and increase Capacity.

- **Striving for Obsoletion**

The ultimate goal in leadership is to become obsolete! However, a belief of contribution is critical to self-esteem, making the notion of obsoletion as a strength profoundly difficult for people to accept. Striving for Obsoletion is not about lacking usefulness but rather not being so critical to the system that any threat to the individual is a threat to the whole. Indispensable individuals are toxic to the system because their removal threatens its viability.

Contingency planning is the bedrock of creating obsoletion. It acknowledges that no-one is infallible and that no individual, no matter how talented, is greater than the whole. Leaders who understand this frequently break the system theoretically to develop a response to the challenge: 'in the event that X is removed, what should be done?' This promotes a distribution of risk mindset when it comes to the human asset countering the threat of centralisation (see 1.4 'Adjust Style': 'De-Centralised versus Centralised'). Through delegation, training, talent management and active succession planning, effective leaders clear the path for a successful handover.

A successful handover is not just about succession but also operating effectively in the current role. It affords leaders the option of pursuing business opportunities, attending training and taking uninterrupted, protected time off without the system grinding to a halt. This healthy self-removal (obsoletion) can only happen through de-centralising the system (i.e. clear communication channels, accountability, empowerment and support) so the leader is no longer critical to every operation, only to those the leader ought to be responsible for. In so doing, the leader's energy is not consumed with lower-level decision making, petty employee grievances, customer complaints and so forth, which shackle the leader to be constantly present. By minimising burnout, Striving for Obsoletion paradoxically *increases* longevity in the leadership role, leaving mental space for the leader to increase Capacity.

Individuals who believe they must be central to all business items and processes cap the growth of the business, as it can only grow as far as their ability to control it allows. Such individuals are so caught up always working *in* the business (management) that they neglect to work *on* the business (leadership), leaving no room for Self-Investment. Sadly, they begin to resent the business they feel chained to and are consumed with worry about the business when not there. This obsessive need to be involved in every action may stem from being the founder and owner (see 1.1 'Raise Self-Awareness': 'Inner Resources'), from feeling out of control due to irresponsible promotion (see 1.2 'Build Mental Toughness') or it may be the vanity of indispensability arising from the corruption of power. Whatever the driver, it is toxic management and an unsustainable model.

The Leader Coach can help coachees Strive for Obsoletion by facilitating coachees to:

o Review the requirements of their role frequently

- *How frequently do you compare your workload with your role's responsibilities? How involved do you like to be? How comfortable are you with others being in control in your absence? What is the threat to you of others filling your shoes? What are the benefits?*

o Differentiate between what they like doing and what they should be doing

- *Doing work you like doing instead of what you should be doing is a major time waster for many people. Would you say you are easily distracted by the jobs you like doing over what you should be doing? Do you default to doing the smaller, easier tasks first to feel a sense of accomplishment?*

- *Which of your responsibilities contribute most to the business? How readily do you invest your efforts in these? If you struggle to focus on these, what could help you to stay on track? How could you make necessary but less attractive work more enjoyable and easier to commit to?*

o Challenge their assumptions about their own and others' capabilities.

- *Where would you rank your ability in relation to that of your team members and/or colleagues? If others are better than you, how does that make you feel? If you perceive them as weaker, how does that make you feel?*

- *Why don't you involve others? What is the worst that will happen if you do/don't? How might others view this lack of involvement? Could you be creating learned helplessness by doing other people's jobs for them or spoon-feeding people? Could you be creating your own chaos by making yourself pivotal or indispensable? How might this be counterproductive for your own progression? Why are you the best or only person to perform a task?*

Simple approaches such as appropriate delegation, Effective Time Management and comprehensive role clarity are all useful ways the Leader Coach can facilitate a leader's Striving for Obsoletion and increase Capacity.

- **Positive Mindset**

Mindset is the dominant paradigm by which an individual interprets the world and events; thus a Positive Mindset results in the dominant interpretation being positive. 'We can choose to change our mental diet and feed our minds on different information that can positively influence how we see ourselves and the world.' (McGee, 2015) Having a Positive Mindset shares many similarities with *self-aware* Mental Toughness (see 1.2 'Build Mental Toughness') and so will only be briefly discussed here, but this does not diminish the role it plays in increasing a leader's Capacity.

Individuals with a Positive Mindset believe they can achieve, apply themselves, are proactive in developing themselves, have a strong sense of agency in their own lives, do not fear failure and always believe they can do better. They value the input and nurture the talents of those around them. Increasing Capacity is fundamental to a Positive Mindset or a growth mindset (Dweck, 2017).

Individuals who have a negative mindset may be viewed as pessimistic, cynical and depressing to be around due to suppressing the moods of others. They believe the application of effort is futile and are overwhelmed by obstacles. Such individuals rarely apply for achievement-focused roles such as leadership; their mindset inhibits such wilful ambition.

Where individuals have a fixed mindset in a powerful leadership role (Dweck, 2017) they are often self-congratulatory, unwilling to accept feedback from others, have a strong tendency to blame others and are inclined to take personal credit for successes. When left unchecked, bullying and dictatorship emerge. In response, employees are unlikely to propose new ideas, offer feedback or invest themselves further but rather go into self-protect mode to avoid the wrath of their toxic boss. Being blinded by their own importance, such individuals believe themselves to be already at a far superior Capacity than is required and don't seek to re-evaluate that opinion.

The Leader Coach can help coachees develop a Positive Mindset by facilitating coachees to:

   o Challenge their self-limiting beliefs and negative self-talk

- *What do you say to yourself and how do you talk about yourself when you are fed up/frustrated/disappointed with your performance? Does this inner talk motivate you to produce a better performance?*

o Appreciate their strengths

- *What do you like about yourself? What do you do well? What do others say you do well? What self-improvements do you feel most proud of? How did you identify, commence and support that self-improvement? Could you use that strategy again to turn your perceived weaknesses into strengths?*

o List the positive attributes of their team members.

- *List three things you like about each team member. Name each member's single most outstanding strength. Name something about each member that they do better than you or that you wish you could do.*

Simple approaches such as reading the mainstream writings from the discipline of Positive Psychology (e.g. those of Carol Dweck, Dan Gilbert and Martin Seligman), recording three things to be grateful for every day (see 1.5 'Transition Roles/Careers': 'The Affirmations Model') and making and reflecting on small constructive changes are all useful ways the Leader Coach can facilitate a leader to develop a Positive Mindset and Increase Capacity.

- **Support Network**

A differentiating factor of resilient individuals is their Support Network. Having people to rely on, with whom problems can be shared and discussed, dramatically reduces the mental load created by a leadership role, thereby increasing Capacity.

A Support Network should be both internal and external to the workplace. An internal Support Network is not just about having a core group of confidantes but should be about actively building the best possible team throughout the organisation. This is what Collins (2001) refers to as having the 'right people on the bus'. When the right people are in place, leaders can realise their own potential because '[t]he best people don't need to be managed. Guided, taught, led – yes. But not tightly managed.' (Collins, 2001, p.56)

A work-related but external Support Network might comprise a mentor or panel of mentors, peers in the industry/sector/same membership body, consultants and the Leader Coach. These will be individuals who have empathy for the pressures the leader is under (peers), can offer guidance (mentor), advice (consultant) or facilitate a structured self-inquiry (Leader Coach). Some of these individuals may operate on a retainer, so the leader has access to their support when required.

An external Support Network comes naturally from an individual's family and circle of friends. However, continuous negative pressure from the workplace can erode loved ones' willingness to be supportive of the frequently distracted individual who is there but not present. Where individuals have created obsoletion for themselves (see above) they are strengthening their social licence to remain in the leadership role because they are not exacting a heavy emotional toll on their Support Network as a result of toxic pressure from their job.

Covey's fourth area for developing self in his seventh habit, 'Sharpen the Saw', is *social/emotional*. He advocates developing the skills of effective communication (particularly listening), empathy and compromise to get the best out of interpersonal relationships. These skills will enhance relations with members of the leader's Support Network and in so doing increase the leader's Capacity.

Individuals who undervalue the importance of a Support Network also tend to undervalue the contribution and satisfaction of others. They are unlikely to perceive that, in the workplace, 'letting all the wrong people hang around is unfair to all the right people as they inevitably find themselves compensating for the inadequacies of the wrong people' (Collins, 2001, p.56). Furthermore, an inability to rely on or value others may be perceived as distrust, being controlling or having a cold lack of empathy. This creates a self-perpetuating downward spiral where the less approachable the individual is perceived to become, the less he/she is approached. Ultimately such individuals shoulder the burden of stress themselves, become isolated and dramatically decrease their Capacity to develop themselves further.

The Leader Coach can help coachees develop a Support Network by facilitating coachees to:

   o Reflect on whose opinions they value

       • *Who do you listen to? Do you respect their opinion? Whose opinion do you value?*

       • *Are these opinion holders in a position to impact your performance (i.e. key stakeholders)? If so, how can you positively influence them? If not, why do you allow their opinions to influence you? What's the worst that could happen if you ignored them?*

- *How might you identify peers/mentors who will give you honest and constructive feedback rather than falsely flattering/sycophantic/malicious feedback? How might you incorporate them into your social Support Network?*

o Define the area they would most like support in

- *Where do you believe is your greatest room for improvement? Can you articulate your preferred outcome and how you will achieve it? Convince me (role play) that it's in my interest to support you?*

o Appreciate that relying on others is not a weakness.

- *How do you feel when asking others for help? Why do you feel that way? Do you perceive other parties as weak when they ask for your help?*

- *When looking at successful individuals, what kind of Support Networks do they have? If that support was removed, where might that person be now?*

Simple approaches such as thought stopping to leave work at work, incorporating casual networking in the work day and scheduling official Support Network meetings are all useful ways the Leader Coach can facilitate a leader to develop a Support Network and increase Capacity.

ACCELERATING CAPACITY WITH COACHEES

Continuous Professional Development (CPD) is one of the most tangible methods an individual can use to increase Capacity. Typically associated with accredited courses through professional bodies, the practise of CPD can and should be embraced by everyone in the workplace and is not restricted to the formal acquisition of knowledge but rather to a continuing need to self-challenge, self-inform and self-develop (Covey's fourth area of 'mental' in Habit 7).

CPD can be viewed as equivalent to Continuous Improvement, as championed by Lean Management, with the CPD Cycle being an edited version of the Deming or PDCA Cycle (Plan, Do, Control, Act). There are various versions of the CPD cycle, but it typically also includes four steps (though there can be as many as six) of an iterative (repeatable) process.

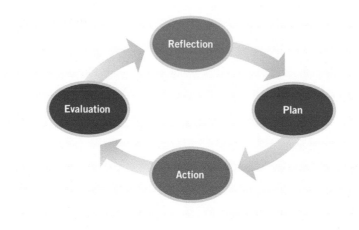

Figure 8: The CPD Cycle

- **Reflection:** This phase is about *knowing* the gaps or developing *conscious incompetence* (see 1.1 'Raise Self-Awareness').

  Here the Leader Coach can:
  - o *Facilitate the coachee to identify his/her most pertinent development need accurately.*

- **Planning:** The coachee develops a strategy to acquire the knowledge identified as the deficit in the reflection phase. CPD can be acquired through courses, in-house training workshops, on the job experience, shadowing others (closely watching others), conferences, symposia, reading books/articles, online resources such as webinars, podcasts and so forth.

  Here the Leader Coach can:
  - o *Help the coachee to incorporate getting the chosen CPD into his/her work schedule optimally.*

- **Action:** This involves doing the selected training/learning.

  Here the Leader Coach can:
  - o *Support the coachee through times of doubt when work demands and/or personal-life issues force the coachee to question the wisdom of committing to another pressure (i.e. CPD).*

- **Evaluation:** The relevance and application of the CPD activity should be recorded and evaluated at this point.

Here the Leader Coach can:

- o *Facilitate the coachee to extract relevance from the newly acquired skill(s) to improve the coachee's role effectiveness.*

QUICK RECAP: LEADER COACHING TO INCREASE CAPACITY

- o **Why?** – Optimise intellectual, physical and emotional 'bandwidth' in critical roles

- o **Main Concepts?** – Self-Investment, Effective Time Management, Striving for Obsoletion, Positive Mindset, Support Network

- o **How?** Coaching Conversations using:
  - Planning
  - Time management (incl. task prioritisation)
  - Reflection
  - Thought stopping
  - Positive affirmations

- o **Accelerate Capacity Coaching? Use:**
  - **Continuous Professional Development**
    - CPD cycle – reflection (spotting the gaps), planning (how to acquire knowledge), action (receiving training), evaluation (assessing the impact)

1.4 COACHING LEADERS TO ADJUST STYLE

For the most part, individuals in leadership roles have expertise in the mechanics of the business, having grown the business themselves or progressed through the industry. The ability to bring others successfully and *continuously* on that journey eludes all but a few, however. Engaging others is a matter of understanding and adjusting leadership Style. The challenge is knowing what Style to adjust to.

While there is an abundance of thinking on leadership Style, global consultancy firms as well as mainstream leadership writing discuss four-to-six different leadership Styles (e.g. Goleman, Murphy). While such approaches are intuitively and anecdotally stimulating, there is a risk that individuals will latch onto the Style they prefer or perceive as better/nicer. Given the dynamic nature of organisational demands and the multifaceted responsibilities of the leadership role, leaders require an array of Styles at their disposal and the ability to fluently slide between those Styles to be influential.

MAIN STYLE COMPONENTS

Since Terman's (1904) seminal paper on school playground leadership skills predicting the likelihood of individuals' having future leadership roles, the discipline of psychology has actively researched leadership. Among this mass of research, the understanding that effective leadership is situationally dependent has not been disputed since the 1960s, with the emergence of Fiedler's (1967) Contingency Theory of Leadership Effectiveness and Hersey and Blanchard's (1969) Situational Leadership Theory (made famous by the Blanchard Corporation's One Minute Manager series). This characteristic of leadership dictates that effective leaders need a repertoire of Styles and the skill to *adjust Style* to fit the situation. We have found that the Integrated Leadership Model (Browne, 2008) provides Leader Coaches with a useful framework for developing this skill in their coachees.

Leadership Styles (The Integrated Leadership Model)

A five-year study of leadership psychology research (Browne, 2008) concluded that virtually all leadership models mapped to twelve components (or six dual constructs) of leadership Style.

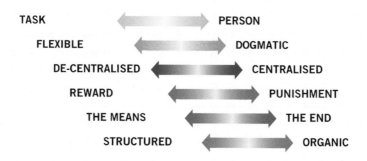

Figure 9: The Integrated Leadership Styles Model

The following are descriptions of each Style with explanations of where each Style is effective or ineffective, and suggestions and questions for the Leader Coach on how the coachee can develop that *Style* to be able to *adjust* to a given situation.

- **Task versus Person**

  This looks at whether the leader is focused on the task or on people. There are pros and cons to each Style.

  o **Task**

    A task Style places emphasis on the completion of individual tasks, daily workloads and performance goals as the business strives to accomplish its vision. The completion of tasks is the basis of the employee contract and needs to be enforced to uphold the transactional agreement between employee and company. Leaders are using a task Style when they oversee the completion of tasks to an agreed standard. Successful task completion has been found to be a workplace motivator.

    Using the Task Style (When Appropriate/Not Appropriate):

    - ✓ Time is limited, e.g. looming deadlines
    - ✓ Someone is new to a task and requires task-related instruction (e.g. training)
    - ✓ Employees engaged in routinised tasks, e.g. on assembly lines (personal interaction does little to enhance production rate and may be disruptive to the operator who can achieve a state of flow (Csikszentmihalyi, 1990) when allowed to work to his/her own rhythm)
    - ✗ Counterproductive if the incorrect tasks are being focused on (making a *task Style* different to the *end Style* described below)
    - ✗ Investing heavily in accomplishing a non-contributing task is energy and morale depleting and loses the respect of colleagues and employees alike
    - ✗ Excessively task-focused individuals may be dismissive on a personal basis, losing the opportunity to build trust and respect with the employee
    - ✗ Telling an expert how to do the task he/she is an expert at can be perceived as micro-managing, thus causing frustration

The Leader Coach can help coachees develop the *task Style* by facilitating coachees to:

o Understand the task responsibilities of each team member

- *How frequently do you review your direct reports' workloads?*

- *How frequently should you review them?*

- *How can you incorporate that routine into your own workload?*

o Set deadlines to ensure focused application

- *When receiving task instructions, are you always clear about the urgency and importance of each task?*

- *How can you influence upwards to ensure sufficient resources to make on-time task completion realistic?*

o Incorporate regular reviews of completed work quality.

- *How regularly do you review your work in line with KPIs? Is this frequent enough?*

- *What do you do if your work and/or the work of others falls short of expected standards?*

- *How do you prevent underperformance of future tasks?*

Simple approaches such as planning, prioritisation and work breakdown structures (from Project Management) are all helpful tools and ways the Leader Coach can support a leader developing the *task Style* and his/her overall ability to *adjust Style.*

o **Person**

A person Style places great importance on developing human relations in the workplace. It involves a genuine concern for employee satisfaction and wellbeing, demonstrated by a deep interest in employees as more than labour units.

Using the Person Style (When Appropriate/Not Appropriate):

- ✓ New employees require high levels of personal support due to confidence issues while 'learning the ropes' (leading to the development of buddying and mentoring programmes in many larger organisations)

- ✓ Employees working on complex tasks (complexity means tasks take longer and are more problematic, resulting in higher risk, causing employees to, at times, doubt themselves; this leads to a need for emotional support and reassurance)

✓ Due to the risk and complexity of change implementation, an overarching *person Style* is necessary (Kotter, 1996; see 3.3 'Spark a Change Culture')

✗ Time constraints (effective leaders *postpone* the personal interaction rather than dismiss it, allowing the leader to be fully present for an appreciative employee when deadline distractions have been managed)

✗ Overly *person* focused individuals may be unwilling to be unpopular and may avoid tough decision making to avoid being perceived as mean (in extreme cases, toxic managers counterproductively neglect the task in favour of employee wellbeing to the detriment of the business strategy and bottom line, leaving employees feeling contempt for the manager's lack of achievement rather than gratitude for his/her concern)

The Leader Coach can help coachees develop an understanding of the *person Style* by facilitating them to:

o Actively get to know employees

- *How well do you know each of your colleagues and direct reports?*
- *What are the barriers to getting to know them better?*
- *What are the risks of getting to know them better? How can you mitigate these risks?*

o Improve communication skills, especially listening

- *How inclusive of others' opinions are you? Who do you listen to and why? Who don't you listen to and why?*
- *On a scale of 1 to 10, how effective are the communication channels in your unit? How can this score be maintained or improved?*
- *Would your team members give the same score? If not, how would you feel? What could you do to improve their rating?*

o View people management as a critical task.

- *What opportunities regularly present themselves that*

could be used to work on the person style? How could you incorporate regular team communication into your work schedule?

- *How could you convert people management into manageable tasks?*
- *How would you measure success?*

Simple approaches such as using psychometrics (e.g. personality questionnaires to demonstrate individual differences), recommending Emotional Intelligence training and the Square of Communication (improve communication skills) are all helpful tools and ways the Leader Coach can support a leader developing the *person Style* and his/her overall ability to *adjust Style*.

Interestingly, in situations of conflict the use of either a *task Style* or a *person Style* may prove more beneficial. In certain conflict situations it may be necessary to temporarily abandon the task and focus on the person issues of the conflicting members to get the team functioning properly again (social cohesion); while avoiding the person issues and focusing on the task as a common goal may prove more effective (task cohesion) elsewhere. The choice of Style is at the discretion of the leader who should consider the individuals involved, the nature of the conflict and the organisational constraints to direct his/her decision.

- **Flexible versus Dogmatic**

  This looks at whether leaders seek the opinions and information of others to make decisions. There are pros and cons to each Style.

  o **Flexible**

    A flexible leadership Style means leaders are willing to listen to and incorporate the opinions of others.

    Using the Flexible Style (When Appropriate/Not Appropriate):

    - ✓ Highly experienced workforce
    - ✓ Allowing knowledgeable employees to contribute their valuable insights enhances employee motivation through recognition (Herzberg, 1959), stimulates ownership of the project their opinion has contributed towards and encourages future engagement
    - ✓ Engaging company expertise reduces the time taken to arrive at a final correct decision

✗ Tight deadlines limit the breadth of any information-gathering exercise

✗ Waiting for perfect certainty before acting (common in perfectionists but the need to act can be more important than the need to get it right in business, especially when it comes to securing market share – e.g. Apple has used early release of products to gain market share)

✗ Individuals may be overly inclusive due to a lack of Self-Confidence in their analytical abilities (promoted prematurely or feel under-supported and exposed)

The Leader Coach can help coachees develop the *flexible Style* by facilitating coachees to:

o Start the information-gathering process sooner/allow it to take longer

- *Reflecting on previous tasks/projects, what is a realistic information-gathering window? How will you apply that knowledge to future information-gathering exercises?*

- *How might you ensure you receive more timely information? Who could you task with following up to help you?*

- *What are the best information-gathering methods? Can you think of others?*

o Include more diversified sources of information

- *Who do you typically include? Why? What is the benefit/ disadvantage?*

- *Who do you typically exclude? Why? What is the benefit/ disadvantage?*

o Rely more on the participation of others.

- *What prevents you being more inclusive? What is the risk with relying more on others? How could you mitigate these risks?*

- *How do you think others would respond to you if you asked for their opinions? How can you assure them their opinion will not be used against them?*

- *What skills do you need to develop to help you communicate more effectively with diverse sources?*

Simple approaches such as challenging the coachee's assumptions about others' abilities, 'what if...?' scenarios (e.g. 'what if you did/didn't include X?') and Mental Toughness interventions (interpersonal confidence) are all helpful tools and ways the Leader Coach can support a leader developing the *flexible Style* and his/her overall ability to *adjust Style*.

o **Dogmatic**

Self-reliance or reliance on a limited group for information exemplifies a dogmatic Style. Leadership popularity polls consistently reveal that decisive leaders confident in their own opinions are the most admired by the general population. This show of personal confidence engenders a sense of security in followers.

Using the Dogmatic Style (When Appropriate/Not Appropriate):

✓ You are the single most informed individual and your information carries the greatest weight

✓ Information sought from a well-informed core/select group (it is foolish to seek the opinions of the inexperienced or uninformed because it creates inappropriate expectations about employee roles or can lead to performance paralysis where individuals feel overwhelmed at being asked to share an opinion they feel ill-equipped to give)

✓ Immediate actions are required, with delays carrying risk or penalties

✗ Limits the quality of the decision by potentially excluding critical information

✗ Disengages employees capable of contributing but who haven't been asked

✗ Poor utilisation of available valuable resources when relevant experts are ignored

✗ Where a select group is being used consistently, this may be perceived as cronyism

✗ During an economic/business crisis, for example a recession or business collapse, the breadth of information gathering dramatically contracts as individuals self-preserve by tightening control to reduce the possibility of being blamed; this is a short term and often destructive mentality

The Leader Coach can help coachees develop the *dogmatic Style* by facilitating coachees to:

o Continuously anticipate informational needs and become well informed

- *How can you improve your understanding of business demands/direction?*
- *What blockages prevent you anticipating informational needs?*
- *Who are the best sources of information to keep you continually informed?*

o Select the most relevant opinions

- *How could you override a default dependence on the opinions of too many parties?*
- *What criteria could you use for selecting opinion relevance?*
- *Visualise excluding someone from providing information. How might that conservation go?*

o Restrict the time spent information gathering.

- *How can you ensure swift and accurate information gathering?*
- *Can you live with the trade-off between speed and inclusiveness? What's the worst that could happen? How can you mitigate this risk?*

Simple approaches such as stakeholder mapping (for selective inclusion; see 2.4 'Align Stakeholders'), assertiveness training (confidently exclude people) and confidence building through decision-making training are all helpful tools and ways the Leader Coach can support a leader developing the *dogmatic Style* and his/her overall ability to *adjust Style*.

- **De-Centralised versus Centralised**

This looks at power distribution or the authority to make decisions. There are pros and cons to each Style.

o **De-centralised**

De-centralising decision-making power reduces the burden on the individual and substantially increases the capacity of the business by allowing decisions to be taken at the lowest possible level. A culture of delegation, empowerment and support, underpinned by role clarity, open communication and delineated decision-making authority, is required to make this Style work properly.

Using the De-Centralised Style (When Appropriate/Not Appropriate):

- ✓ Perceived as trust by employees, who feel recognised for their competence
- ✓ Speeds up performance by removing the bottleneck of having a single decision maker
- ✓ Allows leaders to work to their potential, being no longer central to every decision (see 1.3 'Increase Capacity': 'Striving for Obsoletion').
- ✗ Individuals who prefer or have a fixed *de-centralised Style* may have developed this due to:
  - o Feelings of role incompetence making them incapable of decision making
  - o Fear of blame for a poor outcome in risky situations
  - o A wish to devolve power because they are uncomfortable/embarrassed having it (e.g. promoted over their friends)
- ✗ Taken to the extreme, it may result in the abdication of responsibility or laissez-faire leadership, causing organisational paralysis through lack of role clarity and direction
- ✗ Hides malpractice where there is no delineation of responsibility (cited as one of the main causes of the 2001 Enron scandal)
- ✗ In less extreme cases, employees are reluctant to take the initiative because they don't know on whose authority they can proceed and what the consequence will be if they do

The Leader Coach can help coachees develop the *de-centralised Style* by facilitating coachees to:

- o Train in effective delegation
  - • *How are decisions currently being made? What works? What could be improved?*

- *In the absence of you or other decision makers, what contingencies are in place to ensure work continues?*
- *Is there someone you can mirror/emulate/ask to be your mentor to develop this skill?*

o Create decision-making tolerances (e.g. >£10,000, <£100,000, etc.)

- *What decisions could be broken down into tolerances (e.g. You do not need my go ahead for purchases below £2,000)? Who will you assign to each tolerance level? Why?*

o Regularly review decision-making capacity in line with competencies.

- *What support do decision makers in your team require to feel confident?*
- *What reassurance do you need to prevent you from centralising? How will you articulate this to your team?*

Simple approaches such as Mental Toughness interventions (relinquishing control), visualisation ('what's the worst that could happen') and a delegation training recommendation are all helpful tools and ways the Leader Coach can support a leader developing the *de-centralised Style* and his/her overall ability to *adjust Style.*

o **Centralised**

A centralised Style insists that all decisions go through one person or only a few people. All decision making is a burden because it is a choice between alternatives and so inherently carries risk. Although an uncomfortable truth, it should be acknowledged that not every employee seeks a position of authority but rather feels happy and secure that someone else has taken that responsibility.

Using the Centralised Style (When Appropriate/Not Appropriate):

- ✓ You are the most competent person
- ✓ Creates role clarity
- ✓ Recognisable accountability when the decision carries high risk
- ✗ Used to excess, the style may exert a level of control that is stifling (in such cases, the toxic manager is often termed a 'control freak' – see 1.2 'Build Mental Toughness')

✗ May create overly bureaucratic systems (can result in a slow, grinding machine that is unresponsive to the dynamic demands of the market)

✗ The risk of corruption such as cronyism is high (where one person has all the decision-making power)

The Leader Coach can help coachees develop the *centralised Style* by facilitating coachees to:

o Accept the responsibility granted them by the business

- *Why are you reluctant to accept decision making responsibility?*

o Attend decision-making training

- *How could you safely test out your learning? What resources would you need to this? Who could you ask for guidance on this?*

o Influence upwards for support in the decision-making process.

- *How might you influence upwards to gain decision-making support? What resistance might you experience? How will you overcome this?*

- *Would you like to role play that critical conversation?*

Simple approaches such as assertiveness training, Mental Toughness interventions (developing confidence) and building influencing/persuasion skills are all helpful tools and ways the Leader Coach can support a leader developing the *centralised Style* and his/her overall ability to *adjust Style*.

- **Punishment versus Reward**

This scale looks at whether a leader tends to reward or punish to get the job done. There are pros and cons to each Style.[5]

o **Punishment**

This has always been a controversial topic. However, it is unacceptable for leaders to deny the need for punishment in the leadership role because of the negative publicity it receives. Punishment can take many forms such as withholding rewards including praise, promotion and

---

5   The word 'punishment' is used due its prevalence in the leadership literature. Alternative words have been considered but 'punishment' consistently arises as the antonym of 'reward'. These two Styles are pervasive in the leadership literature thanks to the motivational conundrum 'the carrot or the stick'.

monetary or status rewards. It is ultimately about holding people accountable as part of the transactional nature of employment and is crucial to the productivity and employee satisfaction of any business.

Using the Punishment Style (When Appropriate/Not Appropriate):

✓ Should be systematically meted out for those who breach zero-tolerance standards such as safety (physical and psychological), theft, confidentiality, unfounded reputation damage, lying with destructive consequences, etc. (where the outcome of non-compliance is harmful, punishment is a readily accepted and anticipated leadership Style e.g. in the armed forces, fuel industry, mining, etc.)

✓ Setting expectations particularly in a new role to set precedence e.g. 'kill one to warn one hundred' (Chinese Proverb) to prevent sabotage/mutiny (employees will always push boundaries to establish role clarity – this is natural human behaviour)

✓ Should occur as soon as possible after the fact and should fit the 'crime' (lessons learned should be implemented to prevent reoccurrence of the misdemeanour)

✗ A *punishment Style* has become toxic when it supports/ignores the use of insidious behaviour such as flippant/snide comments, overt and covert bullying, racism, exclusion, etc. (this is hugely destructive to workplace morale and will result in stress-related outcomes such as poor health, absenteeism and personnel attrition)

✗ Unfair punishment such as being in excess of the crime, based on prejudiced evidence (e.g. hearsay) or compiled to be served 'cold, in one dish' (as companies that drastically misunderstand the appraisal process do) is also counterproductive

✗ Challenging poor or unacceptable performance is about challenging the behaviour i.e. it should *never* be a personal assassination or humiliation

The Leader Coach can help coachees develop the *punishment Style* by facilitating coachees to:

o   Identify organisational punishable behaviours

- *Where will you get this information? How will you convey these punishable behaviours to your team?*
- *If you have previously struggled to hold people accountable or challenge behaviour, why? How did it make you feel? Why do you think you feel that way? How can that reluctance be overcome?*

o   Accept that employees respond well to leadership that is strict but fair

- *Can you articulate your understanding of the phrase 'strict but fair'? What does it mean to you? What might fairness look like to others? What might be perceived as unfair?*
- *How can you get your message across without humiliating the other person? Let's role-play that conversation.*

o   Influence upwards to receive support for punishment decisions.

- *Whose authority do you need to support your punishment decisions? How might you engage with that person, so they feel willing to support you? How might you establish 'rules of engagement' so that person knows you won't abdicate and make him/her the villain?*

Simple approaches such as role-playing difficult conversations, reflecting on lessons learned from previously punished/unpunished scenarios and encouraging assertiveness training are all helpful tools and ways the Leader Coach can support a leader developing the *punishment Style* and his/her overall ability to *adjust Style*.

o   **Reward**

A reward Style is viewed as socially more acceptable but, like all leadership Styles, should be judiciously used. Reward includes praise, perks of the job, promotion, and financial remuneration such as a raise or bonus. Less obvious but nonetheless powerful, rewards might include time off, flexible working conditions, autonomy, mentoring, discretionary projects, team selection and management of prestigious client accounts.

Using the Reward Style (When Appropriate/Not Appropriate):

✓ Acknowledge exceptional performance (after the fact is more sustainable than using it to promote exceptional performance as that can incentivise short cuts)

✓ Monotonous jobs to reduce staff turnover (e.g. call centres)

✓ High-risk/unpleasant jobs to attract people (e.g. offshore oil rigs)

✓ Highly competitive, high-burnout environments (e.g. stock trading)

✗ Attracts and retain employees who are extrinsically motivated with loyalty to the highest payer, creating a headhunting or poaching risk

✗ Managers who are uncomfortable holding people accountable may compensate with an excessive *reward Style* (employees should be held accountable for doing the job they are paid for and, where performance is substandard, despite all conditions having been met, incentivising should never be defaulted to)

✗ Use of bonus systems has been found to be problematic across all sectors and should only be used as a one-off strategy with clearly defined parameters where it is not industry common practice (e.g. bonusing and its fallout are acceptable within finance)

The Leader Coach can help coachees develop the *reward Style* by facilitating coachees to:

o Appreciate that people are not always being needy when they seek praise

- *Can you articulate what's praiseworthy daily/weekly/monthly/role specific, etc.? Does everyone on your team have a clear understanding of what's expected of them? Do you?*

- *Why might team members seek praise? How might you praise and reassure them that they are doing their job well?*

- *Who do you seek praise and recognition from and why? How does it make you feel? Could you learn from this to help with praising your team members?*

o Recognise that a well-placed 'thank you' has great value

- *What small gestures do you appreciate? How could you find out what your team members want in terms of praise/recognition?*

o Establish parameters for unacceptable/acceptable/exceptional performances and respond accordingly.

- *What have you the authority to grant (see 2.1 'Motivate Employees': 'Reward and Recognition Model')? Who do you need to influence to get greater rewards for your team?*

Simple approaches such as using motivation models (see 2.1 'Motivate Employees'), creating appreciation and gratitude statements and Appreciative Inquiry are all helpful tools and ways the Leader Coach can support a leader developing the *reward Style* and his/her overall ability to *adjust Style*.

Fascinatingly, the excessive use of punishment and the excessive use of reward have a similar outcome on employees. Once employees realise that regardless of their on-task effort they will be rewarded, there will be little incentive to do more than the necessary minimum. Similarly, if regardless of effort they will be punished, they will default to doing the bare minimum, predicting they will be punished irrespective of their degree of application. In conclusion, an excessive *punishment Style* and an excessive *reward Style* both result in minimal employee effort and engagement, and ultimately lead to employee complacency.

- **The Means versus the End**

This considers sustainability and may be viewed as the conflict of short-term and long-term intentions. There are pros and cons to each Style.

o **The Means**

Following the revelation of corrupt financial practices in banking, securities and finance which led to the Great Recession, a greater leadership focus on the *means* gained traction and is now here to stay. Indeed, the means Style is being used effectively wherever any one of ISO 26000's ('for businesses and organisations committed to operating in a socially responsible way') seven areas (see below) are being actively promoted in the workplace. It is how such sensitive matters are handled that differentiates between correct and incorrect use of the means Style.

Using The Means Style (When Appropriate/Not Appropriate):
- ✓ Organisational governance
- ✓ Human rights
- ✓ Fair labour practices
- ✓ Fair operating practices
- ✓ Community involvement and development
- ✓ Consumer issues
- ✓ The environment
- ✗ Excessive use may lead to overly bureaucratising processes
- ✗ May distract from the core function of business profitability (concern for the *means* is unlikely to be at the forefront of a growing or struggling business's agenda, and even a business set up to be ethical and sustainable needs to be financially viable)
- ✗ Being misused where management avoid making tough but necessary decisions for fear of offending people (for example, redundancies to secure the future of a business will require being unpopular for a time but shouldn't be avoided)

The Leader Coach can help coachees develop the *means Style* by facilitating coachees to:

o Familiarise themselves with corporate social responsibility
- *How familiar am I with the seven areas? What small acts can I do every day that will create meaning for the people around me and in my work?*

o Project into the future to predict long-term impact rather than short-term gain
- *Ask yourself projection questions: Will this matter in a year/5 years'/100 years' time? How might history reflect on this? Is this something I can/will be proud of? Who stands to gain from this and am I happy with that?*

o Improve communication skills for damage limitation of difficult messages.
- *What objections might arise against this course of action? Can we live with those?*
- *What can you offer to offset an uncomfortable process? What can you offer to offset a negative outcome?*

Simple approaches such as visualisation of future outcomes, 'if... then' projections and enhancing communication skills (e.g. Square of Communication) are all helpful tools and ways the Leader Coach can support a leader developing the *means Style* and his/her overall ability to *adjust Style*.

o **The End**

Given that leadership exists to achieve a specified outcome (vision, objective, why, etc.) the end Style is a dominant Style in any high-performing unit. Furthermore, with achievement being one of the leading motivators in the workplace (Herzberg, 1959) employees willingly sanction its use.

The end Style should not be confused with a task Style, which focuses on the execution of the task at hand. Due to misunderstanding the outcome, goal or bigger picture (the *end*), a task-focused individual could achieve nothing through investing in the wrong task.

Where the end Style is used to excess, employees are exploited in terms of working hours and expectations, illegal/fraudulent behaviour is not discouraged, resources are abused and a limited few reap all the rewards.

Using the End Style (When Appropriate/Not Appropriate):

- ✓ Boosts employees' morale through positive self-concept that they are part of a successful entity
- ✓ Critical in times of business volatility such as starting up, economic instability, losing market share, hostile takeovers, mergers, brand damage, employee unrest, internal sabotage, etc.
- ✗ Exploitation of employee working hours and expectations
- ✗ Illegal/fraudulent behaviour in pursuit of the goal
- ✗ Resources abuse
- ✗ A limited few reap all the rewards

However, with the emergence of servant leadership and a wider call for a focus on the means, the social licence for the aggressive pursuit of the *end* has been somewhat revoked. This is evidenced by an increasing expectation of improved corporate governance, the promotion of the circular economy model and the exposure of malpractice via social media.

The Leader Coach can help coachees develop the *end Style* by facilitating coachees to:

o Identify outcome goals

- *How can you gain greater insight into the company's vision? How frequently do you review tasks against the company vision?*

- *Can you articulate the desired outcome succinctly to your team? Can you break it down into its constituents or manageable chunks?*

o Differentiate between distractions and supports to goal completion

- *What are the main distractions that threaten successful completion? How can you counter these? What are the key contributors to successful goal completion? How can you promote these?*

o Remove obstacles to implementing the business strategy.

- *Which aspect of the business strategy meets with greatest resistance? Why?*

- *How can you create a shared deep understanding of the business strategy across the organisation?*

- *How might you inculcate a greater productivity mindset in your team?*

Simple approaches such as thinking about the 'big picture'/ visioning, goal setting and a recommendation of Emotional Intelligence skills training for effective influencing are all helpful tools and ways the Leader Coach can support a leader developing the *end Style* and his/her overall ability to *adjust Style*.

- **Structured versus Organic**

This looks at how individuals approach leadership: as a learnable skill or as an instinctive reaction. There are pros and cons to each Style.

o **Structured**

A structured Style is a formal approach to the acquisition of effective leadership skills. In Western society, business operates within a regulated framework where educational standardisation confers an expectation of what an individual can do (for example, solicitors have recognised legal quali- fications). The use of protected titles in certain professions to ensure these standards also forces a structured route (e.g. auditors). While some industries still harbour a preference for on-the-job experience (e.g. hospitality), progression to the C-Suite is likely to require both experience and formal qualification.

Using the Structured Style (When Appropriate/Not Appropriate):

- ✓ Challenges current thinking
- ✓ Improves understanding
- ✓ Builds networks through participation with others
- ✓ Strengthens your CV
- ✓ Increases capacity (see 1.3 'Increase Capacity': 'CPD')
- ✗ May be perceived as overly academic and not 'real world' enough
- ✗ Despite the strengths of models to distil a vast amount of information, the complexity of people's individual differences fits less neatly in a model, and expecting them to do so may cause frustration and resentment
- ✗ Heavily formulising the thinking process may stifle innovation and creativity (Levitin's (2014) work suggests the opposite, however)

The Leader Coach can help coachees develop the *structured Style* by facilitating coachees to:

- o Challenge any reluctance to taking a formal route (e.g. lacking Self-Confidence)
  - *What is preventing you from learning more/attending training/taking a course/gaining a qualification?*
  - *What will happen if you don't continue learning? What will happen if you do?*
- o Identify training needs
  - *How can you keep current? What area of development would provide the greatest return of investment to you/ the company? Why?*
  - *How will you convince your manager that you are worth the investment? Would you pursue this at a financial/ time cost to yourself? Why/Why not?*
- o Support them on the learning journey.

- *What format will your learning take? How will you schedule the assignments and learning?*

- *What options does your current role provide to enhance this training experience? How will you assimilate your learning into your current role?*

Simple approaches such as a training needs analysis, creating a CPD/personal development plan and working with a CPD cycle (see 1.3 'Increase Capacity') such as the Deming or PDCA cycle are all helpful tools and ways the Leader Coach can support a leader developing the *structured Style* and his/her overall ability to *adjust Style*.

o **Organic**

An organic Style is where individuals rely on intuition, experience and personality for their leadership approach. Entrepreneurs are generally considered to use a more organic Style of leadership. Businesses grow organically in a reactive fashion, where 'firefighting' is a daily occurrence and the need to convince others to commit to the potential of a yet-to-be-manifested vision is not easily encapsulated by a business model. Indeed, entrepreneurs may lack the ability to articulate what it is they are trying to achieve; they just believe that they will recognise it when it happens. Through passion and an almost-maniacal conviction, others are willing to be led blind for the project to be realised.

Using the Organic Style (When Appropriate/Not Appropriate):

- ✓ Entrepreneurial activities

- ✓ New ventures, e.g. product development, diversification, etc.

- ✓ When obvious solutions are not forthcoming and 'thinking outside the box' is required, i.e. creativity

- ✗ Constantly being reactive depletes resources and creates an unstable foundation for coping with new pressures

- ✗ For founding members (entrepreneurs) who thrived in the crisis mode of business creation, formalising business procedures, once the entity has reached a tipping point, can be contentious (founders can become disruptive to the point of being saboteurs)

× The thinking and behaviours that grow a business will not sustain it (a shift from *organic* to *structured* is the natural progression for a growing entity and successful business leaders, understanding this, adjust their Style accordingly)

Of further concern with an *organic Style* is the notion of charisma. Although highly prized by society, charisma should come with a 'toxic' warning label. Charisma is the ability to persuade others through strength of personality rather than merit-worthy actions or results. There is a risk, therefore, that charismatic individuals will manipulate others for personal gain (self-embedded charisma) rather than influence others for the greater good (self-transcendent charisma). Effective leadership should be defined by the journey taken and the results achieved, not how well liked a person is (i.e. referent power).

The Leader Coach can help coachees develop the *organic Style* by facilitating coachees to:

o Schedule brainstorming sessions

- *When choosing people for brainstorming sessions, do you pick those you think like you or do you seek diversity (see 2.3 'Develop Teams': 'Belbin Team Roles')?*

- *What type of thinker might add an extra dimension to the session?*

o Listen to their emotional rather than rational self

- *If there were no limitations on what you could achieve with X, what would be the possibilities? If left to your own devices, all inhibitions removed, what could be achieved with X? Ignore your head when it says what you should be doing and ask yourself what you feel like doing or trying in relation to X.*

o Incorporate less-conventional thinkers in their support network (see 1.3 'Increase Capacity').

- *How would you define 'less conventional'? How do you feel about people who think and see the world differently to you? How do you think their approach might contribute to your existing repertoire? What is the risk of including/excluding them?*

Simple approaches such as encouraging blue-sky thinking, metaphorically wearing De Bono's green hat (creativity – see 3.1 'Clarify Strategy') and challenging fixed-mindset thinking are all helpful tools and ways the Leader Coach can support a leader developing the *organic Style* and his/her overall ability to *adjust Style*.

ACCELERATING LEADERSHIP STYLE ADJUSTMENTS

The ability to *adjust Style* firstly requires that individuals know what Style they are currently using. This may be a favoured Style (one they like using), a preferred/default (most ingrained) Style that expresses itself when individuals are under pressure or it may be that individuals have a range of Styles they move through. Knowing requires the creation of awareness. Using a psychometric creates self-awareness (see 1.1 'Raise Self-Awareness'). Like a snapshot in time, it provides individuals with a starting point to explore the effectiveness of their current Style given the situation, and from there they can work with the Leader Coach to develop different Styles and to adjust Styles in response to situational factors (see above) – a hallmark of effective leadership.

The ILM72

The development of the Integrated Leadership Model (Browne, 2008) led to the development of the 72-question (item) Integrated Leadership Measure, the ILM72 (licensed by AQR International Ltd). The ILM72 is a self-awareness tool that provides a starting point for self-development.

The development report, generated instantly on completion, provides the candidate with two different scoring systems: the six bi-polar Leadership Style sten-graph scales discussed above and shown below again (in Figure 10) and three further global scales of Leader Competence (normative data).

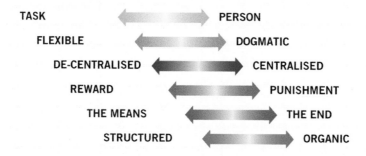

TASK		PERSON
FLEXIBLE		DOGMATIC
DE-CENTRALISED		CENTRALISED
REWARD		PUNISHMENT
THE MEANS		THE END
STRUCTURED		ORGANIC

Figure 10: The ILM Leadership Style Scales

Completion of the questionnaire allows coachees to gain an insight into the leadership Styles they are currently deploying by interpreting the ILM72 report. The reports present the Style scores as 'ipsative' data which:

o   Allows individuals to make comparisons with themselves and draw conclusions (i.e. it is not a comparison with others)

o   Encourages individuals to draw the inferences from their profiles such as 'In this job, I tend to be more dogmatic than flexible in my decision-making Style' or 'I focus more on the task at hand than on the people I work with'.

Backed up with discussion, 360-degree feedback, situational analysis and so forth, the *effectiveness* of the individual leader's Style can be established; and where different Styles would be more appropriate, the Leader Coach can help the coachee:

o   Assess the situational factors

o   Decide on the most appropriate leadership Style

o   Develop that Style and add it to his/her repertoire for use in future appropriate situations (i.e. coach the individual to adjust Style – see above).

The ILM72 Global Factors of Leadership Competence

A further benefit of the ILM72 is that it presents three further higher-order factors or global scales of leadership *competence*: Determination to Deliver, Engagement with the Individual, Engagement with Teams. These factors emerged through further statistical analysis of the six dual constructs of leadership Style that resulted in the development of the Integrated Leadership Model.

FACTOR	CONTRIBUTING STYLES
Determination to Deliver	Task, The End, Centralised, Punishment, Structured, Dogmatic, Reward
Engagement with Individuals*	De-Centralised, Flexible, The Means, Organic, Reward, Task, Structured
Engagement with Teams*	Person, The Means, Organic, De-Centralised, Reward

*The individual items (questions) differentiated between individuals and teams.

Each scale of the three Global Factors produces a score on a scale of 1 to 10. This rating system is representative of the Normal Distribution Curve where 16% of all respondents will score below average, 16% will score above average and 68% will score in the average range.

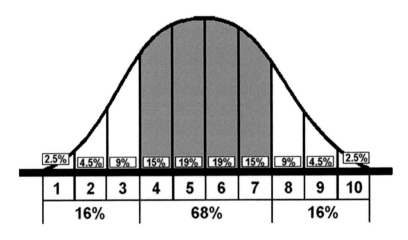

Figure 11: ILM Normal Distribution Curve

Where development is required on any of the Global Factors, the leadership Styles scales can be referred to. For instance, a low score on *Determination to Deliver* may correspond with an excessive resort to the *means Style*, while poor *Engagement with Individuals* might correspond with an overly *dogmatic Style*, indicating limited employee inclusion.

- **Determination to Deliver**

  Regardless of the function of the unit (e.g. sport, charity, social policy, etc.), leaders exist to implement a vision and drive performance. Effective leaders, therefore, are goal-oriented, creating the least path of resistance by anticipating and offsetting potential blockages, tackling any unexpected occurrences along the way and optimising resources. Such leaders are not afraid to make tough/unpopular decisions but, through their Determination to Deliver, communicating effectively, engaging in damage limitation and delivering the outcome they become trusted, admired and supported even by those who may have opposed them.

  Individuals who are not determined to deliver a desired outcome are not, by definition, leaders. Where individuals occupy a position of leadership and fail to deliver, this may be due to several factors such as a lack of resources (including human resources), economic climate, unrealistic expectations and so forth. If, however, the individual has the desire to perform but lacks the capability or confidence, the Leader Coach can be engaged.

  The Leader Coach can help coachees develop their *Determination to Deliver* by facilitating coachees to:
  - o   Reflect on what might be inhibiting their performance
  - o   Identify solutions for improving performance
  - o   Develop a road map for goal accomplishment.

  Simple approaches such as using the ILM72 Style scales scores to interpret the Determination to Deliver score, increasing capacity (see 1.3 'Increase Capacity') and clarifying strategy (see 3.1 'Clarify Strategy') are all helpful tools and ways the Leader Coach can support a leader developing his/her overall Determination to Deliver.

- **Engagement with Individuals**

  Given that the human asset is the limiting factor in all barring blue-chip organisations, follower engagement is key to outcome achievement. Indeed, it is blue-chip organisations' ability to deliver by engaging with their membership that has made them blue chip.

Covey (1989) said treat everyone the same by treating them differently. This is time consuming and easily avoided by addressing teams and groups, but it is an essential aspect of leadership. Effective leaders understand that everyone's contribution creates the whole and invest in maximising each contribution through role clarity, personalised training, mentoring arrangements and career-path support. Bass (1985) termed this Individualised Consideration in his work on Transformational Leadership.

Individuals who do not take the time to understand and engage with employees individually are at risk of stereotyping or falling foul of the cognitive error known as the halo effect (Dobelli, 2013), where everyone is rated the same based on the performance/behaviour of a few (for example, the idea that all accountants are risk averse). Where this occurs, individuals may be under- or over-utilised; both are a misappropriation of a limited asset.

The Leader Coach can help coachees to develop their *Engagement with Individuals* by facilitating coachees to:

- o Reflect on what might be inhibiting their individual engagement
- o Identify solutions for improving individual engagement
- o Develop a road map for greater individual engagement.

Simple approaches such as using the ILM72 Style scales scores to interpret the Engagement with Individuals score, motivating employees (see 2.1 'Motivate Employees') and aligning stakeholders (see 2.4 'Align Stakeholders') are all helpful tools and ways the Leader Coach can support a leader developing his/her overall Engagement with Individuals.

- **Engagement with Teams**

Despite teams being made up of individuals, effectively managing teams requires a separate skillset. Due to the almost alchemical reaction of people's personalities when combined (see 2.3 'Develop Teams') it is not a simple matter of scaling up engagement with the individual. When the combined potential of a group is harnessed correctly, the leader substantially enhances performance capability. This is capitalising on synergy. It results in faster, more accurate, easier-to-implement decisions allowing for agile responses in dynamic environments.

A failure to manage teams results in lower productivity and workplace morale. Inter- and intragroup conflict impede performance and, at worst, the toxic group behaviour of groupthink (Janis, 1972) can result in sabotage capable of collapsing a unit, if not an entire business.

The Leader Coach can help coachees develop their *Engagement with Teams* by facilitating them to:

- o Reflect on what might be inhibiting their team engagement
- o Identify solutions for improving team engagement
- o Develop a road map for greater team engagement.

Simple approaches such as using the ILM72 Style scales scores to interpret the Engagement with Teams, encouraging an active interest in group dynamics and processes, and enabling coachees to inspire teams (see 2.3 'Develop Teams') are all helpful tools and ways the Leader Coach can support a leader developing his/her overall *Engagement with Teams*.

Benefits of using the ILM72:

- · *Looks at leadership Styles and leadership effectiveness*
- · *Draws from 100 years of research in leadership psychology*
- · *Maps to virtually every model of leadership, including all the mainstream theories*
- · *Most leadership models can therefore be used as development interventions*
- · *It can be used in conjunction with existing in-house training programmes*
- · *An organisational profile can be generated by combining the results from every employee who completes the questionnaire*
- · *Pre-intervention test completion and post-intervention test completion differences can be used to demonstrate ROI.*

QUICK RECAP: LEADER COACHING TO ADJUST STYLE

- o **Why?** – The dynamic nature of business requires the leader to display 'situational agility'
- o **Main Concepts?** – Leaderships Styles, Self-Awareness, situational requirements, effective/ineffective leadership responses

- o **How?** Coaching Conversations using:
  - **The Integrated Leadership Model**
  - Task vs. Person
  - Flexible vs. Dogmatic
  - De-Centralised vs. Centralised
  - Punishment vs. Reward
  - The Means vs. The End
  - Structured vs. Organic
- o **Accelerate Style Coaching? Use:**
  - **ILM72 questionnaire (licensed to AQR International Ltd)**
    - o 72-item questionnaire derived from the Integrated Leadership Model
    - o Six bi-polar scales (Task vs. Person, Flexible vs. Dogmatic, De-Centralised vs. Centralised, Reward vs. Punishment, The Means vs. The End, Structured vs. Organic)
    - o Three global factor scales (Determination to Deliver, Engagement with Individuals, Engagement with Teams)
    - o Computer-generated reports provide development suggestions

1.5 COACHING LEADERS TO TRANSITION ROLES/CAREERS

The Leader Coach can help *accelerate coachee personal growth* by raising their Self-Awareness, building Mental Toughness, increasing Capacity and adjusting Styles; these are all behavioural interventions which will undoubtedly assist the coachee as they transition roles. However, given the prevalence and significance of changing their roles or careers, the Leader Coach needs to be *specifically equipped* to help the coachee to successfully handle this *pivotal* chapter of their working lives. It is a period of their career fraught with danger. Egon Zehnder (2017) reported that 38 per cent of *all* external senior-hire appointments result in *outright failure*, with 60 per cent of 'hangers on' experiencing severe *delayed performance*. Why? Based on our combined insight into this area, we pinpoint seven main reasons:

o **Cultural Mismatch** – A failure to move from outsider to insider status through understanding, respecting or fitting in with the norms, nuances, customs and rituals of their new environment

o **Team Conflict** – An inability to gel with direct reports, peers and wider organisational networks

o **Strategic Disagreement** – Serious disagreements over the future short-term and long-term direction of the business and/or functional area

o **Operational Misunderstanding** – Complete lack of understanding of the business model and its key drivers (customers, products and processes)

o **Stakeholder Misalignment** – Lack of clarity (or naivety) about the performance expected of them by key stakeholders

o **Personal Incompetence** – To paraphrase Jim Collins, they find themselves 'on the wrong bus, in the wrong seat, at the wrong time'; in other words, they lack the necessary EQ, IQ and LQ firepower (emotional, intellectual and learning skills) to do the job

o **Assimilation Deficit** – No strategic, formal processes to assimilate fresh senior hires into their function or wider organisation.

Thus, transitioning jobs and/or careers is beset by several potential derailers. It is here that the Leader Coach can be of significant assistance.

MAIN TRANSITIONING CONCEPTS

Most Leader Coaches, at some point or other, will have coached or mentored somebody who is preparing to, or is in the process of, transitioning roles or careers. Smart Leader Coaches will have read up on the area, perhaps absorbing the lessons of Potts's (2015) *The Executive Transition Playbook*, which provides a sequential checklist for the transitioning process; Dotlich et al.'s (2006) *Leadership Passages*, which focuses upon navigating significant transitionary events during careers (joining, moving, stretching, assuming responsibility, dealing with failure, coping with a bad boss, losing your job, being part of an M&A, living in a different culture, finding work–life balance, facing personal upheaval, retiring etc.); and Elsner and Farrands' (2012) *Job Transitioning in New Roles*, which unpacks the 'rhetoric versus the reality' of transitioning roles (exploring the myths, reality, tensions and tools for transition). Reviewing the literature, there are several concepts – which we can group around two main headers (*behavioural* and *process*) – that will help sharpen the Leader Coach's knowledge and effectiveness in this area.

- **Behavioural Concepts** – The first set of concepts relates to how people commonly feel, think and should adjust their style during job/career transitions.

    o **Reality Shock** – Moving from the comfortable and familiar to the new and unknown draws upon *physical, intellectual and emotional resources*, often inducing sensory and neurological overload. In addition, the optimistic expectations that job/career movers have prior to moving might be rudely confounded by harsh reality. Kramer (1974) conceived jobs as involving four stages – honeymoon, shock, recovery and resolution. She defined the 'reality shock' stage as 'the total social, physical and emotional response of a person to the unexpected, unwanted or undesired, and in the most severe degree to the intolerable', citing it as the most common reason for outright failure or delayed performance during job/career transitions.

    o **Imposter Syndrome** – In addition to reality shock, job movers (particularly those moving up to senior levels of responsibility) often suffer from Imposter Syndrome (see 1.1 'Raise Self-Awareness': 'Self-Confidence'). This is a debilitating psychological pattern of feeling and thinking in which they doubt their past accomplishments, experiencing a *persistent* internalised fear of being exposed as a fraud. Despite external evidence of their competence, they secretly attribute their success to luck or deceit. Thus, once the temporary feeling of exuberance from securing the role has passed, many senior hires (especially) will ask themselves: 'am I really good enough to do this job? Have I oversold myself to get it? What will happen to me when I am found out!?' One explanation for this is that, often, *negative drivers* such as raging *self-doubt* and a visceral lack of *Self-Confidence* have resulted in *over-compensatory behaviours* that have led to improbable job/career achievement (Edger, 2019a).

    o **90-Day Dip** – In addition, a lot of research has uncovered a phenomenon that occurs when a newly placed candidate loses motivation over the first 90 days of a new role. Researchers have found that once the honeymoon period has worn off, the reality of what the job *requires* starts to set in and often leads to a fall in motivation and performance. This phenomenon is like reality shock, albeit slightly more delayed; a creeping and gradual realisation that the shoe might not fit!

o **Fit** – Ultimately, however, in addition to resolving psychological and motivational impediments, the leaders that most commonly transition successfully are adept at adjusting their style/behaviour to their new contexts. The *Harvard Business Review* article 'For Senior Leaders, Fit Matters More than Skill' (Martin, 2014) points out that outside hires take twice as long to come up to speed as internal candidates, but that their effectiveness is accelerated if they fit their style and priorities with their new cultural surroundings. Edger (2019a) takes this one stage further, by arguing that hires can only be successful if they are able to adjust their style/behaviours to the 'business lifecycle' requirements of their new surroundings:

- Start-Up – Joining during a *start-up phase*, where there are a lack of rules and procedures, the senior hire must display 'loose' and dextrous behaviours (see 1.4 'Coaching Leaders to Adjust Style')
- Growth – Coming onboard during the *growth phase*, the senior hire needs the energy and discipline to keep up with the relentless pace of the organisation's velocity
- Maturity – If they join during the *maturity phase*, the senior hire must be mentally prepared for the frustrations associated with dealing with multiple decision makers and layers of ossified hierarchy that will try to impede their progress
- Decline – Joining at the *decline stage*, the senior hire will have to adjust to the fact that they need to be geared up to grapple with and find a way through high levels of uncertainty, confusion and chaos, which could either result in triumphant rebirth or annihilation (and job loss)!

• **Process Concepts** – The other body of literature dealing with job/career transitions attempts to offer rational, process-led solutions to smoothing passages between roles.

o **Onboarding** – A substantial body of work in this area concentrates upon the art and science of organising structured induction and immersion events to ameliorate transitions. This onboarding helps 'bring the leader safely on deck', after which they are expected to do things with little guidance. Unfortunately – despite all the best-practice guides – organisations do this process notoriously badly! According to research by Egon Zehnder (2017), only 30 per cent of senior hires believe they receive meaningful support during their transition into a new organisation. Follow-on research completed by Egon Zehnder with 198 HR executives established that whilst they believed that their organisations did *'formal, structured onboarding'* well (administration, processes, procedures and 'business orientation'), they admitted that they *'aligned expectations with teams and bosses'*, *'organised meetings with stakeholders'* and *'facilitated cultural familiarisation'* badly. Factors such as time, money, politics and chaos were blamed for a lack of deep immersive, integrative mechanisms for assimilating senior hires, leading to sub-optimal outcomes (i.e. *outright failure* and *delayed performance*) for both the senior hire and the organisation.

o **Integration** – Research in the *Harvard Business Review* outlined in 'Onboarding isn't Enough' (Byford, Watkins and Triantogiannis, 2017) agreed with these findings, suggesting *integration* ('doing what it takes to make the new person a fully functioning member of the team as quickly as possible') rather than onboarding was a more aspirational goal for organisations. In this article they differentiated between *basic orientation* (information sharing), *active assimilation* (meetings and briefings) and *accelerated integration* (custom-designed experiences). They advanced a notion of deep immersion and integration (including interviewing predecessors, starting early, setting clear expectations, assigning a mentor) as being the most effective way of getting new senior hires to stick and 'produce' quickly!

o **90-Day Plan** – Another stream of writing in this area advocates leaders having a defined '90-Day Plan' on entering new roles. In his book *The First 90 Days*, Watkins (2013) outlines a number of distinct activities and phases that should underpin executive transitions in their first three months in the job, namely: prepare yourself, accelerate your learning, match strategy to situation, negotiate success, secure early wins, achieve alignment, build your team, create alliances, manage yourself and accelerate everyone (see also 2.3 'Develop Teams' and 3.3 'Spark a Change Culture').

KEY TRANSITIONING MODELS

The main behavioural and process transitioning concepts outlined above provide useful background knowledge for Leader Coaches embarking on job/career coaching. But in order to negotiate coachees successfully through role transitions, Leader Coaches require a tried and tested framework that can guide purposeful coaching conversations. Our Big Six Tasks and Six 'R's of Interference Model (see Figure 12 below) provides such a framework (Edger, 2019a):

Figure 12: The Big Six Tasks and Six 'R's of Interference

Essentially, there are two parts to this model: first, the mutually interdependent tasks that new hires must simultaneously conquer and resolve to prevent outright failure or delayed performance; second – and relatedly – the resolution of six main types of interference that can impede the execution of these six tasks. They are both outlined below, accompanied with probing questions that the Leader Coach can use to facilitate value-added coaching conversations.

- **The Big Six Tasks** – In general, successful senior hires tackle *six mutually interdependent tasks* better than their peers (Edger, 2019a). Many of these tasks are dealt with more fully in the 'Business Growth' section of this book, but it is important – with specific regard to transitioning roles – that they are reprised here, alongside some useful Leader Coach questions:

  o **Drive Strategic Clarity** – Often, transitioning leaders are confronted with organisations and functions suffering from groupthink, strategic imprecision and drift. Looking at the problem with a fresh perspective – seizing the window of opportunity in which they are expected to ring changes – smart leaders *drive* a clear strategic direction that inspires *hope* and *confidence* from top to bottom of their new organisation (see also 3.1 'Clarify Strategy'). *Questions that the Leader Coach can use to boost thinking and understanding in this area include:*

    - *What elements of your organisation/function's strategy are fit for purpose?*
    - *What elements need changing to increase its clarity, delivery and INSPIRATIONAL impact?*
    - *Describe the process you will put in place to review and change it QUICKLY – whilst achieving maximum buy-in.*

  o **Achieve Operational Grip** – Frequently, standards slip and organisations lose sight of what they are there to do, namely: satisfy and delight customers. Getting into the business quickly, smart transitioning leaders identify the root causes of operational failure by *listening* to their front-line people and closely *watching* customer behaviour (see also 3.2 'Grip Operations'). Back at base they quickly get a *grip* on the resources, processes and enablers to positively impact the customer experience; producing an immediate discretionary dividend on the front-line.

    - *What do your customers really care about/crave?*
    - *Rate where you think your organisation's quality of products/services sits on a scale of one to ten? Which elements fall short?*
    - *What could you do QUICKLY to make a difference to quality standards?*

o **Navigate Cultural Sensitivities** – Cultural mismatch is the greatest single reason for transitional leader failure. Why? Often newbies find it hard to stomach some of the cultural idiosyncrasies of their new home, taking intemperate steps to change things too quickly. Paternalistic organisations might need toughening up and bureaucratic organisations might need loosening up. The smart transitioning leaders we have worked with have trodden cautiously, *respecting* the traditions, customs, norms and central belief system of their new environments (see 3.3 'Spark a Change Culture'). They diligently avoided the *culture trap* of attempting (and failing!) to change *everything* at once.

- *Describe the culture of your new organisation… How can you improve your knowledge on this?*
- *What elements of culture give it competitive advantage or hold it back?*
- *What elements could you change QUICKLY without losing the organisation?*

o **Shape Team Cohesion** – Often, transitioning leaders are confronted with *resistance* from their new team. Why? Resentment and jealousy from those that didn't get the job and fear of change which might threaten vested interests. Those that succeed have the Emotional Intelligence to co-opt mission-critical teamers quickly, whilst swiftly rooting out toxics and saboteurs (see 2.3 'Develop Teams'). Putting together a strong, united and multi-talented team – quickly! – lies at the heart of new-hire success.

- *Tell me about your team. Rate your key people on a scale of one to ten.*
- *What are you going to do to lock down your best people?*
- *Tell me how you will create a high-performing team QUICKLY!*

o **Create Stakeholder Alignment** – Frequently, transitioning leaders enter highly political, fractious environments riven by secret agendas and self-interest. They quickly map their stakeholder needs and motives, understanding where they can generate *mutuality* and *reciprocity* rather than conflict (see also 2.4 'Align Stakeholders'). They are effective at getting key opinion formers and resource holders onside through win–win solutions, so that they can move things forwards quickly.

- *What do your key stakeholders expect from you now?*
- *What do you require from your key stakeholders?*
- *Tell me about how you will influence key stakeholders QUICKLY!*

o **Optimise Personal Impact** – Finally, smart transitioning leaders are conscious that first impressions make lasting ones. In the early stages of their new appointment they recognise that every word, gesture and deed of theirs will be judged and analysed. They actively seek to convey a sense of *authenticity, humanity, courage and discipline* in their dealings with others, which generates a climate of *trust* – the most important component of successful leadership.

- *What do you really FEEL about X?*
- *How motivational or aspirational is x as an aim? Will it get you out of bed in the morning?*
- *Describe your dream aspiration? Something that really inspires and motivates you!*
- *How would achieving this aim make you feel?*
- *What are you willing to sacrifice to achieve this aim?*
- *Tell me about how much achieving this aim means to you?*
- *What FEELINGS and attitudes do you think you need to change in order to MOVE FORWARDS?*

- **The Six 'R's of Interference** – Having probed and challenged the transitioning leader's goals in the six main impact areas, the Leader Coach will locate a number of generic derailers that threaten to impede progress. We name these the Six 'R's of Interference':

o **Dysfunctional RELATIONSHIPS** – The issue most cited by transitioning leaders is tricky and bothersome relationships with crucial *stakeholders* (particularly peers and bosses) in the early days of their tenure. Why? Many had underestimated or misread the hidden agendas, political motivations and protective self-interest of their new environment. Naively arriving on the scene, expecting collegiality, they were met with depressingly unhelpful (if not sabotaging) behaviour. What does the Leader Coach do? They help them to accept this behaviour as a matter of course, ameliorating it by forging a few solid alliances and advancing win–win solutions (increasing sales or reducing costs) that mutually benefit both parties.

- *How much control do you personally have over the outcome?*
- *Who else has some control over it and how much?*
- *Describe your engagement strategy with key players to date.*
- *I'm impressed that you have recognised that you feel negatively about x! How do you think you could change that feeling?*
- *If I understand you rightly, you really haven't been able to communicate, co-opt, coalition-build, network etc. I wonder what might assist you in forging supportive stakeholder relations?*
- *Tell me about how you are going to develop better relationships with key stakeholders. Give me examples when you have achieved harmonious relations in the past. What were the results? How did you feel?*

o **Stubborn RESISTANCE** – Very often the transitioning leader has been parachuted in to fix functional or operational issues over the heads of an existing cadre of managers. (S)he now must galvanise a *team* that harbours a degree of ambient resentment, its members also fearful for their jobs (realising that newbies often bring in their own people). What is the Leader Coach's job here? To help transitioning leaders see how they can turn resistors into advocates by generating trust. In their early days – with actions being judged more than their words – coachees need to understand how they get people onside by fostering a sense of reciprocity and indebtedness.

- *Where does resistance to you or your plans reside in the organisation?*
- *Which resistors could derail any of your BIG TASKS?*
- *What are the reasons for their opposition to you or your plans?*
- *What else did you see/feel/do when you have been in this situation before?*

- *Who do you know who has encountered similar opposition? What did they do to win people around?*

- *What advice would you give to a friend who faced similar adversity?*

o **Insufficient RESOURCES** – Often, a glowing picture of what lay in wait for the transitioning leader has been painted by the recruiters. Now, having arrived on the scene, the reality sets in! They are expected to deliver improbable *operational* goals with skeletal resources (money, people, capability and time). Having been upsold Elysian Fields only to discover a fetid bog, the transitioning leader has a choice – either cry foul or make do and manage! How can the Leader Coach help? By getting coachees to zone in on a few make-or-break big rocks; trying to focus their attention on *time, cash* and *people capability* that will secure quick wins that will generate momentum. Leader Coaches recognise that coachees who demonstrate early success stand a greater chance of attracting valuable resources more quickly.

  - *What resources do you need to execute your BIG SIX TASKS?*

  - *What resources do you already have at your disposal? (skill, time, enthusiasm, money, support, etc.)*

  - *In order of priority, list the 'show stoppers' that might derail this TASK?*

  - *I am impressed you think it's too costly! How can you make the solution less expensive?*

  - *You say that you don't have the time and resources. What elements of the task could you do with the resources you do have?*

o **Inadequate RECOGNITION** (of the issues/problems) – A major problem that a lot of transitioning leaders cite is an underestimation of how difficult it is to craft some degree of *strategic* clarity. Having been appointed to set a dynamic new direction, it had taken them longer than they thought to see the wood for the trees, despite their due diligence. What they initially perceived to be the root issues and remedies of previous strategic imprecision often turned out to be wrong! The Leader Coach's role here? To get the transitioning leader to do nothing other than watch, listen, enquire and probe as many sources as possible in the early days (i.e. customers, front-line operators, suppliers, etc.). Their three crucial questions? *What should we stop, start or continue to do to create a best-in-class business?*

- *When you say this is a major BARRIER can you be more specific; is it more/less than who/what?*
- *Rate your knowledge of this TASK and how to get it done on a scale of one to ten (one = 'I don't have a clue', ten = 'I am all over it!').*
- *What is holding you back from gaining more knowledge about how to nail this TASK?*
- *If you were advising yourself about getting to the heart of this problem, what would you say?*
- *What would your most-trusted advisor tell you to do NOW to get the roots of this problem?*

o **Lack of RESPECT** – Often, transitioning leaders are told by recruiters that their new position represents a chance for them to contribute to changing the *culture*. Flattered and aroused, they enter their new role with a predetermined disrespect for its norms, customs, values, icons, stories and traditions (see 3.3 'Spark a Change Culture': 'Culture Web'). They are there to make a difference! Unwittingly, they fall straight into the cultural trap and – unless they change their tune pretty quickly – are run out of the organisation. The Leader Coach's role here? To get the leader to acknowledge that, although they have been appointed to govern in prose by their recruiters, they must deftly lead through poetry. Leader Coaches must help the transitioning leader to assimilate and integrate themselves by praising and respecting the cultural aspects of their new home, whilst sensitively ringing a few subtle changes that challenge redundant orthodoxies.

- *How would others describe your level of empathy/understanding for others?*
- *What is your state of mind before and during meetings with a) direct reports, b) other business stakeholders and c) more senior people?*
- *What NEGATIVE thoughts and feelings would the most trusted person you know tell you to change NOW in order to advance and progress?*

- *How are you going to flip your internal conversations about the people and culture around you from negative to positive territory? List three great things that you admire about your new cultural context.*

- *How will you and other people be able to see the difference? How proud would you (AND THEY) be of this achievement?*

o **Collapsing RESOLVE** – Having been sold the dream job, transitioning leaders often discover that they have entered a dystopian nightmare! After a short while in situ they suffer the classic 90-day dip (see above), diluting their *personal impact.* They question why they took the job in the first place and how they can possibly cope with everything. Their inner conversations are becoming increasingly fraught and immobilising. How can the Leader Coach assist? By helping the transitioning leader to modify their expectations/perceptions so that the coachee is either unperturbed when they find chaos or pleasantly surprised when they don't. Second, by facilitating insight into the coachee's levels of Emotional Control and self-management, and how they can exercise a high level of Mental Toughness under pressure (see the preceding four sections).

- *On a scale of 1 to 10 ('not at all' being 1 and 10 being 'a lot') how much is the achievement of this aim related to your personal mindset and behaviour?*

- *If you asked x, what would they say about you? What would they say might really prevent you from achieving this aim?*

- *Tell me about your secret/hidden fears, anxieties and insecurities about the position you are in now and where you want to go in the future.*

- *What are you holding back from me? What do you really think and FEEL? Describe to me what is running through your mind when you get up in the morning or are alone working from home or in the car.*

- *Given all the interference and barriers you face, what do you do to keep going? Tell me about the personal qualities and reserves you currently draw upon to cope with your situation.*

- *If you were to wake up tomorrow and your negative thoughts and insecurities were gone, how would you feel? What do you think you could achieve?*
- *Tell me about all the great PERMANENT INTERNAL QUALITIES you have. How can you leverage them to successfully overcome this TEMPORARY EXTERNAL INTERFERENCE?*

The case study below showcases the BUILD-RAISE Coaching 'reframing questioning method' outlined in 'Courageous Coaching' sections 4.4 and 4.5. In order to bring these concepts alive, the case study practically illustrates how a Leader Coach can help senior business leaders tackle some of the Big Six Tasks outlined above by acknowledging, confronting and potentially overcoming some of the Six 'R's of Interference (particularly relationships and respect) during their transitional stage.

CASE STUDY – TARGETED TRANSITIONAL COACHING (TTC)

Targeted Transitional Coaching (TTC) of a Transitioning Hospitality CEO using the BUILD-RAISE Model

In this case study (which is based on a real-life interaction) the Leader Coach and the newly appointed CEO of a medium-sized multi-brand hospitality company 'Eat Co' (£650m turnover, 16,000 staff, £52m EBITDA) are having their third coaching conversation. The company has been owned by private equity for five years and has had a couple of turbulent years trading, due to increases in input costs (labour, rent, rates, goods) and ferocious competition caused by a wave of new openings. The CEO – who has 32 years' experience in the industry – has now been in-situ for 30 days (facing the so-called '30-day dip'), having been appointed to stabilise and grow Eat Co to provide the private equity owners with an exit route within two years. Prior to joining Eat Co, this CEO had conducted extensive due diligence and, during his first 30 days, had spent a considerable amount of time in the business listening to employees and Eat Co consumer behaviour. During their last two coaching conversations, the Leader Coach established a good rapport with the CEO. The first session concentrated on readiness and the BIG SIX TASKS and the second focused on achieving OPERATIONAL GRIP.

STEP 1 – BUILD RAPPORT

LEADER COACH – Good to see you again! How are the family? How did your daughter get on? [*LEADER COACH facilitates 'problem free talk' to uncover any fresh anxieties and concerns.*]

CEO – Alright, thanks. But I have to say my family aren't seeing a lot of me at the moment! It's pretty full on… the private-equity boys want to know what our plan is!

LEADER COACH – At the end of our last session we agreed that you were going to go after some **OPERATIONAL** 'low-hanging fruit' to improve morale and service. How did you get on? On a scale of 1 to 10, how successful have you been in such a short space of time? [*LEADER COACH recaps last session's BIG SIX TASKS aim.*]

CEO – 8–9! For instance, as we discussed, I went back to my **TEAM** and sold in my idea to get rid of 'daily labour dial-in' meetings between the Area Managers and their GMs… and the sense of relief has been enormous. I've agreed that we'll only expect Area Managers to have dial-ins with the real problem children (about 10 per cent of the estate). This has immediately freed up time for everyone, removed the **CULTURE** of fear, and got people onto the front foot, doing what they should be doing: delighting customers! Early days, but feedback is great.

LEADER COACH – So that session was useful then? [*LEADER COACH establishes utility of the coaching sessions*]

CEO – Yes, it made me focus on something really tangible that would release discretionary effort immediately.

LEADER COACH – [Gets out the BIG SIX TASKS pictorial] We looked at this BIG SIX TASKS Model in the previous couple of sessions. Looking at it now, what would be the **most valuable task or topic** to focus upon? What is bothering you or concerning you now? What will accelerate performance over the next 60 days? You mentioned that the private-equity guys wanted a definitive plan? [*LEADER COACH picks up on the previous cue.*]

CEO – Yes. 30 days in and they want a plan out of me that solves it all and allows them to walk away with a pot of gold. No pressure! So looking at the model, it's all about clarifying **STRATEGY** and aligning **STAKEHOLDERS** at present. [*LEADER COACH has used the BIG SIX TASKS Model to focus discussion.*]

LEADER COACH – That's great. So, to recap: you would find it useful to focus on how you get a STRATEGY together and get your STAKEHOLDERS onboard? [*LEADER COACH checks for understanding and buy-in to a meaningful topic.*]

CEO – Absolutely. Can't hold it off any longer!

STEP 2 – UNCOVER AIM

LEADER COACH – So you want to talk about how you put together a STRATEGIC PLAN that gets the STAKEHOLDERS to where they want to be: exiting within two years. Look at this model [gets out the Strategic Pyramid Model] – take time to have a think. What is the company's strategy at the moment? [*LEADER COACH focuses upon* **STRATEGIC CONTENT** *first – checking the CEO's understanding of the present position by using the Strategic Pyramid pictorial.*]

CEO – Well, I don't have it in front of me at the moment – but broadly... [The CEO articulates the current Vision, Mission, Purpose, Objectives and KPIs of the organisation, with the LEADER COACH checking for understanding.]

LEADER COACH – Thankyou; that was insightful. Look at this model [gets out the Paths to Growth Model]. So what strategy is the company broadly pursuing at the moment: market penetration, new market development, product development and/or diversification? [A discussion ensues where the CEO outlines what the company's growth strategy is.]

CEO – ... So in the end I think it comes down to the fact that although the company talks about new market development (to recruit new customers) and product development (to increase the frequency of existing customers) it actually comes down to the fact that they are obsessed with market penetration (selling more of the same stuff to existing customers). They actually have a price-led strategy rather than an innovation-led strategy that can drive margin and new customer recruitment! This isn't sustainable. We have no real point of difference and we are trying to milk the same customers.

LEADER COACH – OK. To recap: their strategy says one thing but they are actually doing the opposite?

CEO – Yes. I think the previous team were panicked into taking short-term measures – slamming down on labour and pursuing a price-led volume strategy. It is my belief that we will only be able to build equity back into the company by taking a more long-term view. But this a huge task – there's no way that I can get all of this fixed to hit their two-year deadline!

LEADER COACH – That's understandable. What elements could you focus upon now? [*RESISTANCE REFRAMING QUESTION*] If you were advising a friend in a similar situation, what would you advise NOW? [*RELATIONALLY BASED REFRAMING QUESTION*]

CEO – Fix and Grow! Fix the biggest brand in the portfolio (over 300 sites) that's dragging the whole company down (wasting management time and resources)… Grow the two smaller high-velocity brands that are showing real promise by targeting investment at them.

LEADER COACH – So, to recap: your STRATEGIC goal is 'Fix the Big Brand and Grow the Two High-Velocity Brands'?

CEO – Yes. But selling that into the private-equity guys won't be easy!

STEP 3 – IDENTIFY INTERFERENCE

LEADER COACH – You mentioned your key private-equity STAKEHOLDER. You said that they want you to turn the company around so that they can exit in two years? Tell me a bit more about them.

CEO – Basically, they've got three 'advisors' on our Board – the key guy is Tim (he's got the ear of the private-equity owner). He doesn't know anything about leisure and hospitality though. He's a kid who's come up through investment banking! I've already had a couple of tough conversations with him! He seems like a right twat. Thinks we can price-cut our way to victory and knock out the competition. 'Race to the bottom' stuff. Seen it too many times in this industry. Vouchering, couponing, discounting equals disaster. No way back! [***RELATIONSHIP AND RESPECT** issues are starting to emerge!*]

LEADER COACH – And at this early stage – from what you've seen and learnt – you would want the company to run with a more nuanced 'Fix and Grow' strategy.

CEO – Yes. Obviously I'm going to have to get everyone together and thrash it out at a Strategic Review day. But I'm going to have to bring Tim around beforehand because he is the trusted 'eyes and ears' of the owners.

LEADER COACH – On a scale of 1 to 10 (1 being 'non-existent' and 10 being 'excellent') how would you rate your relationship with Tim at the moment and where does it need to be? [*SCALING REFRAMING QUESTION*]

CEO – It's 2 at present. It needs to be at least a 7!

STEP 4 – LOCATE SOLUTION

LEADER COACH – OK [gets out the Points of Powers Model]. Looking at this model, how do you think you will be able to influence your STAKEHOLDERS – and Tim in particular?

CEO – Well obviously, I work for them; so not through *position*. They can sack me; so not through *coercion*. I suppose through *reward* (if I can show how much value I can put on this company), *expertise* (because I can demonstrate that I know what I'm taking about) and good *relations* (by getting on with them). But I just don't think I will ever relate to Tim!

LEADER COACH – So, to date you really haven't been able to communicate in order to develop a relationship with Tim. I wonder what might assist in creating good communications. [*POSSIBILITY REFRAMING QUESTION*]

CEO – Look, I knew when I took the job that I would be dealing with idiots like this. I've been there, done it, got the tee-shirt!

LEADER COACH – So you've worked for owners and people as difficult as Tim in the past! Tell me about the times or situations in which you were able to work well together. What did you do? [*EXCEPTION REFRAMING QUESTION*]

CEO – Looking back on it, I spent a lot of time with them out in the business. Discuss, talk, explain, win over. But with this guy… I don't know…

LEADER COACH – You really have severe reservations based on the couple of conversations you've had with him! Tell me who would be surprised to hear you say that. If you had a friend in a similar situation, what would you advise? [*RELATIONALLY BASED REFRAMING QUESTION*]

CEO – People who know me would say 'Typical – you make snap judgements about people! And just because you don't RESPECT this guy you will let this get in the way of creating a good RELATIONSHIP'. If I was advising a friend I would say 'grow up! There is as much pressure on this guy as there is on you to grow the business – and you can help him learn and understand how we can build this business!'

LEADER COACH – So, to recap: you and Tim have a MUTUAL interest in growing this business. You can build a **RELATIONSHIP** by showing a little more **RESPECT** for his predicament. In the end he might buy-in to your 'Fix and Grow' strategy.

CEO – Yeh. Thinking about it, I really haven't had enough time with Tim. My attitude towards him is based on a couple of chats. I need to bring him onboard with where I think the company needs to go. After all, that's what they brought me in for!

STEP 5 – DETERMINE EXECUTION

LEADER COACH – [Summarises the discussion] … After 30 days you want to get stuck into the STRATEGY but you will need STAKEHOLDER alignment. Your *aim* (at this stage) is to get a 'Fix and Grow' strategy off the ground… You think that the main *interference* to this will come from Tim (the owner's enforcer)… You rate your current relationship with him as being 2/10 but believe that it needs to be 7/10 at least… You recognise that you need to build a **RELATIONSHIP** with him, showing **RESPECT** for the pressures he faces himself! … What will you do next?

CEO – I am going to go out of this meeting and phone Tim up. I'm going to tell him that I want to trigger a quick Strategic Review but I want to spend time with him out in the business beforehand. We will visit the big brand that needs fixing and the two high-velocity, smaller brands that need growing through targeted investment. This – in my view – will form the bedrock of the turnaround.

LEADER COACH – If you could envision a situation where you had got Tim onside and that your relationship had become a 7/10, how would you feel? What would your life be like? [*MIRACLE REFRAMING QUESTION*]

CEO – Bloody relieved. Unstressed! I'd be able to attack the turnaround QUICKLY!

LEADER COACH – Good. Let me know how your call goes and talk to me – if you need to – before you go out into the business with Tim.

ACCELERATING TRANSITIONS WITH COACHEES

The models, concepts and case study above provide valuable guidance and insight for Leader Coaches engaged in accelerating leader job/career transitions. They provide a rational 'targeted transitional coaching' (TTC) framework that the Leader Coach can use to probe and challenge the prejudices, fears and myopic thinking of transitioning leaders. But this is not sufficient. As we have highlighted, major transitioning derailers include Imposter Syndrome and 'reality shock' (see above). Where these feelings are particularly embedded, Leader Coaches will require more sophisticated strategies to reframe attitudes and behaviours. What and how?

It is our contention that individuals who perform consistently well possess an innate belief that they have an ability and capacity to do so. They are blessed with a grounded sense of quiet inner Self-Confidence. However, those who suffer from Imposter Syndrome and experience severe levels of 'reality shock' are – usually – lacking in this regard. How can Leader Coaches help further build (see 1.1 'Raise Self-Awareness' and 1.2 'Build Mental Toughness') coachee inner Self-Confidence to transcend or counteract these feelings? The Affirmations Model (see Figure 13 below) is a useful framework that Leader Coaches can use with transitioning leaders in order to increase their levels of belief, optimism and resilience. Through using this model, Leader Coaches can help transitioning leaders *build up strong affirmations to expect and believe* that what they are aiming for is achievable. In some senses, its antecedents lie in Positive Psychology, namely: people who consciously build up powerful 'positive affirmations' are more likely to succeed than those with negative expectations who subconsciously burden themselves with affirmations of preordained failure (see 1.3 'Increase Capacity': 'Positive Mindset'). Also, as people are generally drawn to 'positive affirmers', they can further boost their Self-Confidence through the cheerleading support and engagement of others.

Thus, the Affirmations Model (Figure 13) – based upon Steele's (1988) theory of self-affirmation – can be used to build optimism, confidence, Mental Toughness and positive expectations, supporting the framing of stretching and demanding goals, resulting in superior outcomes and results.

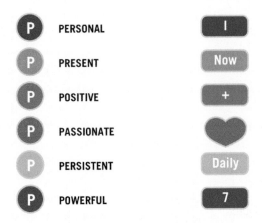

Figure 13: The Affirmations Model

How is it applied? By using the model as a checklist to guide and challenge transitional leaders to *write down positive affirmations that conform to the six 'P' essential rules*:

o **Rule 1 – Personal**: Beginning with the singular, first-person 'I'. This helps create and establish a positive sense of future identity and accountability.

o **Rule 2 – Present**: Written as 'now'; imagining what is desired is already in place. This is the vital disruptive component that causes the subconscious mind to become active and create connections for realising the affirmation. It is the catalyst for making things happen that would not otherwise occur.

o **Rule 3 – Positive**: Written in the positive; doing rather than waiting, winning rather than losing, achieving an opportunity rather than being risk averse.

o **Rule 4 – Passionate**: Written with genuine emotion so that they resonate and mean something to the individual. This raw emotional power will energise the discipline, focus, belief and confidence required to achieve outstanding results.

o **Rule 5 – Persistent**: Invokes the need for discipline. If someone is persistent enough to write down their affirmations for a few minutes every day they will supercharge their journey into outstanding outcomes.

o **Rule 6 – Powerful**: Affirmations will be at their strongest when they strike the right balance and blend. Writing seven affirmations, seven days a week is highly recommended for the most amazing results. If any of the affirmations become less positive or passionate over time, they need to be upgraded to keep motivating.

What do positive affirmations look like within the context of successfully transitioning jobs/careers? Here are some examples:

o TEAM – I have created the most energised, proactive and *customer-loving* team in this organisation

o STAKEHOLDERS – I have reached out to engage and *charm* all our principal stakeholders so that they become our friends

o STRATEGY – I have created a *buzzing*, exciting and bold strategy that will *transform* this organisation

o PERSONAL – I am doing important, *worthwhile work* that I believe in and contributes to the *wellbeing and happiness* of all those around me.

In effect, what the Leader Coach is aiming to do here (with the assistance of the Model of Affirmations and its six golden rules) is to give the transitioning leader the ambition and Self-Confidence to make their aspirations self-fulfilling prophesies. Once thought through and committed to, what is written down will (likely) become reality! It becomes the transitional leader's proxy manifesto – something that is open to review and upgrade should something even more inspiring come to mind.

QUICK RECAP: LEADER COACHING TO TRANSITION ROLES/CAREERS

o **Why?** – Prevent delayed performance or outright failure!

o **Main Concepts?** – Reality shock, Imposter Syndrome, 90-day dip, onboarding, integration, 90 day plan

o **How?** Coaching conversations using:

- **Big Six Tasks Model:**
  - Drive Strategic Clarity
  - Achieve Operational Grip

- Navigate Cultural Sensitivities
- Shape Team Cohesion
- Create Stakeholder Alignment
- Optimise Personal Impact
- **Six 'R's of Interference:**
  - Dysfunctional Relationships
  - Stubborn Resistance
  - Insufficient Resources
  - Inadequate Recognition (of issues)
  - Lack of Respect
  - Febrile Resolve
- o **Accelerate Transitional Coaching? Use:**
  - **Affirmations Model**
    - Reinforce personal affirmations that are personal, present, positive, passionate, persistent and powerful!

BRIEF CHAPTER SUMMARY – ADVANCING PERSONAL GROWTH

This chapter has outlined several strategies and methodologies that Leader Coaches can deploy to help coachees with their personal growth. It is – in our view – the most important chapter of the book. Why? Because leadership starts with personal readiness to lead. If an individual lacks Self-Awareness, Mental Toughness, installed Capacity, an appropriate leadership Style and/ or ability to Transition Roles, (s)he will ultimately be found wanting in highly pressurised leadership positions.

To this extent, in this chapter we have advocated that Leader Coaches:

- **Raise Leader Self-Awareness** by prompting *better Emotional Awareness*, *Accurate Self-Assessment* and *heightened Self-Confidence* through challenging conversations. Real acceleration can be gained through accompanying these conversations with insightful *psychometric test data*.

- **Build Leader Mental Toughness** by helping to reduce their stressors through focusing upon strengthening their Four 'C's (*Control, Challenge, Commitment and Confidence*) levels of resilience. Acceleration in this area can be achieved by using AQR's *MTQ48Plus* test instrument that will facilitate extremely rich dialogue around areas of weakness that require toughening.

- **Increase Leader Capacity** by assisting them to understand how *Self-Investment, Effective Time Management, Striving for Obsoletion,* a *Positive Mindset* and Building a *Support Network* can increase their bandwidth. Accelerated Capacity growth can be facilitated through an in-depth *CPD (continuous professional development)* conversation.

- **Adjust Leader Styles** by analysing what the requirements of their situation are and helping them adjust their Style to suit across six continuums: *task–person, flexible–dogmatic, de-centralised–centralised, reward–punishment, the means–the end* and *structured–organic*. Accelerated interventions that the Leader Coach can use to facilitate adjustments include the ILM72 leadership Style test, which surfaces three 'global factors' of leadership effectiveness: *determination to deliver, engagement with individuals* and *engagement with teams*.

- **Assist Leader Transitions** to prevent delayed performance or outright failure in new roles by having coaching conversations around the *Big Six Tasks* (*strategic clarity, operational grip, cultural sensitivity, team cohesion, stakeholder alignment* and *personal optimisation*) in which the Leader Coach helps ameliorate some or all of the *Six R's of Interference* (*dysfunctional relationships, stubborn resistance, insufficient resources, inadequate recognition of the issues, lack of respect* and *febrile resolve*).

But ultimately, the key point for Leader Coaches is this: leaders will be fully functional and impactful if – as the Advanced Leader Coaching Model highlights – they are able to *think clearly* and *feel positive* about themselves. This will enable them to radiate contagious energy – something that is highly necessary for the next construct in our model, namely, advancing interpersonal growth.

2 ADVANCING LEADER INTERPERSONAL GROWTH

The previous chapter examined and explained how Leader Coaches can help their coachees achieve a degree of personal growth by focusing on several core areas and issues that might be derailing or incapacitating them. To this extent, as the model in Figure 14 shows, they will have focused on assisting coachees improve their *Emotional Intelligence, recognising* and *self-regulating* their attitude, thoughts and feelings in a more proactive, positive manner (Goleman, 1998). As the model demonstrates, the value of this is that it has a behavioural knock-on effect with regards to improving their levels of *social awareness* and *relations* with others.

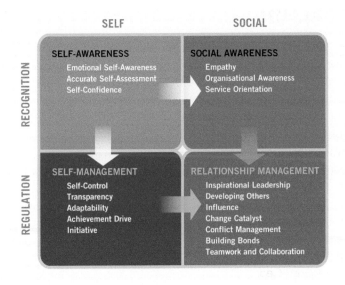

Figure 14: Interpersonal Skills Model

The net result, then, of Leader Coaches actively nurturing personal growth – as our integrated Advanced Leader Coaching Model *also* illustrates – is that coachees will have a better chance of improving their interpersonal skills. Undoubtedly, leaders with high levels of self-awareness and self-management who 'know themselves' stand a far greater chance of knowing (and motivating) others. And this is critical. Leadership is all about galvanising and inspiring organisations/teams to achieve worthwhile and stretching goals in often-adverse circumstances. If leaders are unable to sort their own mindset out, how can they expect to ignite others? Unless, of course, they lazily expect people to get excited on their own behalf!

So, the next area of Advanced Leader Coaching practice that must be mastered by all Leader Coaches is encouraging coachees to hone their levels of inter-personal growth by upping their *Emotional Intelligence*. How? By learning and applying the concepts, key models and coaching techniques that underpin motivating *employees*, igniting *customers*, developing *teams* and aligning *stakeholders*. These will now be considered.

2.1 COACHING LEADERS TO MOTIVATE EMPLOYEES

The first port of call for leaders wishing to embark on a journey of interpersonal growth is reviewing and addressing how they interact with and motivate their people. Why? Businesses amount to nothing without the ignition of human skill, passion and endeavour. Multitudinous books have been written about the importance of adopting a people-centric approach – including *Employees First, Customers Second* (Nayar, 2010) and *Make Your People Before You Make Your Products* (Turner and Kalman, 2014) – and yet it remains surprising (and disconcerting) that so many leaders fail to get this truism.

But what is motivation, its benefits and its reality in the workplace? First, a definition: the word 'motivation' is derived from the Latin root word 'movere', meaning movement, so in this regard it can be defined as '*moving people*'. But in what direction? George and Jones (2008) define employee motivation as 'the (positive) psychological forces that determine the direction of a person's behaviour in an organisation, a person's level of effort and a person's level of persistence', whilst more generally it can be described as the level of energy, commitment and creativity that a company's workers bring to their jobs. Second, what are its benefits? Voluminous study and research has established that, among other things, highly motivated employees are more engaged, committed, satisfied and productive, *more likely* to have better mental health, less inclination to quit, more interest in personal development and involve-ment, *enabling* organisations to reach their goals, increase output, improve efficiency and enhance quality. Third, let's consider the reality. In 2017, after an extensive survey of 10,000 UK workers' perceptions, Gallup revealed that:

just 8% of employed Britons are engaged at work… only one in twelve employees are highly involved in and enthusiastic about their work and workplaces… [and] the bulk of employees in the UK – 73% – are classified as 'not engaged' meaning that they are psychologically unattached and putting little energy or passion into their work… [T]he remaining 19% are 'actively disengaged', resentful that their workplace needs are not being met and likely to be acting out their unhappiness on the job…

(Crabtree, 2017)

These shocking findings run counter to what most leaders we have coached tell us, namely, they rate managing and leading people as their greatest strength! Clearly – as the Gallup survey showed – there is vast room for improvement for swathes of British management, who clearly do not understand how to satisfy the *needs, feelings and aspirations* of their employees, by applying a range of motivational mechanisms that will positively move, shift and supercharge behaviours! Quite the contrary, more often than not they are inclined (whatever they might say) to apply *Theory X transactional* techniques rather than *Theory Y transformational* approaches to achieve their objectives. Undoubtedly, the Leader Coach has a significant role to play in helping many coachees to modify their motivational style to get the best out of their people.

MAIN MOTIVATION CONCEPTS

All Leader Coaches will have their own view, formed from practice, experience and education, as to what constitutes employee-motivation best practice. Prior to embarking on coaching conversations in this area, however, it would do them no harm to remind themselves as to the main concepts underpinning this critical area:

- ***Internal and External Motivators*** – Motivation is conceived by psychologists as being internal (intrinsic) and external (extrinsic), with the former being regarded as far more powerful and long-lasting than the latter.

  - *Intrinsic Motivation* describes human behaviour that is driven by *internal rewards* (Deci, 1972). Hence, people are intrinsically motivated to engage in tasks and goals from within, because of the *naturally satisfying nature of the task to the individual*. Basic psychological needs that are satisfied by this driver include autonomy, knowledge, competence/mastery, social relatedness and meaning.

- *Extrinsic Motivation* refers to behaviour that is driven by *external rewards*, where personal goals are *focused purely on outcomes* and don't (necessarily) satisfy basic psychological needs. Goals here include external gains such as money, fame, power, praise or avoiding punishment!

- **Hierarchy** – In contrast to this binary view of motivation, Maslow's (1943) Hierarchy of Needs, outlined in 'A Theory of Human Motivation', argues that people's needs are satisfied *progressively*. Basic needs must be met within humans prior to the setting and satisfaction of higher-order goals and aspirations. According to Maslow, these most basic needs are *physiological needs* (having enough to eat and drink, warmth, shelter and rest), followed by *safety needs and protection* (job security and good health). Beyond that, Maslow described *social needs* (associated with working in groups and other people), then *psychological ego needs* (how other people acknowledge you and what you do) and, finally, the pinnacle of *self-actualisation needs* (how you regard yourself and how you are regarded). Quite simply, people need to attain *physiological* safety and security before they attain *psychological and social* enrichment.

- **Expectancy** – But to others, human motivation is not only a factor of internal, external or progressive drivers; it is also a function of the *expectation of desired outcomes*. Vroom's Expectancy Theory (1973) posits that people will expend effort when they sincerely believe their goals are worthwhile, achievable and will lead to desired rewards. To this end, he constructed a motivational equation encompassing four concepts: $f = v + e + i$, meaning **force** (a person's motivation to perform) is contingent upon **valence** (the attractiveness of potential rewards) plus **expectancy** (a person's belief that the performance goals are attainable) plus **instrumentality** (a belief that good performance will be well rewarded).

- **Goals** – This belief that motivation is connected to the perceived fairness, equity and achievability of goals is extended by Locke's Goal Theory (1968). This conceives that employers who set realistic and challenging goals for their staff not only generate employee motivation (enabling employees to engage in their job and achieve satisfaction in achieving a goal) but that also, this allows them to progressively set more ambitious new goals that will propel business momentum. Later he expanded his theory to encompass five key principles which underpin the motivation and accomplishment and completion of a goal, namely: *clarity* (unambiguous), *challenge* (significant), *commitment* (buy-in), *feedback* (on progress and recognition) and *complexity* (stretching not overwhelming). Subsequent models have followed these principles such as SMARTER (Doran, 1981) where goals are conceived as motivational when they are *specific, measurable, assignable, relevant, timely, evaluated and reviewed*.

- **Best Practice** – Following on from the Human Relations School of enquiry into motivation, the field of HRM in the 1990s attempted to identify and categorise key employee motivators. Researchers attempted to prove the efficacy of 'best fit HRM', 'best practice HRM' and 'bundles of high-performance work practices' upon employee motivation. Their conclusion? Employee motivation is situational (based upon the needs and desires of the individual and the performance of the organisation) but certain practices are motivational whatever their context, such as Pfeffer's (1998) '7 Practices for Building Profits by Putting People First', namely: *employment security, selective hiring, self-managed teams or team working, high pay contingent on company performance, extensive training, reduction of status differences and information sharing*. Basically, a combination of the intrinsic and extrinsic motivators outlined above!

KEY MOTIVATION MODELS

Having reminded themselves about or digested the core concepts surrounding employee motivation, the Leader Coach requires a couple of models with which they can frame coaching conversations to probe, challenge and reframe perspectives. Which ones should they use? We would advocate Herzberg's (1987) Two Factor Model of Motivation (which illustrates and simplifies the concepts of intrinsic and extrinsic motivation) and our own Reward and Recognition Model (Edger, 2015). What are the principles and factors underlying these models and how can Leader Coaches use them?

First, let's consider Herzberg's seminal Two Factor Motivation Model (TFMM). In this model (see Figure 15) Herzberg sought to illustrate what drove human behaviour in the workplace, proposing a 'two factor' motivator-hygiene theory as an explanation for satisfaction/motivation. Its underlying assumption is that the two main drivers which shape satisfaction at work are completely different and, as such, require specific practice and policy responses from management, namely *hygiene factors* and *motivators*.

- **Hygiene Factors** – These *'context'* factors need to be in place first to prevent dissatisfaction. Although (for most people) they do not motivate behaviours, their improvement minimises the chances of 'base' dissatisfaction and can increase productivity/work outputs. Importantly, *motivators* (see below) will not work properly unless hygiene factors are properly accounted for, for individuals and/or teams. Hence organisations should ensure that hygiene factors such as equitable reward, good working conditions, transparent/fair company policies, healthy boss–subordinate relations and sufficient resources to do the job (Maslow's so-called physiological and security-based 'motivational needs') are in place so that workers are not *extrinsically* detached and demotivated.

- **Motivators** – These *'content'* factors are 'positive satisfiers' when they are present at work, leading to enhanced levels of discretionary effort by workers. They are only effective if they are underscored by appropriate hygiene factors. Elements in this motivational category include opportunities to feel a sense of achievement, meritocratic chances of promotion, due recognition for effort, the ability to display some self-expression and interesting dimensions to the job. These so-called *intrinsic* motivators also accord with Maslow's notions of 'higher level' human motivational requirement for 'self-actualisation'.

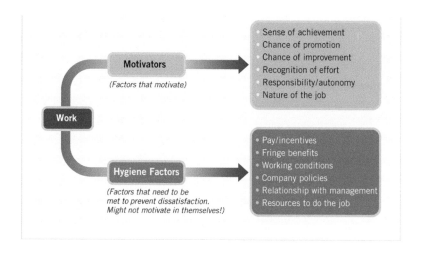

Figure 15: Two Factor Motivation Model

Thus leaders should pay attention to whether *hygiene* factors are in place before they apply/drive *motivator* factors; otherwise, they could be wasting precious time and effort. For instance, efforts to *satisfy* will be compromised by constant gripes/carping concerning poor working conditions and a lack of resources to do the job.

How can the Leader Coach use this model with coachees? Having explained the TFMM, the Leader Coach can ask a series of questions around each construct to probe understanding and effectiveness in this vital area:

- **Hygiene Factors**
  - *Pay/Incentives: To what extent do these meet your employees' basic needs and aspirations?*
  - *Fringe benefits: Tell me how they add to the overall employment brand and employee experience?*
  - *Working conditions: How safe, secure, clean and tolerable are they? How do they meet the needs and wellbeing of your employees?*
  - *Company policies: How fair, equitable and transparent are your employee policies (as regards to sickness, grievances, disciplinary, rules of attendance, etc.)?*
  - *Relationship with management: How collegiate and harmonious are your relationships with your people?*
  - *Resources to do the job: What tools do you provide your employees to do their work to time and specification? What are they lacking?*

- **Motivators**
  - *Sense of achievement: How do you ensure that your people feel a real sense of achievement from the work that they do?*
  - *Chance of promotion: How transparent are the progression paths within your unit/organisation?*
  - *Chance of improvement: What training and development programmes do you have in place to increase skills, capability and competence?*
  - *Recognition of effort: What formal/informal practices do you deploy to recognise attitude, effort and/or performance?*
  - *Responsibility/autonomy: How do you empower your people to do the best possible job for their internal/external customer?*
  - *Nature of the job: What aspects of your employees' roles give them a sense of meaning and fulfilment?*

The second model we advocate that Leader Coaches use to raise awareness and critical reflection around employee motivation is our Reward and Recognition Model (RRM – Figure 16). This posits two layers of reward and recognition organisations, one determined by *company policy* and the other (subdivided into formal and informal categories) which can be driven by 'local' *leader discretion*:

- **Company Discretion** – At the centre of the RRM lies the company's total reward and recognition practices, including important hygiene factors such as its base-pay parameters and benefits package. These are generally fixed and cannot be influenced by the leader per se.

- **Leader Discretion –**

  - *Local Formal Recognition* – Leaders have a bundle of recognition tools that they can deploy at the workplace level to motivate their team/subordinates. These are usually *tangible* and *visible* (see model below).

  - *Local Informal Recognition* – These are less formal, more intangible, but nonetheless just as important. Leaders use *currencies of exchange* with followers that build up emotional *bank accounts* amongst employees which they can 'draw down' at critical times. This type of informal recognition generates powerful reciprocity and *indebtedness* from recipients resulting in enhanced exchanges of discretionary effort, loyalty and engagement which helps the leader to achieve operational excellence and business growth without direct daily supervision.

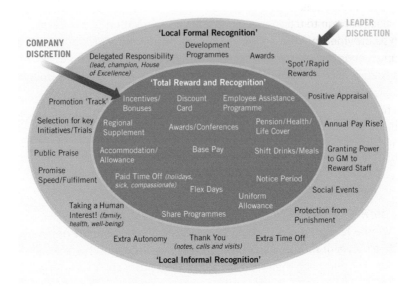

Figure 16: Reward and Recognition Model

How can Leader Coaches use this model with coachees? They can use it as a proxy checklist to review the reward and recognition toolkit at the coachee's disposal, checking that their 'deployed practices' fit with the behavioural outcomes they wish to stimulate from certain individuals and cohorts of employees (i.e. matching interventions and practices to specific needs, feelings and desires). For instance, 'Star' employees will most likely value development/progression opportunities whilst 'Pillar' employees might value responsibility, autonomy, protection from punishment or a heartfelt 'thank you' more highly! In all probability – and certainly in our experience – the RRM will allow the Leader Coach to have a rich coaching conversation to unpack what practices they perceive they use to motivate people and how effective/appropriate these might be.

ACCELERATING EMPLOYEE MOTIVATION WITH COACHEES

The models above will undoubtedly prompt some stimulating coaching conversations, helping the coachee to question whether they are deploying the right motivational techniques, to the right people, at the right time! But this is not enough to truly accelerate interpersonal growth. Why? Because the analysis provided by the coachee on their motivational techniques is largely circumstantial, drawn from *their own perceptions* of their effectiveness rather than from the *recipients* of those impacted by their motivational techniques. Real progress can be made when – in addition to the above – the Leader Coach has access to fresh 180- or 360-degree Employee Engagement or Leadership Development data that yields empirical information about their motivational prowess. Using valuable data from such sources (accounting for 'outlier' and 'contaminated' scores) improves the validity, reliability and impact of coaching conversations in this area.

How do we suggest Leader Coaches facilitate conversations on raw 180- or 360-degree feedback data on how direct reports and line managers rate a coachee's level of motivational powers?

- *Understand – Check that the coachee understands the model and constructs underlying the 180- or 360-degree survey*
- *Buy-In – Establish that the coachee believes in the veracity and importance of the survey feedback (crucial if progress is going to be made on altering behaviours)*
- *Evaluation – Get the coachee themselves to say what they think the data means (this will allow the Leader Coach to identify and locate self-justifying attitudes and behaviours)*
- *Reflection – Having got the coachee to explain what they believe the data says and means, the Leader Coach can ask a number of probing questions in a structured conversation (following the framework provided by the survey instrument), unpacking some of the gaps, discrepancies, anomalies or examples of poor practice*
- *Action – Having finally garnered an accurate interpretation of the survey feedback, the Leader Coach needs to elicit a commitment to seriously address perceived gaps and shortcomings so that the coachee can improve their employee motivation techniques*
- *Review – In further coaching conversations, the Leader Coach can ask for tangible evidence of rectifying behaviours. In an ideal world, the Leader Coach would be able to inspect a timely follow-up survey to measure progress!*

But what sort of questions and constructs in 180- or 360-degree Employee Engagement or Leadership Development surveys really count? Often these surveys have a battery of questions that are related to multiple factors (such as company strategy and organisational reward policy) that are not necessarily connected to the coachee's *personal* capacity to motivate employees. In previous research we conducted (Edger, 2012, p.128) we located a specific set of questions in employee surveys which *linked leader behaviour to positive performance outcomes*. We found that leaders who scored well on the questions below were empirically proven to outperform their peers:

- *My manager and I regularly discuss how I could improve through training, coaching or development*
- *My manager involves me in setting our team's goals*
- *The manager of our team gives us clear guidance*
- *I feel as though I get fair recognition for a job well done*
- *I have the resources I need to do my job to the best of my ability*
- *There is a good spirit in our team*
- *My manager is open, respectful and honest with me.*

Clearly the bundle of questions above – which we found to be statistically significant predictors of high-performance leader practice – are a combination of some of the intrinsic/motivator and extrinsic/hygiene factors outlined above; although they tilt more towards intrinsic than extrinsic drivers (actions and signals that the leader really *cares* about their people). What the Leader Coach can do – where the coachee might be displaying 'gaps' against the norm – is, during Stage 4 of the coaching conversation (see above), probe more deeply as to why their score might be deviating from the mean. Taking '*I feel as though I get fair recognition for a job well done*', for instance, they might ask:

- *Tell me about your employees' current feelings concerning how you recognise their attitude, effort and performance. How do you know that your perceptions are correct? When did you last ask them how they felt and what they required from you to improve their general sense of motivation?*
- *How do you practically show that you recognise their attitude, effort and performance? Give me examples.*
- *How sensitive to their feelings, needs and aspiration for recognition do you think you are? HOW DO YOU SHOW YOU GENUINELY CARE ABOUT THEM? Give me examples.*
- *How does your line manager recognise you? How does that make you feel?*
- *Based on the survey feedback and your reflections upon how you recognise your people's attitude, effort and performance, what will you:*

- STOP DOING *NOW*!?
- CONTINUE DOING?
- START DOING *NOW*!?

- *Write it down and we'll review the impact of your remedial actions in subsequent sessions.*

QUICK RECAP: LEADER COACHING TO MOTIVATE EMPLOYEES

- **Why?** – Highly engaged, motivated and productive employees are a source of competitive advantage
- **Main Concepts?** – Intrinsic and extrinsic motivation, hierarchy of needs, expectancy theory (force = valence + expectancy + instrumentality), goal theory and best practice/best fit HRM
- **How?** Coaching Conversations using:
  - **Two Factor Motivation Model**
    - Hygiene Factors (pay, incentives, benefits, working conditions, company policies, managerial relationships, resources to do the job?)
    - Motivators (achievement, promotion, improvement, recognition, responsibility, autonomy, fulfilling role?)
  - **Reward and Recognition Model**
    - Company discretion (centrally conceived)?
    - Leader discretion (personal and local)?
- **Accelerating Employee Motivation with Coachees? Use:**
  - **Feedback Data**
    - **Employee Survey**: 180-degree feedback on leadership style and approach
    - **Leadership Development Survey**: 360-degree feedback from team, peers, bosses that gives a holistic view on strengths and weaknesses

2.2 COACHING LEADERS TO IGNITE CUSTOMERS

Why do companies fundamentally exist? To provide goods and services to customers. How do great companies stand out? By anticipating customer needs and providing what customers and markets *crave*, faster and better than their competitive set. As Berry, the high priest of service branding, observed:

> A strong service company stands for something that is important to targeted customers: the brand not only differs from competitive brands, it also represents a valuable market offer...

> (Berry, 2000, p.132)

The vital role that business leaders play in galvanising organisations to provide memorable and outstanding service has been written about and commentated upon in the huge amount of literature on service operations and customer service. But today their role in igniting customer service has never been more important. Why? The rise of digital communication over the past fifteen years has made company transactions with customers more transparent, with factors such as quality, speed and value being scrutinised and commented upon in real time. Customers can roam for information, check and spontaneously comment and interact with the 'world' on products and services. The digital phenomenon has also subtly altered customer behaviour (Edger and Hughes, 2016) intensifying trends such as:

- *'Immediacy and impatience'* (a need for instant rather than deferred gratification)
- *'Promiscuity'* (greater 'switching' behaviours caused by access to digital 'real-time' comparative data and willingness to trial, moving up or down the 'brand hierarchy')
- *'Sovereignty'* (enhanced perceived customer power due to more information and the ability to make 'spontaneous' public, online comments about service performance).

What are the implications of this for business leaders? They can no longer just rely on allowing other people in their organisation to get excited about customers on their behalf. They must try and achieve a higher degree of intimacy and a deeper understanding – working backwards from the customer – of how their organisation is designed, geared and motivated to deliver exceptional customer experiences every time. To do this, they need to display higher levels of curiosity and empathy; traits that are not always associated with careerist managers who have (relished) been detached and distant from the operational front line, where the rubber hits the road.

This is where the Leader Coach can help. How? By really challenging the business leader's received orthodoxies on what their customers' feelings, needs, expectations and aspirations really are and how their organisation is geared up to satisfy and exceed them. And based on our experience of coaching business leaders in this area, we would say this: it is vital that the Leader Coach really does have fierce conversations about the level of their organisation's customer-centricity. Why? Because if business leaders don't keep on top of or ahead of the customer demand curve, they will be out of a job and/or their company will fail.

MAIN CUSTOMER IGNITION CONCEPTS

The Leader Coach will be well acquainted with concepts relating to customer-service excellence, derived both from their experiences as a customer and their acquired learning. However, prior to embarking on a coaching conversation on the matter with their coachee, it would do them no harm to refresh or bolster their knowledge relating to service *design*, *execution* and *measurement*.

- **Brand Equity Drivers** – The start point for all business leaders in this area is understanding what drives service excellence in the minds of consumers. The most widely cited article on service branding – Leonard Berry's 'Cultivating Service Brand Equity' (2000) – argues that strong service branding is important in service industries because it increases the *customer's trust* of the invisible purchase, enables consumers to visualise intangible products, reduces customers' perceived monetary, social or safety risk, and provides owners an opportunity to differentiate in a homogenised market (where most service is indifferently perceived as equal!). Berry argues that to increase service brand power and *customer 'mind share'*, owners need to focus on four drivers:
  - *Dare to be Different* – Seek to continually 'defy convention' (an advance on Levitt's (1980) distinctions between generic, expected and augmented products in 'Marketing Success through Differentiation – of Anything' where he argues that firms must continually augment their marketing mix in order to maintain competitive advantage)

- *Determine Your Own Fame* – Provide a valuable market offer that focuses upon unserved market needs

- *Make an Emotional Connection* – Seize customer hearts by sparking feelings of closeness, affection and trust

- *Internalise the Brand* – Make sure the brand is clearly defined for, and understood by, service providers; they articulate and exemplify your brand (a point extended by de Chernatony (2001) in 'A Model for Strategically Building Brands' in which he argues that staff are the fundamental 'brand builders' within service brand contexts).

- **Brand Success Criteria** – In addition, 'cut through' with customers can be achieved if companies adopt a laser-like approach to addressable markets. In 'The Criteria for Successful Service Brands' (2003), de Chernatony and Segal Horn – having interviewed 28 leading-edge service brand consultants – conclude that strong service brands must have three fundamental properties:

  - *Focused Position* – Ruthless clarity for what the brand stands for in the *minds of the consumers* (service brand owners should beware of over-communication and too much information as there are limits to consumers' cognitive capacity)

  - *Consistency* – Perceived brand consistency (with regards to execution and 'delivering on the promise') among all stakeholders (employees, suppliers, investors, customers, communities, etc.)

  - *Values* – Unified internal belief systems and shared values that are underpinned by genuine conviction, which result in commitment, loyalty and clear brand understanding.

- **Service Excellence** – Having *designed* the foundations of the brand (ensuring its salience, relevance, focus and emotional connection) another body of literature in this area addresses the fundamental props of flawless *execution*:

  - **Service Profit Chain** – Extending the notions of consistency and values set out above, this body of work examines how to improve *customer service execution* within branded service environments. Heskett et al.'s 'Putting the Service Profit Chain to Work' (1994) stresses the importance of the *alignment between internally and externally facing service systems*, advancing the notion that perceived levels of external service provision will never exceed internal levels of service (suggesting that companies should pay due attention to investment in people, technology, machinery and concept design if they want to achieve positive customer and profit outcomes). His central philosophical argument in this model is that a well-designed service concept *plus* motivated, happy workers will *result in* increased customer satisfaction and profit.

- **Total Service Approach** – In a similar vein, Albrecht (1992) and Albrecht and Zemke (1995) argue that organisations that provide excellent service take a Service Management View (SMV) comprising three vital components. *First*, they take a *long-term* perspective to generating enduring customer relationships and are focused upon realising substantial lifetime customer value. *Second*, such organisations adopt a *total service approach* in which the organisational values and objectives are directed towards superior service provision. *Third*, such an approach is underpinned by a *management focus*, whereby the organisational systems are designed to elicit maximum commitment and effort from front-line service providers. Such systems include the following characteristics:

    - *Resource Availability* – Appropriate resources are provided to service providers to provide superior customer satisfaction
    - *Local Decision Making* – Service providers are granted the autonomy to deal efficiently and effectively with customer complaints and service faults
    - *Service Skills* – Supervisors are granted the necessary materials and time to concentrate on upskilling front-line staff to improve service levels and release discretionary effort
    - *Aligned Reward* – Incentive systems are customer orientated, with disproportionate emphasis on satisfying key customer service metrics (i.e. speed, quality, politeness, knowledge, rectification, etc.)
    - *Two-Way Feedback* – Mechanisms are provided for effective two-way feedback from service providers to managers (i.e. pre and end of session briefings, team meetings, forums, focus groups and confidential surveys).

- **Service Personality Framework** – Extending the Service Profit Chain and Total Service concepts, the best practice Service Personality Framework (SPF) conceived by Johnston (2001) – the result of empirical analysis of hundreds of organisations – views the Service Personality of a Firm (*i.e.* the *functional and emotional* attributes of excellent service) as framed by three significant contingent variables: *a service culture* (shared values and 'in touch' leadership), *committed staff* (positive attitude and adult/mature behaviours) and *customer-focused systems* (best-in-class communications, feedback, training, reward, recognition and complaint management systems). By investing time and effort in these three areas, Johnson and his colleagues – as a result of their empirical observations – claim that organisations which *create identifiable service personalities in the minds of consumers reap higher profits, margins and total return on assets.*

- **Moment of Truth Investment** – In addition to these perspectives on constructing service excellence, the notion of pivotal 'make or break' moments of truth in the customer relationship is particularly important. Two of McKinsey's most widely read papers, 'The "Moment of Truth" in Customer Service' (2006) and 'Maintaining the Customer Experience' (2008), make the argument that service firms rarely review what customers really want (*properly discriminating between what they say and what they do and feel*). Service firms should scientifically evaluate where the true *'breakpoints', 'sensitivities' and 'patience thresholds'* lie within their service delivery systems to determine where high and low perceived value lies. Companies should eliminate cost and effort in servicing non-value-added elements of the service chain and *focus investment in areas of high perceived customer value.* Also, *isolating emotionally charged moments of truth* which might affect the repeat purchase intentions of customers is vital, with emotions most commonly running high during 'problem events'; those that provide instant solutions will increase their emotional bonds with their customers and achieve a fair degree of differentiation. Staff are the key lever here, with McKinsey suggesting that service companies should commit resources to hiring *emotionally intelligent staff, creating real meaning* (that addresses thoughts, feelings, values, beliefs and emotional needs), *training to improve capabilities and mindsets, proper reward and resourcing structures/processes* and *exemplar modelling from front-line leaders* (who particularly serve as role models for emotionally intelligent behaviour).

- **Experiential Measurement** – Having designed the concept and service delivery mechanisms to deliver outstanding customer experiences, organisations need to measure their impact. How? By measuring perceived benefits and their impact upon detractors or advocates.

  - **Perceived Benefits Analysis** – It is important to business leaders that their brand/company appears unique to customers, offering benefits that others don't. Business leaders can achieve clarity in this process by measuring the distinctive functional and emotional attributes of their business that make tangible and intangible impacts upon customer perceptions:

    - *Functional benefits*: Product-based (quality and process speed) and economic (price and value proposition)
    - *Emotional benefits*: Psychological (needs, feelings and aspirational fulfilment) and sociological (affiliation, community and sociability).

- **Net Promoter** – Over the past twenty years, articles and books focusing upon enhancing the customer experience have stressed the importance of getting customer perceptions to exceed their initial (or pre-formed) expectations, in order to generate loyalty and raving advocacy. Reichheld's argument in his seminal article 'The One Number You Need to Grow' (2003) stresses the need for companies to focus their efforts upon measuring Net Promoters. These are 'strong advocates' who will readily 'recommend the brand to friends and family' to 'drown out' tepid supporters or detractors. But how should they achieve this? Wilkinson in his *The Ten Principles Behind Great Customer Experiences* (2013; winner of the prestigious 2014 CMI Book of the Year) argues that *raving advocacy* is achieved when customer experiences are carefully designed to *reflect the customer's identity, satisfy higher objectives, leave nothing to chance, more than meet expectations, be effortless, stress free, indulge the senses, socially engaging, put the customer in control and always consider emotions.*

- **Spontaneous** – However, over the last ten years, customer experience measurement has become less of a company-led science. The rise of digital and social media has provided a means of measuring unexpurgated, 'authentic', spontaneous feedback. Furthermore, companies/brands that actually engage with customers in these forums – assuming a 'human personality' – can actually strengthen consumer perceptions of the brand.

KEY CUSTOMER IGNITION MODELS

Having updated and refreshed their knowledge on key customer excellence concepts, the Leader Coach has recharged their vocabulary and level of insight. Now they must facilitate a coaching conversation with the business leader about their organisation/SBU's level of internal and/or external service. We advocate two models that can be used by the Leader Coach to challenge and probe business-leader understanding and reflection, namely: the Value Proposition Model (which looks at the business's 'offer balance' with regard to customer needs) and the Service Culture Wheel (which provides an analytical tool to examine 'front-line' service provider readiness). Both will now be considered in turn.

First, the Value Proposition model (Edger, 2016). What is its purpose? Quite simply, it is a diagnostic tool, illustrating the four main 'experiential' attributes of a standard service-based business that requires *balanced alignment* to achieve positive customer advocacy and commercial success; whatever the differentiated positioning of the brand (in premium, mid or discount-led segments of the market). Its central argument is that once all the main cornerstones of the business are in place (price, environment, product and service), it is the way that they are kept within relative balance with one another that is the main determinant of success or failure.

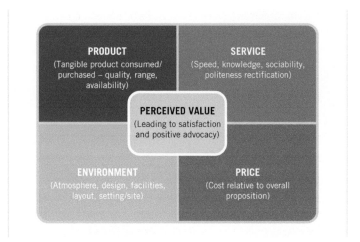

Figure 17: Value Proposition Model

Furthermore, the model is underpinned by the following equation:

$$PA = CSftPVft(£p,p,e,s)$$

PA (Positive Advocacy) is an outcome of CS (Customer Satisfaction)
which is a ft (function) of PV (Perceived Value)
which is a ft (function) of £p (price), p (product), e (environment) and s (service)

The central premise of this equation is that positive advocacy by existing customers (by both word-of-mouth and 'mouse') results from high levels of customer satisfaction derived from high levels of perceived value (conscious and unconscious feelings of a 'good deal') derived from an experiential combination of:

- **Product** – This encompasses the tangible served product (for instance, food and beverages in food service) including aspects such as quality, range, availability, etc.

- **Service** – Including 'appropriate' speed during all aspects of the chain of service (so-called 'touches'), combined with sociability, knowledge, politeness and the ability to immediately resolve/rectify breakdowns

- **Environment** – Factors include the actual site (location and accessibility), design, facilities, layout and atmosphere

- **£Price** – Incorporating the 'unbundled' or 'bundled' experience in which price should be relative to other VPM factors such as product, service and environmental quality.

What the Leader Coach can do, using this model, is ask the coachee to consider how 'balanced' they think their proposition currently is in the eyes of their consumers. Further probing questions might include:

- *Needs – What matters most to your customers (don't just look at what they say – look at how they act!)? What distinctive benefits do you currently offer to satisfy their needs, desires, aspirations and feelings?*

- *Deadly Combinations – Is there any evidence of the 'deadly combination' effect at play; for instance, where customers feel that current levels of service or environmental quality do not justify the price?*

- *Sensitivity Points – What elements are degrading the current 'experiential equation'? What are the current 'break/sensitivity points'? How can they be fixed? How can you eliminate costs of serve that don't matter and finance the ones that do?*

- *Controllables – What immediate controllables (EMOTIONAL service being the obvious lever) can you drive to impact impressions of perceived value and, consequently, rates of customer satisfaction? How do you ensure customer perceptions exceed expectations leading to high levels of attraction, loyalty and advocacy?*

This latter point is pivotal. Obviously, what the Leader Coach is trying to do is get the coachee to understand what their customers *expect* from their brand and how these *expectations* are being met or exceeded. It is worth remembering that it is far more expensive to recruit a customer than to retain one, so great efforts must be made to understand 'core customer preferences'! However, it is fruitful if the Leader Coach poses questions not only about core customers, but also about infrequent, lapsed and non-users as well. This will get the business leader to ponder upon how they might be able to increase sales penetration and profitability.

- *Core Users ('hard core loyals') – What is your core demographic? Which group constitutes 20 per cent of customers but 80 per cent of your sales/visits? What do they seek from the brand? How can you reward their patronage? What 'communication' media do they prefer? What are the core messages that mobilise them?*

- *Infrequent Users ('split loyals') – What is the secondary demographic in this brand? What are their preferences? Why are they so 'disloyal'? What are their other brands giving them? How can you increase their frequency of purchase/visits? What messages do they respond to? How can you mobilise them?*
- *Lapsed ('switchers')/Non-Users – Why don't they visit? Where can you reach them to 'sell' your message and encourage (re)trial?*

The second model the Leader Coach can use with the coachee is our Service Culture Wheel (Edger, 2016). In the core concepts section above, we cited commentators who have empirically observed that many successful organisations have instilled a vibrant front-line service culture. This will inevitably be strengthened if there is an unambiguous and explicit focus upon hiring front-line staff with great 'service personalities' who are able to bring the brand to life in front of the customer. Our Service Culture Wheel in Figure 18 is a representation of the key elements that lead to a positive service culture at operational level within service-led companies. Its sequential stages represent the various interdependent attributes of service cultures that will result in satisfying/memorable service experiences for guests/users and thus lead to retention, loyalty, advocacy and new user recruitment; which in turn lead, hypothetically, to higher sales and a better reputation.

Figure 18: Service Culture Wheel

Referring to the five interlinked stages involved in constructing a front-line service culture, the Leader Coach can challenge and probe the coachee, using some of the questions below.

- *Clear Service Cycle – Describe your chain of service (customer 'touches' from welcome to exit). How simple and easily understood are they by your service providers involved at key moments of the customer-order-fulfilment process? How is your chain of service documented in simple terms for your front-line service providers?*

- *Service Personality Staff – What percentage of your staff are recruited into your business based on the basis of 'will' – not purely 'skill'? Tell me about how you identify and recruit staff who gain pleasure from serving others (generating 'emotional contagion' with customers) and working as a team.*

- *Organised, Trained and Motivated – How do you train, develop, deploy, reward and resource your teams with the tools to do their jobs with passion and efficiency? What is their core job purpose?*

- *Empowered to Resolve Complaints – Tell me about the customer competency levels within your business (high or low maintenance behaviours). How do you empower your teams to rectify service break-downs on the spot? How well informed are your front-line staff on your service recovery or problem rectification protocol?*

- *Celebrate Success – How do you publicly recognise great service moments with individuals or teams? Furthermore, how do you recognise employees with rewards that they can show or boast about to their friends and families (thereby increasing their levels of pride and self-esteem)?*

ACCELERATING CUSTOMER IGNITION WITH COACHEES

The models above provide the Leader Coach with good frameworks to work with coachees on upping their customer insight and impact. They can also get the business leader to commit to conduct further research by:

- *Mining for big data on their customers' expectations and perceptions (triangulating quantitative and qualitative sources of data)*

- *Asking their customers directly what the business should stop, start or continue doing*

- *Quizzing their employees and teams on a single (and poignant) question: 'if you had the autonomy to change one thing that would improve the customer experience, what would it be?'*
- *Going 'back to the floor' to experience the reality of the point of impact of their organisation's customer service and its effect on overall customer experiences*
- *Re-routing the organisation's customer experience team to report directly into them.*

Having done some of this, further coaching sessions might be built around the results of this enquiry and the resulting solutions and actions. But this is not enough.

Most of what is proposed above is internally rather than externally focused. To *jolt* the coachee, the Leader Coach needs to get the business leader to examine best practice outside their organisation. In extreme examples (where the business leader's organisation has really poor levels of service), this will show up how risible their customer service is and, more importantly, give them some ideas concerning how they can fix it. How can the Leader Coach go about this? In an ideal world, they might get their coachees to do their independent research into examples of best practice (exemplar/competitor visits and meetings with customer-service experts) but these interventions are outside of the Leader Coach's control. One thing that they can do is get the coachee to read, digest and comment upon a case study, such as the one we have commonly used – based upon Justin King's customer-led recovery of Sainsbury's between 2004 and 2014 (contained in Edger and Hughes, 2017) – to spark a discussion on how service change can be ignited within organisations.

CASE STUDY – JUSTIN KING, FORMER CEO, SAINSBURY'S

Justin King, former CEO, Sainsbury's – 'Making Sainsbury's Great Again'

Justin King was CEO of Sainsbury's, one of the UK's top-three grocery chains, for ten years. When he took over in 2004, there were doubts over whether the chain would survive, given its catastrophic collapse in profit and market share under previous management. Implementing his turnaround plan, 'Making Sainsbury's Great Again', King increased sales during his tenure from £16.5bn to £26.3bn, profit from £249m to £798m and customer transactions from 14m to 24m per week. In 2014, he was voted 'Most Admired Leader' by his peers in the Management Today Most Admired Companies Award. Previously, Justin had occupied senior positions at M&S Food, Häagen-Dazs, Asda, PepsiCo and Mars.

Sainsbury's had truly *once* been a great business! If one goes back to the mid-1980s, it would have been seen, by common consent, as one of, if not *the*, leading grocery businesses in the world. John Sainsbury, the CEO and chairman at the time, would have been regarded as the leading light of his generation. **He was an *inspirational leader* who really got the customer and had a knack of getting the customer before the customer got themselves!**

But it became a business that lost its way because it had *stopped putting customers at the heart of everything it did.* Why? In the 1990s, a new management regime concluded that Sainsbury's had the best sites, that 30k sq ft was the optimal supermarket footprint and that the UK grocery market was becoming saturated; so they looked at diversifying abroad and into non-food. But their analysis was wrong. While Sainsbury's were 'aiming off', Tesco reinvented the supermarket over a period of ten years, with Tesco surpassing Sainsbury's as the number-one grocer in the UK in 1995.

So when I arrived at Sainsbury's in 2004, the business had lost market share for about 14 years in a row because – I would argue – **first, it had lost consumer focus** (at least partly through the loss of its inspirational leader, John Sainsbury); *second*, it had diverted resources away from the core of the business so **it was satisfying customers less well over time**; *third*, in an attempt to address that failure over time, it set about a journey around 1999 to 2000 **in a way that customers *couldn't* accept**…

There wasn't a lot wrong with the turnaround plan that the business originally started in 2000 in terms of the identification of the issues that the business faced but they [made the mistake] of promising. **So the idea of 'Making Sainsbury's Great Again' really came from listening to how our customers and colleagues in the business were *feeling* at that time. Customers *felt* that 'this was once a great place to shop where I *loved* doing my weekly grocery shop and I'd really *love* to come back and do that again'.** Now that kind of change – if it's at no expense to shareholders – must be at the expense of customers. So, prices were less sharp, availability was poor… availability was poor because the systems changes were being done in a rapid way, which meant that the service levels couldn't be maintained and the business was overly tight on cost because the top line had stopped growing as a result of all those changes! The way I like to describe it is that what we had basically done is *ask our customers to indulge us through this very difficult period* of change and **our customers said to us: 'we might come back when you've sorted it out, but in the meantime there's lots of other places we can do our shopping, thanks very much!' ...**

And our colleagues felt that they 'used to be **proud** to work here. I **loved** working here. I'd tell my friends that I was here and I would envisage the rest of my career here. But now I hope nobody asks me where I work because I don't want to admit it'. **So the 'Making Sainsbury's Great Again' was all about 'we're going to take the business back to that *feeling* for you! – our customers and colleagues!' So how did we do it?**

- **Senior Leadership Change** – The top-leader group in our business – 1,000 or so leaders (including the Store Managers) – stayed largely as I had found it. Four years into our turnaround, 95 per cent of the people were still there. There was a very simple reason for that. I had found a lot of really good people who knew how to do their jobs really well but there had been a real failure of senior leadership; and so most of the 40 or so senior people changed. That was pretty much all of the Plc Board and Operating Board. But beyond that, there was no more than natural turnover in the ranks below. Some people went naturally on to do other things and we recruited some great people in their stead. And by providing that *clarity of direction*, some good personal leadership as well (I'd like to claim my part, if you like, in this success!) we re-energised what was actually a fantastic team that had been badly led.

- **Shareholder Buy-In** – In October 2004 we articulated to share-holders how we thought we could grow sales and how long it would take profits to recover because of the money we needed to invest in the customer-service offer – in pricing and in quality. By laying it out over time with key stage posts, shareholders could check in along the way, monitoring that we were achieving what we'd said we'd do. I found shareholders were very supportive. I think that management has to be very clear that, in the end, *they* manage the business and I would say that one of the first steps on the slippery road to disaster is management starting to do things because they believe that shareholders want them to do it rather than management believing that it's the right thing to do. As you'll gather from my view of the world, *as long as you're focused on customers and colleagues*, then that's almost inevitably going to reap rewards for the corporation and therefore serve the best interests of the shareholders!

- **Legendary Behaviour** – The only place you service customers in grocery (including online and digital) is in your shops. How did I instil this passion back into the business? I became reasonably *famous* for my first day at Sainsbury's! I didn't turn up at what Sainsbury's called Head Office, I turned up at a shop – the number-one store in the company. At about 9 a.m., I got a call on my mobile from the HR Director saying 'Er, Justin it's the 28th March and you appear not to have turned up for work!' I said 'I have, I'm in a shop and – by the way – I've been here a couple of hours and been expecting your phone call!' Now clearly I was – symbolically – trying to send a message. It was a point that needed to be made. '*The only place we serve customers is in our shops. The only people serving customers were our colleagues within those shops!*' And in truth, the organisation was doing a lamentable job of equipping colleagues to serve customers and we needed to change the centre of gravity of the business. I understood this and empowering the operating side of the business was a key part of the change we made. The message was in my actions on that first day. Many of the store managers subsequently said to me that that behaviour alone (visiting a store on the first minute of my first day) made them *feel* stronger than they'd *felt* for a long time in the organisation.

- **Potent Symbolism** – We also set about changing the names of our offices. They were all called Head Office or a Regional Office; they were all changed to be called *Store Support Centres* – a place where we support the stores! But we didn't just change the plaque over the door, we said 'when you achieve these things and are rated for providing support to the stores then you have earned the right to be called a Store Support Centre'. So for example, we set targets about how quickly and frequently phones were answered when a store called, how soon an answer to the store question was provided… and so our depots, regional offices and Head Office in Holborn all earned the right to be called a Store Support Centre…

- **Communicating and Listening** – I set up mechanisms whereby I met with every store manager every quarter for my entire ten years, at 20 or 30 at a time, plus getting the 600 of them together once a year as part of the National Conference. So I met with 20 to 30 of them face to face, with none of their Regional Management present – just them – telling them a bit about what I was thinking about, giving them a chance to ask me questions, but also as an opportunity to tell me about what was going on. Famously, in one of the very first meetings (and this is in a book by Gurnek Bains, who was with me at the time because we were using him as a consultant on culture) after I'd joined and I'd had 15 or so meetings across the country, I had got to the last one and I remember saying to Gurnek 'I'm not getting this, because I'm just not hearing the *anger*, bile and frustration that I should be on behalf of the colleagues and customers – and these are who our store managers represent!' I was quite worried. If our store managers aren't shouting, how am I going to get this business 'up for it'! And to this day I'm absolutely convinced it was deliberate but… as the last group left, placed on the front row was a piece of paper and I walked over and picked it up; and it was an email from one of the Regional Managers (who wasn't in the room, of course) and it said 'following our conference call today – here are the questions we've agreed to ask Justin'! It was then I realised that even the people responsible for the regional operations of the business had become part of the problem.

- **Empowering Colleagues** – So we had to empower the store managers, which I did through regular contact and *also* empower our colleagues in the stores through a suggestion scheme called 'Tell Justin'. During my tenure we had about 70,000 or so suggestions from colleagues! For the first six months I answered every one personally. For the rest of my time there these were answered by a director but I promised that *I* would answer every customer and colleague letter that came *directly* addressed to me. My team told me – as I left – that I'd answered 20 letters a day for every day in the previous ten years. There were some great ideas and you always find out stuff that had not been brought to the attention of the Board.

- **Taming Bureaucracy** – The final point I'd make is that, structurally, Operations had equal representation around the Operational Board (with Finance, HR, Marketing, etc.). Obviously, all the divisions had their part to fulfil and the job of directors was to ensure that 'games' were not played further down the organisation. Because bureaucracy, by its very nature, will tend to do the types of things one would imagine – humans are that way inclined and one needs to be mindful of it. For instance, in the early days we had logistics and retail as two separate divisions. But I couldn't get to the bottom as to why they appeared to be separate divisions at all, when I thought they should be lining up together to serve customers. So I decided that what we would have to do is put them into the same director and it solved the problem overnight!

> Because once both divisions knew that they were marching to the beat of the same director, it's amazing the difference that it made! Sometimes if there are unnecessary arguments, you make sure the structure of the organisation is right because there's this natural tendency to defend your piece of turf even if the whole is more important than the sum of its parts...

Once the coachee has read the case study (either this one or something similar on a customer service turnaround), the Leader Coach can stimulate discussion and reflection by asking the following questions:

- *Why had Sainsbury's lost its way in 2004? (See 'Brand Equity Drivers' in 'Main Customer Ignition Concepts' above)*
- *Why did Justin King focus upon the customer as being the central thrust of 'Making Sainsbury's Great Again'? (See 'Brand Success Criteria' in 'Main Customer Ignition Concepts' above)*
- *What specific issues were customers experiencing in his stores in 2004? (See 'Value Proposition Model' in the 'Key Customer Ignition Models' section above)*
- *How did Justin King galvanise Sainsbury's to re-ignite its customer base, recapturing lapsed users? (See 'Service Excellence' in 'Main Customer Ignition Concepts' and 'Service Culture Wheel' in 'Key Customer Ignition Models' above)*
- *What inspired you most about this case study?*
- *What comparisons can you draw between this case study and your own organisation?*
- *What actions can you take quickly to re-ignite your customers?*

QUICK RECAP: LEADER COACHING TO IGNITE CUSTOMERS

- **Why?** – Without customers who crave their products and services, leaders have no business!
- **Main Concepts?** – Brand equity drivers and success criteria, service excellence, total service approach, service personality framework, moment of truth investment, experiential measurement, sensitivity analysis, perceived benefits evaluation (net promoter and spontaneous 'word of mouse'), user types (loyals, lapsed, switchers and non-users)

- **How?** Coaching Conversations using:
  - **Value Proposition Model**
    - PA = CSftPVft(£p,p,e,s)
    - Positive Advocacy (PA) is an outcome of Customer Satisfaction (CS) which is a function (ft) Perceived Value (PV) which is a function (ft) of price (£p), product (p), environment (e) and service (s)
  - **Service Culture Wheel**
    - Clear Service Cycle?
    - Service Personality Staff?
    - Organised, Trained and Motivated?
    - Empowered to Resolve Complaints?
    - Celebrate Success?
- **Accelerating Employee Motivation with Coachees? Use:**
  - **Case Studies**
    - Exemplary Leadership and Service-based Case Studies of outstanding examples of Customer Ignition (see the Justin King case study, 'Making Sainsbury's Great Again', above)
    - Use these to prompt comparison-based discussions

2.3 COACHING LEADERS TO DEVELOP TEAMS

Leadership is at its zenith when it inspires, develops and motivates a group of individuals, through their combined effort, to an exponentially better performance than could have happened at an individual level. Organisations that effectively build, facilitate and leverage teams create a dramatic market advantage. Their productivity is increased, their problem solving and decision making are superior, they are more agile when responding to market demand/turbulence and they become very desirable to work for. Where businesses fail to maximise teamwork, the opposite occurs.

The productivity of high-performance teams is so compelling that organisations have become addicted to chasing the concept of teams. This has led to the concept being overused, abused and frequently resented by employees who know they are only members of teams in name, but nothing like it in practice. Effective leaders, however, adhere to a well-known but mainly ignored truth about teams: they are task-specific entities with a limited performance window. They further understand that most work in organisations is carried out in a co-actional manner (independent activities that sequentially combine to create an outcome), requiring management not teamwork. This makes the pursuit of teams to accomplish this work costly, disruptive and, overall, futile.

For teams to work to their full potential, therefore, they should not be an everyday solution but rather an elite unit with a well-resourced, specifically defined objective that requires focused facilitation. Where leaders protect the concept of teams as an exceptional tool rather than a worn-out reactive measure, they will not only inspire teams but have inspiring teams. The Leader Coach is in an ideal position to help coachees to reinvigorate the notion and effectiveness of teams in their organisations.

MAIN TEAM DEVELOPMENT CONCEPTS

When leaders have established that a project needs to be carried out in addition to the organisation's routine requirements, it is time to build a team to accomplish that objective.

Tuckman's Stages of Team Formation

Bruce Tuckman's (1965) enduring model of team formation is an ideal approach to building and facilitating teams. Originally including four stages, its five stages (Tuckman and Jensen, 1977) track the transition from a group of individuals (forming) to an accomplished but disbanding team returning to normality or moving onto the next project (adjourning). Consciously steering and supporting teams through these stages not only ensures that leaders deliver projects on time and on target but motivates employees to aspire towards team projects and inspires future quality performances.

Figure 19: Team Development Lifecycle Model

What are the various dimensions of each stage of the Team Lifecycle and what questions can the Leader Coach use to probe coachee awareness, understanding and capability in this area?

- **Forming**

  Forming is the initial gathering of members chosen for the team. Leaders should brief each member as to why they have been selected (e.g. 'you've delivered similar projects before') prior to the initial team meeting. Stating to employees that they have been specifically co-opted usually means they feel a sense of anticipation at this stage and are intrigued to know who else they will be working with. Where team members have not been given due notice or feel at a loss as to why they are being summoned to a team meeting, feelings of trepidation and suspicion may take hold. This may create a poor first impression, putting the team at a disadvantage straight away.

  The *forming* stage requires directive leadership to explain the team's function, the reason for individuals' selection, distribution of roles, resources allocation, schedule of work and impact on related work. This corresponds with the telling phase of Situational Leadership Theory (SLT – Hersey and Blanchard, 1969) where commitment is high but competence in terms of working as a team is low. At this point, similarity in normal job roles such as authority should also be specifically dealt with. Role similarity is a source of contention and will become divisive when vague or left open to interpretation (e.g. who supersedes who). This may appear petty, but this is fundamental to role clarity and effective functioning of the team.

Where teams are sub-units within the members' existing roles, the team's priority should be clearly established – in other words, does it take precedence or is it subservient to their existing workload? Where it takes precedence, has the normal line manager been informed of the employees' shifted focus and – where it is subservient – how is the team member expected to assimilate the team's assignment into their daily task list? If there is time in the system, *forming* may involve some networking opportunities such as meetings and breakfast/lunch gatherings where people have an opportunity to meet and get to know each other prior to project engagement. This may be in the form of conference or video calls for virtual teams. Where time is limited, in an emergency or by a tight deadline, distributing team profiles to every member of the group, to familiarise them with one another, is a useful strategy.

This stage should be carefully planned and as much information given as possible to mitigate disruption further along the team's lifespan. Where leaders have done their homework, having carefully considered the make-up of the team and articulated this well to both the team members and other stakeholders, the team will apply themselves faster, working harder and harmoniously so that the team can flourish, while also managing their other obligations. The Leader Coach can facilitate the coachee to comprehensively prepare for this stage of team formation by challenging the need for the team and the inclusion of its different members so that the coachee learns to articulate his/her intentions clearly. Questions that the Leader Coach can pose to facilitate this might include:

- *Is your team new or inherited? What are the implications of this? (i.e. it is easier for a leader to mould their own team rather than an inherited one, where loyalties and ties might remain with the previous leader)*
- *Were you previously a member of this team? What are the implications of this? (i.e. need for a different – more detached – relationship with team members and the difficulties of managing your ex-peers)*

- *What blend of personalities and talents will you need in your team (see Belbin below)? How will you assess who has which complementary skills, capabilities and behavioural preferences?*
- *How will you make best use of the team, not only as a whole but in specific break-out or 'task group' formations?*

- **Storming**

This stage occurs in all animal groups and is an attempt to create clarity by establishing a pecking order. During the idea generation and discussion phase of how best to deliver the proposed assignment, clashes occur and tension escalates. The greater the degree of planning prior to team formation and the amount of information provided in the forming stage about relationship structure, communication and authority, the shorter lived this phase will be.

Challenges may be overt, such as questioning, disagreeing and arguing. More malicious behaviour such as derogatory comments, shouting down, physical posturing and blatant ignoring may also be witnessed. More subtle behaviours such as staying quiet, avoidance and subdivisions into political alliances or cliques are no less concerning. Active intervention is critical from the beginning of this stage and transactional leadership in the form of management by exception or laissez-faire leadership (Bass and Avolio, 1991) should not be defaulted to here. SLT's selling style of leadership is ideally suited here as there is still project-related incompetence but now also anxiety and disillusionment, as some team members strive for dominance and others retreat from the confrontation. The leader needs to coax team members to stay committed to the project and to focus on combined potential rather than on differences.

Carron's considerable body of research on team cohesion is influential here and, depending on team member preferences, 'cohesion around the task' or 'social cohesion' may be preferable (see 1.4 'Adjust Style' for a similar discussion of task style versus person style in conflict situations). Where task cohesion is considered a better strategy, getting people to lay aside their differences and unify around the task at hand as a common goal can reduce tension. Social cohesion involves working on managing the team relationships through conflict management, negotiation and improved communication. Time plays a factor in the selection of task or social cohesion as the best approach. Where time allows, strengthening social bonds can create longer-lasting relationships, while time pressure typically promotes a task cohesion focus.

In general, it is best to assume that a power play will occur. Leaders will need to develop strategies to mitigate this by investing heavily in team preparation and formation. Where toxic behaviour festers in the *storming* phase, the team is more likely to implode having achieved little to nothing. Indeed, the use of the word 'team' here would be completely inaccurate. The fallout from such a scenario undermines the leader's reputation, creates a resistance to future team formation and, where the team has an interdepartmental membership, may result in larger-scale schisms within the organisation as members disseminate their biased version of events. Whilst most team failures are traceable to poor definition and planning, their physical disintegration is more likely to happen during this stage. Here the Leader Coach can help the coachee to anticipate potential clashes and develop strategies for limiting 'storm damage' by asking the following probing questions:

- *How are you going to overcome inevitable conflict between individual team members or factional groups?*

- *How will you spot and neutralise 'bystanding' or 'social loafing' behaviour (i.e. detachment and avoidance)?*

- *How will you overcome challenges to your authority from the 'big dogs' or 'toxics' within the team? (Especially if the team was formed by someone else before you arrived.)*

- **Norming**

When team members start fitting in and accepting their respective roles, things can proceed productively. Decision making is achieved through consensus and no longer derailed by personality clashes and power plays. Initial project tasks are completed and a shared identity develops, as team members come to value the strengths and contributions of each member and unify. A pattern or norm emerges.

This normalising of behaviour will include when, where and how often the team meets and how those meetings proceed, for example with/without pleasantries, including/excluding coffee, how information is shared, turn-taking and so forth. It also refers to the style of language used which may come to include team-specific jargon. Where time allows, jokes, stories and even nicknames may become part of the team's ritualistic/normalised behaviour. While this behaviour strengthens the intra-team relationships, it may result in outsiders feeling excluded and result in the team being perceived as exclusive or elite, creating inter-group tension. If anything, this serves to reinforce the member's behaviour and they might consciously use it to demonstrate their status to others. This in-group/out-group behaviour is comprehensively considered in Leader-Member Exchange (LMX) theory (Dansereau, Graen and Haga, 1975).

If a team's group behaviour becomes truly self-embedded and toxic it is termed groupthink (Janis, 1972). Where groupthink takes hold, such mob-like tendencies as an illusion of invulnerability (group is untouchable), tendency to moralise (belief of being better), feeling of unanimity (of one mind), pressure to conform (dissention punished), opposing ideas dismissed and risky shift (greater risks than an individual would take on their own) may be witnessed. Effective leadership prevents teams devolving into such negative entities through industrial/deep democracy, where everyone has their say to negate the disproportionate influence of strong personalities, holding all team members responsible for their input and managing disruptive politics as soon as possible.

By now the team has a high level of competence and requires more of a supportive role (SLT) from the leader, who intervenes and guides where necessary. The Leader Coach can support the coachee to develop this style by asking the following probing questions:

- *What ground rules and 'modus operandi' are you going to try and establish with your new team to regulate behaviours? (i.e. 'leave egos outside the door', 'everyone can express a mature opinion', 'raise issue but FIND SOLUTIONS!', etc.)*

- *What techniques and approaches can you apply so that behaviour becomes self-policing and regulating amongst team members? (N.B. This is crucial: if team members start holding one another to account according to their agreed code of conduct, the leader's job is made so much easier!)*

- **Performing**

Up to this point the leader is in team-building mode but now a tactical swap to team working is required. Working from a defined and stable platform, team members can apply the skills they were chosen for and work in earnest towards achieving the team's outcome goal or objective. Although team building is initially time consuming, once the team optimises or works synergistically (Covey, 1989) the results can be truly exceptional; the 1969 Apollo moon landing being the ultimate team performance example!

Team members at the *performing* stage are completely comfortable with each other and view disagreement as productive feedback rather than conflict such as happened in the storming stage. As a result, the team is fun to be part of and the classic workplace motivator of achievement (Herzberg, 1959) begins to inspire further achievement and becomes self-perpetuating. The SLT style of delegation is the most appropriate style now that the team is highly committed and highly competent. The leader continues to facilitate in terms of resources, support and problem solving but in a less hands-on manner.

Leaders should always aspire to have high-performing teams. Blanchard, Carew and Parisi Carew (2004) list purpose and values, empowerment, relationships and communication, flexibility, optimal performance, recognition and appreciation, and morale as the characteristics of high-performing teams. These characteristics are more people oriented than task specific and demonstrate the need for leaders to have high levels of Emotional Intelligence, as well as an agenda to develop soft skills throughout the organisation. In doing so, leaders accelerate the likelihood of teams moving from 'functioning' to 'high performing'.

- *Now your team is highly trusting and performing well, consider how you can make their work and interactions more FUN.*

- *Think about how you can spontaneously reward examples of great team-member performance more regularly (i.e. catching someone doing it right!).*

- *How can you craft or capture TRIBAL stories, symbols and icons which will perpetuate the team's momentum, creating a sense of identity, belonging and sustained cohesion?*

- **Adjourning**

The final and subsequently (Tuckman and Jensen, 1977) added stage of *adjourning* is sometimes referred to as the mourning stage. The inclusion of this stage demonstrates the finiteness of teams, something conveniently omitted by commercial teambuilding businesses that imply effective teams have an infinite lifespan.

For many reasons, teams cannot endure interminably and are short lived. Mainly teams are task specific and task completion signifies a team's redundancy. Changes to the task but more specifically changes to the team (common occurrences in dynamic workplaces) mean the current team *should* adjourn and recommence the cycle.

Where an addition or a replacement has been well thought out, disruption is minimised and the team fast-tracks to the performing stage. Often, however, new members are bolted on rather than slotted in and the team regresses to the storming phase.

A major difficulty with the *adjourning* process is that successful teams will have an intuitive desire to stick together. This becomes an acute issue where the leader/business encourages this, perceiving it to be an obvious, easy solution. For the most part this is a fallacy, however, and subsequent underperformance can erode any memory of former glory.

Overall, the leader should terminate the team with good grace. A process and outcome review with learnings for future projects should be documented. Team members should be thanked for their input, congratulated on successful completion and, if agreed, outstanding individual contributions acknowledged (being mindful that public recognition can be distressing and viewed as punishment by some individuals). This should all take place during work time and not on team members' personal time. Team members' normal work units and especially line managers should also be thanked for facilitating the employees' inclusion on the team. Not to do so can cause resentment, especially where colleagues must carry the burden of extra work in their absence.

The *adjourning* phase re-establishes role clarity by tying up loose ends and releasing team members to pursue other projects or fulfil their job role. When done well, the whole organisation feels motivated and engaged to be part of the next high-performing unit and to test what can be achieved through the synergistic effort of combined and facilitated talent.

Questions the Leader Coach can use to probe coachees around the adjournment stage might include:

- *How will you know when the team's work is 'done'?*
- *How will you ensure that its collective work is adjourned before the 'downcurve'?*
- *How will you celebrate its achievements and accomplishments?*
- *How can you ensure that your high-performance team members are redeployed in other projects or roles? (This is critical – the Leader must always look out for his/her charges once the work is done, otherwise people will feel that they have been duped or used.)*

ACCELERATING TEAM DEVELOPMENT WITH COACHEES

Meredith Belbin was fascinated to discover that intelligence was not enough to create a high-performing team and devised an in-depth study while working for the Industrial Training Research Unit in Cambridge at the Administrative Staff College and later the Henley Management College to investigate effective team composition. This led to the development of the now famous Belbin Team Roles (1981).

Despite receiving criticism from an academic rigour perspective, Belbin's Team Roles remain in popular use and provide an excellent insight into the need for diverse skillsets when it comes to team formation. There are nine role profiles and while, ideally, each of the roles is filled by a person with a behavioural preference for that role, practically this is unlikely to be possible. In the absence of the full complement of nine persons, Belbin's work advocates that individuals take on several roles to account for the nine necessary roles. In so doing, the team is likely to cover all angles and improve effectiveness. The roles are divided into thinkers, doers and relationship managers, which intuitively appeals to businesses' understanding that thinking without action and thinking without action or human regard tend to result in poor outcomes. Working with the Belbin Team Roles model and related questionnaire (licensed to Belbin), the Leader Coach can facilitate the coachee to gain a greater understanding of the human element of team formation and inspire teams to greater productivity, satisfaction and enjoyment.

	Team Role	Behavioural Description
Action-Oriented Roles	Shaper (SH)	Anxious dominant extrovert
		Task-focused, energetic, strident individuals
		May be perceived as overly pushy or aggressive
	Implementer (IMP)	Stable, low dominance, low anxiety
		Dependable, practical, methodical individuals
		May lack flexibility and imagination
	Completer Finisher (CF)	Anxious extrovert
		Dedicated, pedantic, self-driven individuals
		May overly focus on and worry about minor details
People-Oriented Roles	Co-Ordinator (CO)	Stable dominant extrovert
		Facilitative (assume chairperson's role), discerning and supportive individuals
		May abdicate under the guise of delegation
	Team Worker (TW)	Stable extrovert, low dominance
		Diplomatic, inclusive, people person
		May be indecisive and overly anxious to please people
	Resource Investigator (RI)	Stable dominant extrovert
		Networker, sociable, energetic
		May get distracted, lack attention to detail and staying power

Thought-Oriented Roles	Plant (PL)	Dominant introvert, high IQ
		Intelligent, creative, excellent problem solver
		May be individualistic, unpredictable and argumentative
	Monitor-Evaluator (ME)	Stable introvert, high IQ
		Rational, strategic, analytical
		May be perceived as dull, can be slow due to thoroughness
	Specialist (SP)	Introvert
		Knowledgeable, passionate, focused
		May be too narrow in focus and only interested in own speciality

Figure 20: Belbin Team Roles

Questions that Leader Coaches can ask coachees who have used the Belbin Team Questionnaire with their team:

- *Given the goals and tasks confronting the team, do you have the right balance and blend of behavioural preferences and skill sets within your group?*
- *If there is an imbalance (i.e. an overrepresentation of certain behavioural types) how are you going to prevent 'groupthink'?*
- *How are you going to MATCH specific tasks and roles to specific personality types?*
- *How will you get a diverse collection of personalities, with differing skill sets, to work harmoniously and respectfully together? (See Tuckman's Team Development Model above)*

QUICK RECAP: LEADER COACHING TO DEVELOP TEAMS

- **Why?** – Combining people's talents enhances workplace performance
- **Main Concepts?** – Team formation, task cohesion, social cohesion, synergy, Emotional Intelligence
- **How?** Coaching Conversations using:
  - **Tuckman's Model of Team Formation**
    - Forming
    - Storming
    - Norming
    - Performing
    - Adjourning
  - **Leadership Styles**
- **Accelerate Team Coaching? Use:**
  - **Belbin Team Roles**
    - Team Roles Questionnaire (licensed to Belbin)
    - Assess team composition
    - Check coverage of the Nine Team Roles (Shaper, Implementer, Completer Finisher, Co-ordinator, Team Worker, Resource Investigator, Plant, Monitor-Evaluator, Specialist)

2.4 COACHING LEADERS TO ALIGN STAKEHOLDERS

In addition to inspiring their team – creating a sense of shared purpose and meaning amongst *direct reports* over whom they have *direct control* – business leaders also have to work hard at influencing stakeholders over whom they may have *no formal authority*. What stakeholders are we talking about? For CEOs, these will include their board, shareholders, industry bodies, consumer groups, local communities, customers and suppliers. For functional and operational leaders, these might include peers and other support functions. What the business leader must do is to try and ensure their agenda becomes their stakeholders' agenda. This requires a sophisticated interpretation of what the needs, wants and desires of their stakeholder network are, and how they might gain traction through mutuality, reciprocity and *alignment*. However irritating managing expectations and aligning the objectives of multiple constituencies can seem to the business leader, it is far better than the alternative: emotionally draining and/or financially costly *conflict*. The problem is that all too often, business leaders underestimate the time, attention and effort they have to make co-opting multiple stakeholders to help achieve their aims. Too often we have coached executives who have arrogantly dismissed the importance and contributions of other vested interests. This behaviour is extremely misguided and often leads to delayed performance or outright failure. Thus, Leader Coaches can provide a great service to business leaders in this area, alerting them to the danger of neglecting important stakeholders and helping them to classify and prioritise their surrounding network to assist driving their growth agenda.

MAIN STAKEHOLDER CONCEPTS

Most Leader Coaches recognise how important establishing and maintaining good stakeholder relationships are for business leaders. Prior to conducting stakeholder-focused coaching sessions, however, a quick recap on the core concepts surrounding this area will increase their confidence and vocabulary:

- *Stakeholder Theory* – Based on a burgeoning area of research, this proposition holds that *wider stakeholder interests should be placed at the forefront of any organisational initiative, policy or action*. The significant growth in CSR (corporate social responsibility) policies amongst corporate entities over the past twenty years is confirmation that organisations increasingly recognise their obligation towards multiple constituencies that are directly or indirectly affected by their operations, given the *catastrophic reputational consequences* of neglecting these wider duties (see 1.4 'Adjust Style': 'The Means versus the End')!

- *Stakeholder Analysis* – The formal process of assessing relevant and interested parties in a project, programme or any other action where business leaders are required to *weigh up and balance the demands and interests of all affected parties*.

- *Stakeholder Types* – These are typically denominated in descending order of importance, namely: *key stakeholder* (those with significant influence upon a decision/action within the organisation), *primary stakeholder* (those parties most affected by actions), *secondary stakeholder* (those indirectly affected) and *tertiary stakeholder* (those impacted the least). More complex denominations can be completed using the covalence model (a Venn diagram segmenting stakeholders according to legitimacy/power/urgency), highlighting: discretionary, dormant, demanding, dominant, dangerous, dependent or definitive stakeholders.

- *Stakeholder Mapping* – This is a process whereby stakeholders are split into key, primary, secondary and tertiary types by ranking them in order of priority/importance using either two dimensional matrixes (i.e. *power/interest, support/attitude or power/influence*) and/or other factors such as *needs, relative importance, legitimacy, urgency of claim, threat and potential for co-operation.*

- *Stakeholder Engagement* – The process of communicating, co-opting and aligning key stakeholder groups to the business leader's objectives. A thorough benefits analysis will assist the business leader to identify areas of mutual interest and possible exchange. These exchange mechanisms will either be transactional (money, services or goods) or relational (love, status or information). Building indebtedness through practical emotional, social or financial currencies of exchange should lead to reciprocation and alignment. Wise business leaders acknowledge the fundamental *law of all human relationships,* outlined in the Bible: *'unto whomsoever much is given, of him shall be much expected'* (Luke 12:48).

- *Actor Networks* – In addition to these stakeholder definitions, categorisations and strategies, Leader Coaches also need to be cognisant of the power of formal and informal networks *between* stakeholders. Actor Network Theory (ANT) posits that everything in the social world exists in constantly shifting networks of relationships bound together by a *series of relational ties.* The dependencies and connectedness of these ties differ in strength and intensity, and are often hidden! Leader Coaches who grasp the fact that organisations are a *complex web of interconnected formal and informal networks* with competing alliances, demands and agendas are going to be of more utility to their coachees, helping them to make sense of the complex stakeholder terrain within which they are trying to drive their agendas.

- *Information Asymmetry* – In addition to attempting to understand the strength of ties and dependencies between various parties, another issue is the fact that business leaders will often find themselves disadvantaged in relation to some key constituents. Why? Business leaders never – despite neo-classical economic teaching – have 'perfect information'. Often the parties they are dealing with have more or better information than they do, an informational asymmetry which creates an imbalance of power leading to adverse decision-making 'selection', causing their plans, projects or programmes to go awry. Again, the Leader Coach has a role to play here, helping the coachees to pinpoint where these asymmetries lie, what their consequences could be and how they might redress this imbalance.

KEY STAKEHOLDER MODELS

Clearly the business leader needs to influence and co-opt multiple constituencies to expedite their business objectives and plans. But often they have not thought very deeply about *who* they need to get on board, *why* they need to and *how* they can craft a high level of mutuality and alignment. A lot of business leaders suffer from the delusion that all their previous successes can be credited solely to themselves! They discount the notion that many of their 'best-selling books' have had multiple rather than single authors. The Leader Coach needs to help them break this misconception by helping them understand the complex stakeholder terrain they inhabit (using the Enabling Networks Model in Figure 21 below) and the strategies/approaches which will help them gain leverage over powerful key stakeholders (using the Five Bases of Power Model and the Influencing without Authority Model in figures 22 and 23 below) to accelerate business growth.

As stated in the section above, the Leader Coach's first port of call is to map out the various stakeholder categories with coachees. How? Taking a *midranking operational business leader as an illustrative example*, the Leader Coach can use the Enabling Networks Model (in Figure 21 below) to categorise stakeholders within their coachee's operational universe based on their level of *power/interest* and the level/depth of relationship they should pursue with each cohort. In operational contexts there are a vast number of people who can help the business leader and his/her team expedite their jobs more effectively. It is the role of the Leader Coach (using this model) to help the coachee recognise how they can leverage a virtual team and coalition of enabling forces to help them achieve their key performance objectives more quickly.

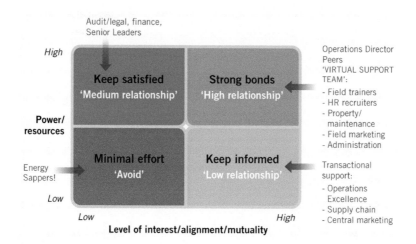

Figure 21: Enabling Networks Model

Thus, using the Enabling Networks Model the Leader Coach helps the coachee (in this case an operational leader) to categorise various organisational stakeholders according to power/resource and interest, in order to explore the level/depth of relationship they need to pursue (ensuring they get better outcomes than other 'competing' managers) through:

- **Strong Bonds (high relationship)** – Here the operational leader must create strong bonds with *key/primary stakeholders* that have a high degree of direct power (such as their boss) and extensive resource access (such as their peers and virtual team from support functions: HR business partners, recruitment and training officers, marketing assistants, property/maintenance managers) who are intrinsically aligned – for the purposes of their own KPI fulfilment – to their business performance. These personnel help drive important inputs on the scorecard so are high value added to the operational leader and his/her team. Given the high power/interest of this group, the Leader Coach can advance coachee insight with the following questions:

  - *What financial or emotional interest do they have in the outcome of your work? Is it positive or negative? What motivates them most of all?*

157

- *What information do they want from you?*
- *How do they want to receive information from you? What is the best way of communicating your message to them?*
- *What is their current opinion of your work? Is it based on good information?*
- *Who influences their opinions generally and who influences their opinion of you? Do some of these influencers therefore become important stakeholders in their own right?*
- *If they are not likely to be positive, what will win them around to support your project? How can you make your agenda their agenda?*
- *If you don't think you will be able to win them around, how will you manage their opposition?*
- *Who else might be influenced by their opinions? Do these people become stakeholders in their own right?*

- **Keep Satisfied (medium relationship)** – This *secondary* stakeholder group has high power/resources but, for practical and operational reasons, possesses a middling degree of mutuality with the operational leader and his/her team (being more detached from day-to-day operations). This cohort – which largely monitors outputs centrally – needs to be kept satisfied, through formal and informal updates, that the operational leader is performing acceptably. A couple of questions the Leader Coach can ask here are:
  - *What effort do you make to update notable people in your organisation about your progress?*
  - *Give me tangible evidence that notable people in your organisation know about you and rate your contribution.*

- **Keep Informed (low relationship)** – This *tertiary* group has a high level of alignment/interest in what the business leader and his team are doing but a low level of power resource to affect outcomes. Personnel fitting into this category might include supply chain (purchasing), central marketing and operational excellence (productivity specialists). However, despite low power, their level of interest in what the operational leader is trying to achieve might prompt the Leader Coach to ask the following questions:
  - *How can you leverage the support of this category of stakeholders given the high interest they have in your success?*
  - *Can you delegate to, or draw down resources from, this cohort more successfully given their level of interest?*

- **_Minimal Effort (no relationship)_** – This cohort has low levels of power resource and low levels of alignment with the business leader and his/her team. The Leader Coach must get the coachee to acknowledge that they should avoid anybody in this category that might include energy sappers and self-interested opportunists who will fail to reciprocate or add value.

The example above conceives the Leader Coach facilitating a stakeholder-mapping exercise with an operational leader, focusing upon internal constituencies that help them achieve their business objectives. But what actual sources of power do business leaders have to deploy in their relationships with others? Sometimes it is useful if coachees are encouraged to review their power resources to distinguish how they will engage with others to achieve win–win outcomes. How can the Leader Coach help? The Five Bases of Power Model was conceived by social psychologists French and Raven (1959) to articulate the five distinct 'bases' of authority possessed by humans during their interactions with others. Understanding which bases fit which 'stakeholder situations' enables business leaders to expedite their own personal agendas and objectives effectively, particularly in relation to key stakeholders.

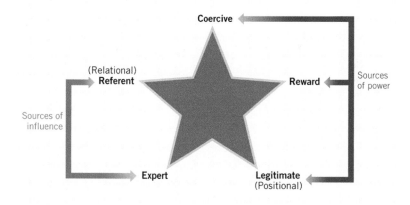

Figure 22: Five Bases of Power Model

Using this model, the Leader Coach can firstly articulate what sources of power the business leader possesses in their relations with stakeholders, following this with a number of probing questions:

- **Coercive** – This source of power is derived from a business leader's ability to utilise the threat of force and punishment to coerce stakeholders to comply with their demands. This power should be used sparingly, given its possible consequences (fear, resistance and conflict). Questions the Leader Coach can ask here include:
  - *Under what circumstances can you threaten certain stakeholders with sanctions? What short-term and long-term effects will this have?*
  - *What 'loss' will stakeholders suffer if you punish them? What 'benefit' will you receive?*

- **Reward** – This base of power is derived from a business leader's capacity to compensate others for compliance with their objectives, either tangibly (i.e. monetarily) or intangibly (i.e. socio-emotional recognition). However, the rewards that are exchanged by the business leader must be of sufficiently high perceived value by stakeholders to guide purposeful behavioural outcomes.
  - *What rewards do you have at your disposal for stakeholders?*
  - *Which ones are likely to be the best fit for your stakeholders?*
  - *How can you get the biggest bang for your buck with low-cost but high-return rewards?*

- **Legitimate** – This power source comes from an understanding and belief amongst others that the business leader has assigned formal authority (principally due to their dominant positional status within the hierarchy) to make demands and oblige obedience.
  - *Will pulling rank really motivate and align or will it irritate and inflame?*
  - *In which circumstances can you subtly use your positional status to align stakeholders?*

- **Expert** – Here a business leader's power and authority are derived from their credibility within the organisation, connected to their perceived superior knowledge, skills and talents. This is a particularly useful power resource for business leaders who need to influence others who are far more powerful than themselves.
  - *Tell me about how you can use your explicit and tacit knowledge of this subject area to influence key stakeholder opinion.*
  - *What do you need to do to increase your expert power resource?*

- **Referent** – This relational source of power refers to high levels of personal likability, worthiness and charm resulting in bonding affiliation and attachment responses from others. This is an exceptionally important power resource for business leaders who invariably must rely on their charm and personality to get stakeholders to 'go the extra mile' in extremely challenging times and circumstances.

- *Tell me about how you create strong relational ties with key stakeholders.*
- *How would others describe your levels of charm and likeability?*

ACCELERATING STAKEHOLDER ALIGNMENT WITH COACHEES

Helping the business leader to understand their different stakeholder categories and personal power sources will be of great benefit to coachees who are on 'receive'. But coachee performance in this area is greatly accelerated if they acquire and master *techniques* to *influence* categories of stakeholders who are likely to be the hardest to be won over. How can the Leader Coach help here? In the past we have found using Cohen and Bradford's (1989) IWA (influencing without authority) technique with coachees particularly helpful.

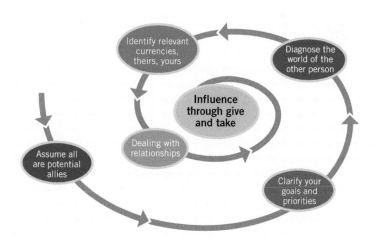

Figure 23: Influencing Without Authority Model

What the Leader Coach can do here is get the coachee to identify a particularly challenging stakeholder and follow the IWA technique, posing several probing questions:

- *Assume all Stakeholders are Potential Allies – Instead of advocating a confrontational ('why the hell can't you do it?') stance, the Leader Coach will ponder: what are your mutual interests? How can you get on?*

- *Clarify your Goals and Priorities – Smart Leader Coaches look for commonalities, asking the coachee: what common goals do you have? What are your non-negotiables? What are their non-negotiables?*

- *Diagnose the World of the Other Stakeholder – Leader Coaches get coachees to 'seek first to understand', asking them: how much pressure is your stakeholder subject to? How are they incentivised and/or coerced and punished? What false preconceptions do you have about their world – how can you put these to one side?*

- *Identify Relevant Currencies (theirs and yours) – In the light of the currencies coachees have that are of high exchange value (expertise, emotional support, information, etc.), Leader Coaches will ask the following: what does this stakeholder care about? How can you help them achieve what they want – making sure that they feel that they are getting something out of the relationship? What hidden value can you find for this person (i.e. something they get of high value that they didn't know existed)?*

- *Dealing with Relationships – Following an imagined state of engagement, Leader Coaches will pose the following questions: how will the relationship evolve – will it be positive, neutral or negative? If it is the latter, how can you make it more constructive?*

- *Influence Stakeholder through Give and Take – As the coachee starts working with the stakeholder, the Leader Coach can ask: are you reciprocating? Are you building indebtedness? Is this relationship now based on long-term mutual trust and alignment?*

QUICK RECAP: LEADER COACHING TO ALIGN STAKEHOLDERS

- **Why?** – Positively influencing and aligning vested interests over whom you have no formal authority is crucial to long-term leader success! Creating mutuality and reciprocity is a higher-order leader skill.

- **Main Concepts?** – Stakeholder theory, analysis, types, mapping and engagement, plus actor networks and information asymmetry
- **How?** Coaching Conversations using:
  - **Enabling Networks Model**
    - High Power/High Mutuality = High Relationship (bond!)
    - High Power/Low Mutuality = Medium Relationship (satisfy!)
    - Low Power/High Mutuality = Low Relationship (inform!)
    - Lower Power/Low Mutuality = Avoid (minimal effort)
  - **Five Bases of Power Model**
    - Coercive?
    - Reward?
    - Legitimate? (positional)
    - Expert?
    - Referent? (relational)
- **Accelerating Stakeholder Alignment with Coachees? Use:**
  - **Influencing Without Authority Model**
    - Assume all stakeholders are allies > clarify your goals and priorities > diagnose the world of the other stakeholder > identify relevant currencies (theirs and yours) > deal with relationships > influence stakeholders through give and take

BRIEF CHAPTER SUMMARY – ADVANCING INTERPERSONAL GROWTH

This chapter has highlighted a range of techniques and approaches that Leader Coaches can deploy to help coachees with their interpersonal growth. As the introduction to the chapter highlighted, it presupposes, of course, that the coachees will already have acquired or developed a fair degree of self-awareness and social awareness in order to exercise the degree of self-management to form productive and co-operative relationships with others. Hence, this chapter is important because all businesses are – basically – a confection of human effort and endeavour. An inability to communicate, motivate and inspire will result in an inevitable decline in effort, engagement and momentum, with disastrous business consequences.

To that end, in this chapter we have advocated that Leader Coaches are equipped to coach leaders to:

- **Motivate Employees** by understanding the key concepts underlying motivation (*intrinsic and extrinsic needs, the hierarchy of needs, expectancy theory, goal theory and best practice/fit HRM*) and using key models (i.e. *Two Factor Motivation and Reward and Recognition*) to raise coachee levels of empathy and capability. Accelerated learning in this area can be facilitated by Leader Coaches using *180- or 360-degree employee engagement or leadership development survey data* to spark challenging conversations with coachees.

- **Ignite Customers** by absorbing the key constructs (*brand equity drivers, brand success criteria, total service approach, service personality framework, moment of truth investment, experiential measurement, etc.*) and using two key models (i.e. *Value Proposition Model and Service Culture Wheel*) as proxy lenses to extend coachee understanding and insight. Accelerated coaching in this area can be facilitated by *exemplar case studies of outstanding leadership practice*, supplemented by a range of probing questions.

- **Develop Teams** by elucidating *Tuckman's Stages of Team Formation (forming, storming, norming, performing and adjourning)* and accelerating coachee competence in this area through using *Belbin's Team Roles Model* to help the coachee gain a better insight into the human dimensions of team bonding and productivity.

- **Align Stakeholders** through understanding various stakeholder-related concepts (theory, analysis, mapping, engagement, etc.) and utilising two key models (*Enabling Networks* and *Five Bases of Power*) to elevate coachee appreciation of their ties, responsibilities and necessary approaches to creating mutuality and reciprocity. Accelerating coachee insight in this area can be facilitated by using the *Influencing Without Authority Model*, posing a number of key questions around how traction and buy-in might be gained with 'hard to win over' stakeholder categories.

But the main message underlying this chapter is this: to get things done in business, leaders must rely on others. No leader is an island unto themselves! There are those that think they are, and they will inevitably fail in the end. The capacity for leaders to build relationships with employees, customers, teams and stakeholders is vital if they are to achieve the third objective of the Advanced Leader Coaching Model, namely, business growth. Again, this is another area in which the Leader Coach can be of great assistance.

3 ADVANCING LEADER BUSINESS GROWTH

The final part of our Leader Coaching Practice Model (LCPM) focuses upon accelerating business growth with coachees. Of course, as the previous chapters have highlighted, this is made far easier if personal and interpersonal challenges are addressed beforehand! Assuming that these have been tackled, the Leader Coach can channel their efforts into helping their charges achieve what businesses are all about: growing sales whilst minimising costs.

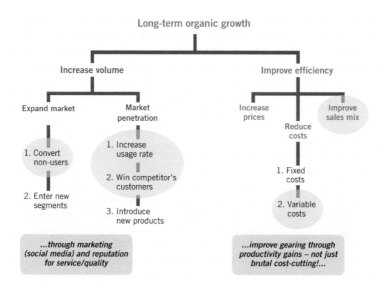

Figure 24: Strategic Growth Focus Model

As the model above highlights (see Edger, 2016, p.67), the primary aim of business leaders is to increase volumes (through market expansion and penetration) whilst improving efficiencies (through cost control, pricing or sales mix management). In order to 'crisis proof' the business, it is also essential that C-Suite leaders build strong cash flows and a robustly capitalised balance sheet in order to ensure their organisations can survive and thrive after so-called 'black swan' events. But to do so, in addition to understanding 'the numbers', they must clarify their *strategy*, gain *operational* grip, inculcate a *change culture* and drive *innovation*. How can the Leader Coach assist? By understanding the concepts and key models underlying each factor, alongside some useful tools, techniques and questions that will accelerate coachee *technical and cognitive thinking capability* in these areas.

3.1 COACHING LEADERS TO CLARIFY STRATEGY

The starting point for leaders wishing to accelerate business growth is Strategic Clarity. Why? Without complete transparency and constancy of purpose and direction, organisations are rendered rudderless and (potentially) ineffective. But many organisations suffer from strategic imprecision, 'drift' and confusion. Their people have no idea *why* their SBU/organisation exists, *what* it is trying to achieve or *how* it is going to get there. It is here that the Leader Coach can greatly assist their coachee. As an independent 'challenger and prober', the Leader Coach can spark a dialogue that enables the coachee to explore new perspectives and tactics, reviewing the *'why, where and how'* of their SBU/organisation's strategy and how it can be implemented/communicated for optimal impact.

MAIN STRATEGIC CONCEPTS

Most Leader Coaches will have a working knowledge of strategy. But before they embark on strategic coaching sessions they would do well – to increase their confidence and credibility – to refresh and sharpen their knowledge of the core concepts and frameworks in this area.

- *What is Strategy?* The word 'strategy' is an ancient concept derived from the Greek word *'strategos'*, incorporating the meanings *'stratus'* (army) and *'ago'* (leading and moving). In contemporary times it is generally defined as a *purposeful direction established for the organisation and its constituent parts to achieve a long-term desired state, by focusing, synthesising and integrating effort, activities and scarce resources*. The emphases on 'long-term', 'integration', 'desired state' and 'scarce resources' are important – implying sustainability, congruence and optimal asset utilisation. Put more simply, Porter (1985) defined strategy as the *'the determination of the basic long-term goals of an enterprise and the adoption of courses of action and the allocation of resources necessary for carrying out those goals'*.

Totally boiled down, strategy can be conceived *as a well-defined route map for the organisation which bridges the gap from 'where we are' to 'where we want to be'* – the setting of a CLEAR direction in order to drive constancy of effort and purpose.

- *What is Strategic Management?* The domain of Strategic Management – developed by several managerial schools of thought over the past century – defines the activity as *the identification and description of the strategies that leaders carry out to achieve better performance, superior growth and competitive advantage for their organisation.* In doing so, leaders actively seek to capitalise upon opportunities and minimise risk, through the inter-related activities of rigorous *analytical strategic planning* and *cognitive strategic thinking.* And the benefits of outstanding Strategic Management? Several studies demonstrate that high-performing firms are more likely to strategise, showing stronger *financial* and *non-financial* outcomes. Strategising organisations are more likely to make better informed decisions, creating greater strategic CLARITY and direction which enable the firm to align its efforts and resources towards optimising its market and consumers, thereby increasing profitability. Intangible outcomes include better employee well-being, engagement and productivity, coupled with less resistance to change.

- *How do Organisations Create Competitive Advantage?* But within the Strategic Management process, how do academics and commentators believe that leaders (based on their research and observations) craft a state of sustainable competitive advantage? What are the *classic* strategic concepts that the Leader Coach needs to familiarise themselves with to be an effective strategic coach?

    - **Clarity**: To the high priest of strategy, Michael Porter (1985 and 1987), clarity, focus and fit were key to achieving competitive advantage through:

        - Creating a *'unique and valuable (market) position'*
        - Making trade-offs by choosing *'what not to do'*
        - Creating fit by aligning organisational activities with one another to support the chosen strategy and, moreover (Porter, 1987), leveraging the processes and activities performed in the firm's *value chain* as the foundations of profound competitive advantage.

    - **Choice**: Choosing the *right strategic path to growth* is also conceived of by Drucker, Ansoff and Porter as a major determinant of competitive advantage:

- Drucker (1955): *'the first responsibility of top management is to ask the question "what is our business" and to make sure it is carefully studied and correctly answered'*
- Ansoff (1968): choosing to pursue the growth strategies of *market penetration* (growth with existing customers), *product development* (growth through new products), *new market development* (growth by recruiting new customers) or *diversification* (growth through unrelated products) would enable organisations to drive competitive advantage
- Porter (1985 and 1987): essentially organisations can make one of three strategic choices about the competitive advantage they seek to achieve – *low cost, differentiation or focus.*

- **Core Competencies**: In addition to the growth choices which organisations can make, leaders should take a *Resource Based View (RBV)* of the *'distinctive competence'* (Selznick, 1957), *'core competency'* (Hamel and Prahalad, 1990) or *'strategic capability'* of their organisation in order to distinguish how they can excel. Their tacit expertise in certain areas is likely to be difficult to duplicate, so firms that wish to gain competitive advantage relentlessly leverage opportunities arising from their own intangible, inimitable characteristics.

- **Co-ordination** – But strategies need to be operationalised! Chandler's (1962) famous dictat, *'structure follows strategy'*, urges leaders to pay close attention to how they organise resources behind a strategy if they wish to bring it alive.

- **Commanding Heights** – In order to gain industry ascendancy, Henderson's (1972) notions of the *'experience curve'* and *'economies of scale'* (doubling production decreases unit costs by 20-to-30 per cent), McKinsey's PIMS (profit increase through market share) and Boston Consulting's Grid (which juxtaposes size against share) suggest that – in order to gain competitive advantage – firms should attend to scale and market share growth for sustained dominance.

- **Complexity** – But strategy cannot just be conceived of as a rational, sequential, planned activity. In reality, strategic planning must be conceived of as *highly complex, emergent, fluid and unpredictable* (Mintzberg, 1987). In disruptive and dynamic environments, according to Mintzberg, 'strategy is a force that resists change, not encourages it!' If firms are to avoid strategic 'drift' and 'convergence', they require agile strategic responsiveness.

- **Calling** – Finally, in a departure from seeing strategy as a dry, inert, rational pursuit, Collins (2001) and Collins and Porras (1994) suggested that companies should ask the existential question *'why'* they exist (with a marketing focus) rather than *'what'* they produce (with a production focus). In his view, companies that achieve competitive advantage address four key questions successfully. *What is our calling? What are we passionate about? What can we be the best in the world at? What drives our economic engine?*

KEY STRATEGIC MODELS

In order to frame their strategic conversations with coachees, Leader Coaches require *process* and *content* models that can stimulate value-added conversations. The two models that we have used successfully in the past as overarching frameworks are the Strategy Process Model (see Figure 25) and the Strategic Pyramid Model (see Figure 26). These act as coat hangers, proxy *guides or navigational tools to bring into play a plethora of other models and frameworks*, all of which can be used to challenge, probe and advance the coachee's strategic thinking and understanding.

The Strategic Process Model (SPM) envisages a rational strategic planning path consisting of four key stages:

Figure 25: Strategic Process Model (SPM)

The stages are conceived as sequential, with feedback loops that occur at each stage of the strategic planning and thinking process. The Strategic Pyramid Model (SPM) falls into the pivotal formulation ('cognitive thinking') stage of the process and is highlighted below.

STAGE 1 – ENVIRONMENT SCANNING

At the beginning of the strategic debate, Leader Coaches must establish if the coachee knows *'where their organisation is now'*. Have they completed an *analytical* process of collecting, scrutinising and interpreting data to understand the prevailing environment in which the organisation operates? Classically, the Leader Coach will be looking to see whether the coachee has mined information relating to patterns, trends and relationships within an organisations' internal and external environment.

- *Organisational Analysis* – Does the coachee understand the prevailing logic and capabilities of the organisation, including its culture, structure (informal and formal), processes, competencies, strategic assets and operational capacity? Models that can aid the Leader Coach in facilitating this discussion include SWOT (the strengths and weaknesses elements), the Cultural Web Model and the Lifecycle of the Firm Model (Edger, 2016 and 2019b).

- *External Analysis* – Examine whether the coachee has got a proper appreciation of the organisation's:
    - Industry Environment – including the competitive structure of the organisation's industry and its relative positioning. Useful models that can generate debate around this element include the BCG Matrix, Porter's Five Forces, Competitive Radar, SWOT (opportunities and threats), Balanced Equation Model and Product Differentiation Model (Edger, 2016 and 2018).
    - Macro Socio-Economic Environment – including an understanding of socio-economic trends, demographics and the regulatory environment. Here the PESTLIED Model (analysing political, economic, social, technological, legal, international, environmental and demographic forces) is particularly illuminating (Edger, 2016).

Pertinent questions that the Leader Coach can use to prompt coachee understanding, insight and knowledge in this area might include:

- *What are the inimitable strategic competencies or capabilities of your organisation? List its key (differentiated) strategic assets. [Here the Leader Coach is trying to get the coachee to establish what their SBU/organisation's core strengths are – leveraging these, rather than building new ones, will yield quicker results.]*

- *Looking at your external competitive environment, which competitor <u>weaknesses</u> and consumer <u>opportunities</u> stand to be exploited at this time and in the future?*

STAGE 2 – STRATEGY FORMULATION

Following on from this *analytical* stage comes the *cognitive* thinking part of the process. Having scanned the environment, the Leader Coach must facilitate a discussion probing the best course of action for accomplishing high performance, growth and competitive advantage. The coachee must reflect upon a series of decisions relating to how the organisation will compete; a *thinking* process described by Mintzberg et al. (1998) as 'synthesis' ('connecting the dots') rather than analysis ('joining the dots') and Beaufre (1963) as 'a mental process, at once abstract and rational, which must be capable of synthesising both psychological and material data'! Usually this incorporates two distinct steps:

- **STEP 1 Decide Strategic Path** – In order to provoke the coachee into taking a series of decisions on how the SBU or organisation will compete, the Leader Coach can use models such as Paths to Growth or the Strategic Growth Focus Model (Edger, 2016 and 2018). By doing so, strategic decisions will be aligned to insights from their environmental assessment. Useful questions from the Leader Coach which will synthesise both *analysis* and *thinking* at this stage include:
  - *What is your organisation's business?*
  - *Who is the target customer for your products/services? Where are your markets?*
  - *What are your points of differentiation in the eyes of the customer?*
  - *How should your portfolio be constructed (by brand, product, category or geography)?*
  - *What skills and capabilities do you require?*
  - *How do you generate more value for investors?*

- *How do you optimise opportunities and minimise risks?*
- **STEP 2 Formulate Coherent Strategy** – Having formulated an intellectually coherent path to growth/mode of competing, the Leader Coach can help the coachee construct an integrated set of goals, objectives and KPIs which bind the 'route map' together combining long-term *aspirations* with short-term *specific* actions. The model we would advocate in order to achieve this is the Strategic Pyramid Model, which serves as an excellent tool for ensuring congruence between all the constituent parts of the strategic plan.

Figure 26: Strategic Pyramid Model

Using the Strategic Pyramid, the Leader Coach can ask the coachee questions that are highlighted in the model, namely:

- *Values: What does your organisation stand for? What are its ethics, principles and beliefs? How are these articulated?*
- *Vision: Where is your organisation going? What does it aspire to achieve? What are its hopes and ambitions?*
- *Purpose: Why do you exist? What is your noble cause? What is its emotional meaning to people?*
- *Mission: What does your business do? Which business are you in? What are your core products, services and customers?*
- *Strategy: How are you going to progress your vision? What are your long-term plans and goals to get you there?*

- *Actions and KPIs: What do you have to do now? What short-term objectives (with specified actions, owners, timeframes, resources and specified outcomes) do you have in place to progress your strategy?*

STAGE 3 – STRATEGY IMPLEMENTATION

Having facilitated an *analysis* of the organisation's internal and external environment and the most impactful *route map* to advance organisational growth and performance, attention turns to putting the organisation's chosen strategy into action (see also 3.3 'Spark a Change Culture'). This is an important stage, much underestimated by leaders and strategy makers. Excellently formulated strategies will fail if they are not properly implemented. Significant organisational re-engineering might be required – for instance, eliminating layers of management and non-value-added processes and structures – that will have a major contingent effect on whether the strategy succeeds or fails. Major considerations that the Leader Coach should raise with the coachee at this stage should include:

- *Congruence – is there perfect alignment between the strategy and each of its dimensions and components?*
- *Articulation – how are you going to communicate the new strategy to capture the hearts and minds of all key stakeholders?*
- *Change Readiness – how 'change ready' is your SBU/organisation – does it have (or need) an embedded CPI, Kaizen, TQM, Six Sigma culture?*
- *Operational Bandwidth – does it possess the operational leadership and capacity to deliver the strategy or do you need to commit, real-locate, animate or 'buy-in' more resources?*

STAGE 4 – STRATEGY EVALUATION

Of course, as Mintzberg observed, strategy analysis, formulation and implementation is a fundamentally 'emergent' process. The best laid strategies and plans can turn to dust because of disruptive shocks. That is why an organisation's strategic 'route map' should be constantly reviewed, evaluated and monitored so that urgent remedial action can be taken if required. What mechanisms and measures should be put in place to act as early warning signals? Questions that Leader Coaches can ask coachees here might include:

- *Do you have a fixed benchmark of <u>desired</u> strategic performance?*
- *What measures of <u>actual</u> strategic performance do you have in place?*
- *How will you monitor the <u>variance</u> between desired and actual strategic performance?*
- *How will you take purposeful and swift corrective action to close the '<u>strategic gap</u>'?*

ACCELERATING STRATEGIC CLARITY WITH COACHEES

The SPM above provides an excellent template with which Leader Coaches can facilitate a challenging discussion with the coachee, enabling the leader to achieve a sense of greater strategic clarity. Admittedly – and obviously – it is not a panacea. It will not provide perfect answers and, indeed, the leader is most likely going to involve their wider team and other stakeholders in the strategy formulation and implementation process. But it provides a valuable starting point. So, how can Leader Coaches really accelerate coachee Strategic Clarity using more thought-provoking and 'left-field' mechanisms?

We advocate that Leader Coaches who really want to accelerate leader development in this area try utilising de Bono's (1985) Six Thinking Hats as a means of challenging and resetting perceptions, prejudices and inert thinking. So, what is it and how can Leader Coaches use it?

De Bono conceived his Six Hat Thinking technique for overloaded managers, creating an imaginative process that would enable them to look at decisions from a number of key perspectives, forcing them to step outside their *habitual thinking style* in order to gain a more rounded, balanced view of a situation. To quote De Bono: *'the main difficulty of thinking is confusion. We try to do too much at once. Emotions, information, logic, hope and creativity all crowd in on us. It's like juggling too many balls'* (1985, p.55). In this statement he could have been talking purely about strategising; this is a hugely complex and messy activity in which leaders have to unbundle multiple data, thoughts and feelings to achieve value-added insights and decisions. In order to *reduce confusion and increase CLARITY* of thought, De Bono advocated that individuals metaphorically wear coloured hats to represent six different types of thinking (see Figure 27): *blue* (managing and process control thinking), *white* (fact-based thinking), *green* (creative thinking), *black* (discerning, cautious thinking), *yellow* (optimistic benefits-based thinking) and *red* (emotionally based feelings and intuition).

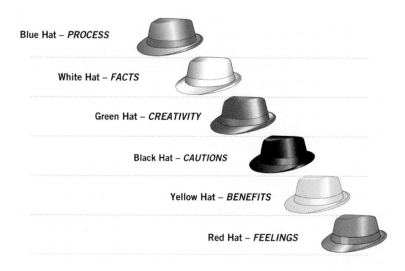

Blue Hat – *PROCESS*

White Hat – *FACTS*

Green Hat – *CREATIVITY*

Black Hat – *CAUTIONS*

Yellow Hat – *BENEFITS*

Red Hat – *FEELINGS*

Figure 27: De Bono's Six Thinking Hats

In terms of using this during a strategic coaching conversation, the Leader Coach can get the coachee to rotate the metaphorical (or actual!) wearing of the hats to adopt specific thinking styles, signposted above.

- ***Blue Hat 'Process'*** – Here the Leader Coach will be concerned with the 'process control' thinking. In the specific case of strategic coaching, this is a 'chairperson' role that can be adopted by the Leader Coach to facilitate the conversation and take notes – rotating and moving the coachee around the hats in order to challenge and expand the coachee's thinking.

- ***White Hat*** **'Facts'** – Asking the coachee to wear the white hat, the Leader Coach will request them to examine a strategic topic or issue by purely focusing on *rational facts and information* (particularly useful when unpacking Stage 1 of the SPM: Environmental Scanning).

  - *What Information do you have about this strategic issue?*
  - *What does it tell you?*
  - *What information do you lack?*
  - *What information would you like to have?*

- *How are you going to get it?*

- **Green Hat 'Creativity'** – Having considered the facts surrounding a particular challenge, the Leader Coach can ask the coachee to wear the green hat, symbolising *creativity, new ideas and possibilities*. Here, the Leader Coach encourages the coachee to come up with creative solutions to a strategic issue – however outlandish or improbable they might seem (this is particularly useful for stages 2 and 3 of the SPM: Formulation and Implementation).

  - *Given the facts at hand, is there a new way you can do this?*

  - *What about approaching the issue from a fundamentally opposing viewpoint?*

  - *Are there any alternatives that you haven't already considered?*

- **Black Hat 'Cautions'** – Now the Leader Coach can help the coachee kick the tyres on their creative thinking by asking them to adopt a *cautious, critical thinking, risk-based thinking frame*. It goes without saying that this hat should be used fleetingly and sparingly (leaders wear it enough in their everyday life as it is!).

  - *What are the weaknesses with some of your ideas?*

  - *What are the risks?*

  - *Where will resistance lie?*

  - *How can it be mitigated/avoided?*

- **Yellow Hat 'Benefits'** – Bringing the coachee back to creative solutions that have been subsequently 'risk assessed', the Leader Coach might get them to *optimistically review the benefits and feasibility* of some of the original ideas that 'stand up'.

  - *What are the strengths of your ideas?*

  - *How can you get them to succeed?*

  - *Who else do you need to sell their benefits to?*

- **Red Hat 'Feelings'** – Finally, the Leader Coach might encourage *intuition, feelings and emotions to come to the fore*, to test whether the coachee actually has any passion for the strategic solutions they are advocating (perhaps the strongest indicator that they will actually 'make it happen').

  - *Why do you have a hunch that this will work?*

  - *Why do you have a good feeling that this will fly?*

  - *On a scale of one to ten, how passionate do you feel about the way forward?*

QUICK RECAP: LEADER COACHING TO CLARIFY STRATEGY

- **Why?** – Setting a clear direction and purpose enables the organisation to *physically and emotionally commit* to a noble cause that has meaning and resonance.

- **Main Concepts?** – Strategic management and competitive advantage (clarity, choice, core competencies, co-ordination, commanding heights and complexity)

- **How?** Coaching Conversations using:
  - **Strategic Process Model**
    - Environment Scanning (organisational and external analysis)
    - Strategy Formulation (decide path and formulate coherent strategy)
    - Strategy Implementation (congruence, articulation, change readiness, operational bandwidth?)
    - Strategy Evaluation (benchmarking, variance analysis and corrective action)

- **Accelerating Stakeholder Alignment with Coachees?** Use:
  - **De Bono's Six Thinking Hats**
    - Blue Hat (process): 'chairperson'
    - White Hat (facts): 'empiricist'
    - Green Hat (creativity): 'innovator'
    - Black Hat (cautions): 'rationalist'
    - Yellow Hat (benefits): 'optimist'
    - Red Hat (feelings): 'intuitive biases'

3.2 COACHING LEADERS TO GRIP OPERATIONS

Having assisted the leader to clarify their strategic intent and its means of implementation, Leader Coaches are often called upon to facilitate conversations relating to operational excellence. Why? Very often an organisation's strategy fails not because it is wrong per se, but because it is not translated into action by the operational 'black box' of the organisation. In order to accelerate business growth, leaders must be able to have some grip over their operational machine so that their intended direction is turned into purposeful and impactful outcomes. Organisations exist to produce *distinctive* goods and services that address viable markets with needs that cannot be *completely* fulfilled by competitors. Their reputation hinges on their ability to meet their specific *customer promises* relating to quality, consistency, speed, memorability and efficiency. To that extent, the SBU/organisational leader has to have an organisational machine in place that, first, they can rely on to deliver on customer expectations and, second, is agile enough to respond to changing demand.

MAIN OPERATIONAL GRIP CONCEPTS

How is operational grip conceptualised in terms of 'form' and 'purpose'? What do Leader Coaches need to know about how business leaders can control operations? This section will provide a brief reprise of some of the typologies that exist within the *operational control literature* that will advance their understanding of the domain. Seven 'forms' of control will be considered:

- *Direct* – Direct or simple forms of operational control are characteristic of workplaces that rely upon singular forms power or authority (e.g. nineteenth-century factory owner–managers, small and medium enterprise – SME – owners). In this context, due to the business scale and type of ownership, one person *informally* interacts (sometimes autocratically) directly with employees. As the firm grows and control cannot be vested purely in one person, levels of hierarchy are built and systems established to ensure conformance.

- *Technical/systems* – Here operational control is achieved through prescribed standards being delivered through operatives whose outputs are measured and monitored by 'controllers'. In this form, especially in production contexts, there is Tayloristic *scientific control* of process systems, stages and throughputs by both measurement and machines.

- *Bureaucratic* – This form of operational control relies upon the use of Weberian *formal rules and laws* to regulate outputs. In this paradigm, business leaders are bound by specified rules and cannot (in theory) act in an arbitrary manner as sanctions for misdemeanours and rewards for success are 'officially prescribed'.

- *Multi-layered* – This approach, favoured within the 'field' operations environments of multi-unit enterprises (as opposed to generic MNCs), conceives of *mutually interdependent systems, standards and service controls* being cascaded throughout the operational line to ensure 'line of sight' alignment and co-ordinated effort (Garvin and Levesque, 2008; Edger, 2012). Hence performance metrics relating to outputs such as sales, margin, safety compliance, labour ratios and customer service are applied at every level of 'field' hierarchy, albeit these measures are tailored to each level of strategic business unit (SBU).

- *Concertive* – In this post-bureaucratic conception, the frontier of control in organisations is moved to employees through mechanisms such as *self-managed teams* (assisted by Kaizen, Six Sigma or Deming principles of continuous improvement). Here groups of employees are conceived of as being socially self-regulating 'clans' where continuous improvement initiatives are generated consensually amongst co-workers. The benefits of this form of control for organisations are that it reduces costs through managerial delayering and (theoretically) increases worker discretionary effort (Barker, 2005).

- *Chimerical* – This is a hybrid form of operational control where vertical control is achieved by means of surveillance through machinery and technology (Sewell, 1998). Horizontal control is achieved in socialised, interdependent work contexts through teamwork and co-worker assessment.

- *Socio-ideological* – These forms of operational control are derived from purposefully designed organisational norms and values. Vision, mission and value statements which designate the 'way in which we do business' are calculated managerial attempts to ensure ideological adherence to senior management will occur through constructing 'meaning' within the organisation through a set of narratives. Ideology co-opts mindsets, underpinning certain laws and rules, prescribing what are acceptable/unacceptable behaviours (Alvesson and Karreman, 2004). Such approaches are not mutually independent from bureaucratic, technical and multi-layered types of organisational control; rather, they work in tandem with them. Its benefit to senior management is that it guides individual decision making and choices into *purposeful action* in complex, ambiguous and uncertain situations where mandated rules might be lacking (e.g. during a hitherto-unexperienced organisational crisis).

KEY OPERATIONAL MODELS

The key overarching model we use for helping leaders to grip operations – incorporating four key pillars – is shown in Figure 28 below.

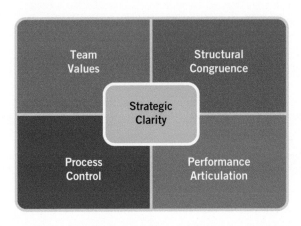

Figure 28: Operational Excellence Model (OEM)

It is our contention that leaders lacking grip in any of the four main pillars in the OEM above will fail to operationalise their strategy (which sits at the heart of the model). Team development and motivation has been dealt with in Sections 2.1 and 2.3, but how does the Leader Coach create value-added coaching conversations around these key pillars? And furthermore, which models prove particularly useful 'conversational anchors' in these areas?

STRUCTURAL CONGRUENCE

In order to achieve operational grip, the first question the Leader Coach needs to ask the coachee is *'how well does your current structure fit your strategy?'* The Internal Value Chain Model in Figure 29 illustrates how internal functions should 'prop up' and feed into the operational line, and how *all* elements of the structure should be aligned behind the main point of *direct customer interface* in leisure and retail businesses, namely: the units and their service-providing teams.

Figure 29: Internal Value Chain Model

Using Figure 29 to probe and challenge the coachee on congruence, the Leader Coach might ask:

- *Strategic Leadership – To what extent are your strategic decision makers – those responsible for the strategic direction of the firm, resource allocation and external stakeholder management – 'in' the business (reaching down and touching/feeling the pulse of the front line) rather than sat 'on' the business in a detached, dispassionate and disengaged manner?*

- *Technocracy – To what extent do you have resource holders and policy makers who are expert functionaries (in property/maintenance, finance/legal/audit, IT, marketing/new product development/supply chain and HR/talent management) rather than enthusiastic amateurs? Also, how do you encourage functions to abandon their silo mentality and work together?*

- *Administration and Support – To what extent are enabling support personnel available 24/7 to the front line? Tell me about your*

> *Operational Excellence personnel (experts in operational efficiency and effectiveness) who regulate the flow of information/communication/initiatives between the technocracy and the line – do they exist and (if they do) how effective are they?*

- *Operational Line – How do you organise the operational line (by geography, product, brand, category, etc.)? What is their span of control? How often does it touch customer-facing staff?*

- *Units and Service Providers – To what extent are your front-line units and service providers provided with the administrative, technical and practical support to delight customers?*

Useful as it is for Leader Coaches in facilitating discussions with coachees on structural congruence, this model is inevitably fairly normative and descriptive, concentrating on *tangible* issues of alignment. It does not deal with *intangible* issues such as competence, power, ideology, politics and culture – all important elements that contribute to success and failure within organisations (issues that are dealt with elsewhere in this book). But one thing that the Leader Coach can probe with the coachee is the *destabilising extent* to which strategic leaders and technocrats in their SBU/organisation might have a preference for *efficiency* ('doing it right') rather than the operational line's focus (due to their closeness to customers) on *effectiveness* ('doing the right thing').

PERFORMANCE ARTICULATION

Leader Coaches understand that 'what gets measured, gets managed' – all the better if what is being measured and incentivised reflects and incorporates the core objectives of the organisation, and if these are ARTICULATED all the way through the organisation to *shift level*. The KPI Cascade Model in Figure 30 below provides a framework for Leader Coaches to probe the coachee on levels of articulation, alignment and 'line of sight' from the strategic apex of the organisation to the operational point of contact!

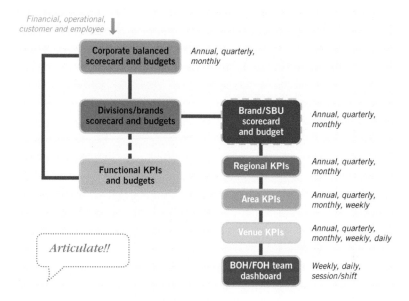

Figure 30: KPI Cascade Model

Coherent, clearly articulated performance-measurement systems (backed up by appraisals, incentives and communications) are critical – particularly in dispersed multi-site national and international organisations. Using this framework, the Leader Coach can probe the coachee, asking:

- *Corporate Balanced Scorecard/Budget – Tell me how it incorporates financial and customer outputs, with people and operational process inputs? How do they fit with your organisation/SBU's top-line strategy and objectives?*

- *Divisional/Brand Scorecard/Budget – To what extent do targets at this level mirror the corporate scorecard? How are targets proportionately adjusted for their respective business-model needs (according to brand, unit, geography)?*

- *Functional KPIs/Budget – How are these made relevant to the overall objectives of the organisation? How do they meld with the needs of the business? (Very often, functional KPIs are totally detached from the body politic of the organisation!)*

- *Operational Line – How are financial, customer, operational and people targets 'articulated' annually, quarterly and monthly, weekly, daily and BY SHIFT/SESSION (where the 'rubber hits the road')? Are they delusional stretch targets or are they achievable and motivational?*

What the Leader Coach is really focussing on here with the coachee is the degree to which their SBU/organisation really is pushing in one direction, rather than pulling itself apart! But there is one further question that a Leader Coach should also ask the Coachee: *tell me about the 'the one number that counts in your organisation that everybody buys into?'* This will provide the basis for a sobering conversation if it is not customer related!

PROCESS CONTROL

Great businesses leave very little to chance. In Operational Process Improvement terminology, they are expert at co-ordinating 'transforming inputs' (staff, technology, facilities and machinery) to shape 'transformed inputs' (materials, information and customers) through several value-added process stages, to create valuable outputs (i.e. quality, safety, speed, satisfaction, sales and profit). The degree to which businesses invest in the enablers (i.e. staff, technology, machinery and facilities) will determine how efficient their processes are; although one should never underestimate the degree to which cultural issues, political infighting, lack of tacit knowledge and personal agendas can undermine the operation of important core processes in businesses. Questions the Leader Coach can ask coachees here might include:

- *How well do core processes (i.e. customer, production, employee, etc.) work in your organisation (as measured in terms of quality, speed, consistency, transparency and safety)?*
- *Where they don't work effectively, highlight the major pinch points and blockages for me.*
- *How do you measure and calibrate the debilitating effects of these bottlenecks? What would be the upside of reducing the number of non-value-added process stages and/or reducing the number of blockages?*
- *How can you eliminate these non-value-added rate limiters? (By increasing your focus on or investment in the 'enablers', namely: people, technology, machinery and facilities!)*

TEAM ALIGNMENT

In order to establish operational grip, alongside structure, performance management and process control – which might be termed as hard *bureaucratic controls* – successful leaders deploy a soft *socio-ideological* approach exemplified through a 'values system'. This mandates a set of required behaviours that will be the basis for practical/ethical action. These are intended to shape attitudes and/or guide practices that provide the moral standards for permissible conduct within the SBU/organisation. In some instances – most pertinently within international contexts – these serve as a corrective against ingrained personal or cultural values which might subvert how people are treated and/or day-to-day business is transacted. These espoused leader value systems are *bounded* statements of 'the way we do things around here' intended to ensure that, in the absence of explicit instructions, their teams and followers are *ideologically programmed* 'to do the right thing' in most circumstances. Figure 31 below (the Values Transfer Model) provides the Leader Coach with a useful framework with which they can challenge, probe and test a coachee's understanding and effectiveness in this area.

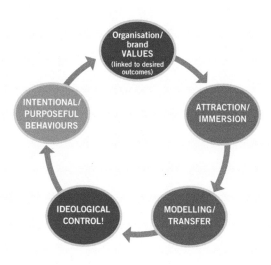

Figure 31: Values Transfer Model

Obviously, the attraction of binding values systems is that they are a cheaper form of control mechanism than bureaucratic ones! Also, given the fact that as one leader once said to us 'you can't take the Operations Manual onto the trading floor!', they provide the leader with some comfort that their teams will act properly in most circumstances – thereby protecting the operational integrity/reputation of their organisation. Questions that the Leader Coach can use in relation to this model with coachees might include:

- *Coherent logic* – *Do the values you espouse to your team have a coherent logic (i.e. do they resonate with why the organisation exists and what it stands for)?*

- *Simplicity* – *Are they emotionally impactful and easy to understand?*

- *Archaeology* – *Are they connected with the organisation's history and DNA? (For instance, Ray Kroc's 'quality, value, service and cleanliness' were devised over fifty years ago and still guide behaviours within McDonald's today!)*

- *Intrinsic alignment* – *Are your values embedded (and tested for) in your recruitment/immersion and communication processes?*

- *Modelling* – *Give me examples of how your values are modelled in both 'word and deed' by you and your team?*

- *Self-regulation* – *How do you ensure that not only do your people live the values but 'self-regulate' others that don't (particularly when you're not around!)?*

- *Intentional/purposeful behaviours* – *Give me examples of how your values lead to intentional/purposeful behaviours from those around you? How do your values act as 'cultural binds', possibly transcending debilitating counter-cultural norms (such as self-protective leadership and nepotism)?*

ACCELERATING OPERATIONAL GRIP WITH COACHEES

The Operational Excellence Model – and its constituent parts and models outlined above – provide an extremely useful entry point for Leader Coaches in facilitating conversations with coachees around achieving operational grip. But these are *'macro'* frameworks that provide overarching organisation/team-wide solutions. What if the leader themselves has to take a *'micro'* approach, solving operational problems themselves? Very often, the best leaders take both a *macro and micro approach*, creating the climate for operational grip to occur by setting up and modelling the correct structures, measures and behaviours BUT they also 'get into the detail' by solving operational issues directly themselves! By taking direct action they can both accelerate business growth and set an example to the rest of the organisation as to what good looks like. The models that the Leader Coach can use here are our GAPPAR model that helps coachees accelerate their thinking and approach to solving operational issues and the Ishikawa Diagram which conducts a *root-cause analysis* on the origins of deep-seated operational issues.

First, let's consider the GAPPAR Model (Figure 32). This can be used by Leader Coaches in two ways to help coachees accelerate operational grip: either as a coaching tool during conversations to unpack and (potentially solve) operational problematics *or* as a framework that can be offered up to coachees to take away and use with their teams.

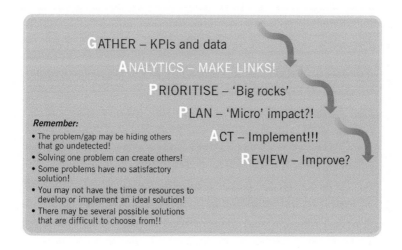

Figure 32: The GAPPAR Model

The GAPPAR framework is fairly logical and self-explanatory, but some added-value questions Leader Coaches can use to probe and challenge coachee thinking might include:

- *Gather – Tell me about how you are 'in' the business rather than 'on' it. Give me examples! How do you triangulate quantitative* data (including customer, quality, financial, product, portfolio, pricing, services, markets, structure, technology, locations, resources, human capital, processes, practices, procedures, micro-operational, engagement, service delivery speed, operational resilience, etc.) with your own qualitative investigation (listening, observing and doing)?

- Analytics – How do you join the dots between multiple data sources? How do you make linkages and connections between what you have read, seen, heard and experienced to make qualified judgements on what you would like to maintain, cease or improve within the operational domain? (This is a prime skill. These advanced cognitive thinking capabilities enable high performers to 'think then do' rather than 'do then think' – marking them out as being superior to their competitive set!) The Ishikawa Diagram in figures 33a, b and c below is an additional tool that the Leader Coach can use in this area to accelerate root-cause analysis.

- Prioritise – Have you located the causes rather than symptoms of operational breakdowns? What are the short-term 'low hanging fruit' fixes, 'easy to do's with quick paybacks? Given everything you have read about and observed first hand, what are the three operational improvements you could activate which would immediately enhance the customer experience?

- Plan – How are you going to co-opt your team and other resource holders within the organisation to formulate and activate a viable plan? Where will resistance lie? How will you overcome it? Who around you has got the will and skill to fix these issues quickly?

- Act – How are you going to drive implementation whilst continuing to SELL the plan and benefits to all stakeholders within the organisation?

- Review – How are you going to constantly monitor and measure performance outcomes, to nudge, incrementally improve and land? How will you celebrate and cheerlead successes with your team?

The common mistake that leaders make, attempting to solve operational issues, is targeting SYMPTOMS rather the true CAUSES of operational malfunctions. In the analytics section of the GAPPAR Model above, Leader Coaches will encourage coachees to think analytically, making linkages and connections to join the dots. Often, the coachee will be able to describe the EFFECT of an operational issue but not its ROOT CAUSE. What can the Leader Coach do here? We advocate use of the Ishikawa Diagram (otherwise known as Fishbone Analysis) with coachees to help them get to the heart of an issue. The example below – where the leader is grappling with poor-food-quality issues in their chain of restaurants – provides a template for conversations using Ishikawa.

STEP 1 – *Materials*: The Leader Coach has a variety of materials at their disposal for this task (white board, flipchart, post-it notes and software packages that can be useful in creating fishbone diagrams: EngineRoom, Excel, etc.).

STEP 2 – *The Effect*: The Leader Coach brainstorms the operational issue that needs solving (THE EFFECT) with the coachee. This should be as descriptive as possible. In this example, the coachee highlights POOR FOOD QUALITY SCORES in their restaurant chain. This is placed on the right-hand side of the *backbone* of the *illustrative fish*.

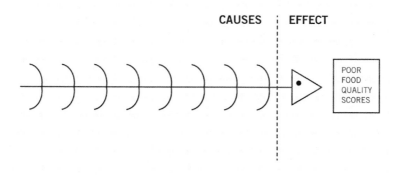

Figure 33a: Ishikawa Diagram

STEP 3 – *Causal Categories*: Having identified an effect (POOR FOOD QUALITY SCORES), the next step involves the Leader Coach facilitating a discussion around the primary causes, which is achieved either by *categorising* by function or process sequence. In manufacturing contexts, the categories are often 'method', 'machine', 'materials', 'measurement', 'people' and 'environment'. In service settings, 'machine' and 'method' are often replaced by 'policies' (rules) and 'procedures' (tasks). In the case of determining causal categories for poor food quality, it is highly likely that the categories and their descriptors will be as follows:

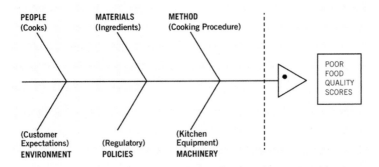

Figure 33b: Ishikawa Diagram

STEP 4 – *Causal Sub-Categories*: In themselves, the casual categories and descriptors will not be sufficient to locate ROOT CAUSES. Now the Leader Coach needs to probe these categories by brainstorming using the 'Five-Why' approach (drilling down by asking 'why?' five times) and then adding additional root causes to the fishbone, as detailed below.

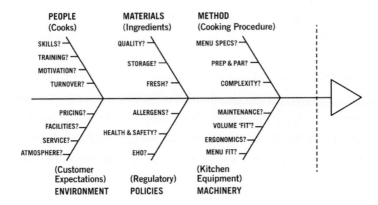

Figure 33c: Ishikawa Diagram

STEP 5 – *Correlation*: Having completed the fishbone, the Leader Coach needs to establish the level of correlation between cause and effect. As it is unlikely that the Leader Coach is trained in regression analysis and/or the coachee has the time and resources to complete designed experiments, the Leader Coach should help the coachee to identify the three-to-five primary root causes which can be the subject of further investigation outside of the coaching conversation. In this instance, three causal sub-categories were identified as the three root causes of poor food-quality scores: *cooking complexity, turnover and pricing* (expectations based on price being degraded by actual experience). But in the end, if the Leader Coach has achieved nothing else, at least they have highlighted to coachees the importance of conducting detailed root-cause analysis rather than surface symptom speculation!

QUICK RECAP: LEADER COACHING TO GRIP OPERATIONS

- **Why?** – Having a deep tacit understanding and 'grip' of the operational 'black box' enables leaders to get things done quicker and smarter, with better quality outcomes – great leaders are 'in' the business not 'on' it
- **Main Concepts?** – Direct/simple control, technical/systems control, bureaucratic, multi-layered, concertive, chimerical and socio-ideological
- **How?** Coaching Conversations using:
    - **Operational Excellence Model**
        - Strategic Clarity (direction and purpose)?
        - Structural Congruence (Internal Value Chain Model)?
        - Performance Articulation (KPI Cascade Model)?
        - Process Control (transforming inputs into value-added outputs)?
        - Team Alignment (Values Transfer Model)?
- **Accelerating Operational Grip with Coachees? Use:**
    - **GAPPAR Model**
        - **G**ather (KPIs and Data), **A**nalytics (make linkages), **P**rioritise ('big rocks'), **P**lan ('micro' impact?), **A**ct (implement), **R**eview (improve?)

- **Ishikawa Method** (establishing root causes!)
  - Step 1 – Materials
  - Step 2 – The Effect
  - Step 3 – Causal Categories
  - Step 4 – Causal Sub-Categories
  - Step 5 – Correlation

3.3 COACHING LEADERS TO SPARK A CHANGE CULTURE

While humans are the most adaptable animal on the planet, people as individuals tend to dislike change. Commercial change-management companies and consultants have exploited this: selling the fear of change and change management as a package offering is big business. Of course, there are also plenty of people in organisations, often in positions of authority, who use the fear of uncertainty for personal gain, while others thrive on fuelling the rumour mill with terrible predictions of what the change means for everyone.

Effective leaders are not fear mongers in any regard, least of all about change, which they understand is already viewed with trepidation. To be clear, they do not hide from tough truths but rather define the issue, discuss the solution and give genuine support during implementation. They fully understand that some people will be less willing to comply and some may even resist but they are not derailed, just mindful that the human condition is not as straightforward as rational decision makers would like it to be, free will being what it is.

Effective leadership notwithstanding, change initiatives regularly fail in organisations because the environment is not conducive for them to succeed. A business's readiness to adapt, assimilate and grow is critical to its survival, therefore leaders need to develop and nurture a Change Culture proactively. Organisations with a Change Culture do not discuss change initiatives but rather incremental/continuous improvements. Implicit in the incremental approach is that much is already being done very well and small adjustments are easily made to a solid foundation. It has a totally different tone to the fear-inducing war cry 'there are going to be some big changes around here!'

This positive and appreciative approach creates a receptive, motivated and solutions-focused workforce ready to drive the business forward together, taking obstacles in its stride and using momentum to push the organisation to the next performance level. Consequently, where the Leader Coach facilitates leaders to spark a Change Culture, the return on investment in the coaching process is exponential.

MAIN CHANGE CULTURE CONCEPTS

Understanding Culture

'Culture refers to norms of behaviour and shared values among a group of people' (Kotter, 1996, p.36). Culture of any kind is circular or self-sustaining. People join the culture based on perceived similarities and, by behaving the same way for acceptance, reaffirm the culture of the group. Through ongoing iterations of joining, conforming and affirming, culture becomes a deeply ingrained framework or group mindset that is highly influential, complex and pervasive (i.e. it permeates everything). Peer pressure and group sanctions leading to toxic teams and groupthink are discussed elsewhere (see 2.3 'Develop Teams').

A Change Culture is one in which embracing change is a group preference (shared value); everyone is thus expected to engage positively with change initiatives. Objection to change programmes will not be frowned upon but ongoing resistance in the absence of a solutions-focused or compromise approach is unlikely to be tolerated.

Sparking a Change Culture for incumbent leaders probably requires the undermining of the current culture. This is no easy feat, as the following figure illustrates, showing culture at the top of the Change Difficulty Pyramid.

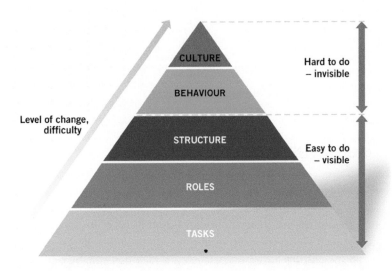

Figure 34: Change Difficulty Pyramid

Change resistance is frequently due to previous bad experiences of change implementation where perhaps much was promised, little delivered and much discomfort experienced along the way. Developing a track record as an effective change implementer is a useful way for leaders to gain credibility with employees, increasing the likelihood of future buy-in. The Leader Coach can work with the coachee to establish a reputation as an effective leader for change and in so doing *spark a Change Culture*.

Sparking a Change Culture

While there are many change-management models in circulation, Kotter's (1996) Eight Step Process for Leading Change (elucidated in the Eight Phases of Change Model in Figure 35) is one of the most popular and comprehensive, and a steadfast approach for many coaches. What does it advocate and what questions can Leader Coaches ask to raise coachee capability and insight in this area?

Implementing
and sustaining
the change
8) Make it stick
7) Don't let-up

6) Create short-term wins
Engaging and
enabling the
organisation
5) Enable action
4) Communication for buy-in

3) Get the vision right
Creating a
climate for
change
2) Build guiding teams
1) Increase urgency

Figure 35: Eight Phases of Change Model

1. Establishing a sense of urgency

Effective leaders are continuously evaluating the long-term viability of their businesses, anticipating change and proactively responding. As a result, effective leaders are typically engaging in incremental rather than radical change. However, radical change is often easier to lead because the imperative to change is obvious (i.e. severe consequences or undesirable alternatives, such as business closure, large-scale redundancies, large fines, etc.). In the absence of a crisis, on the other hand, the use of quantitative information derived from rational business models (Porter's Five Forces, sales-forecasting, profit margin analysis, etc.) is an established method of creating urgency and greatly appeals to the rational decision makers that frequently occupy the C-Suite. However, rational models may fail to engage employees who do not always judge a change based on the bottom line but rather on the perceived inconvenience to themselves (Kahneman, 2012).

Social psychologist Kurt Lewin's (1951) Force Field Analysis is a more encompassing model for demonstrating the imperative to change. It illustrates the conflict between rational driving forces for change and emotional restraining forces resisting the change.

Figure 36: Force-Field Analysis of Change Model

To use the model, both the driving and restraining forces are listed and weighted (assigned a value). Where the total value of the driving forces exceeds the total value of the restraining forces, change is warranted. Where the total values are equal, the issue being analysed is said to be in a state of equilibrium (not requiring change). Questions that Leader Coaches can ask coachees to prompt awareness, insight and competence in this area might include:

- *How do you create a burning platform for this change (i.e. an overwhelming case for change that will be understood by key constituents)?*

- *Where do you think resistance will lie in the organisation and how will you overcome it? (IN EXTREMIS) How will you change the culture of your SBU/Organisation to make this change happen?*

- *How are you going to demonstrate personally (through personal sacrifice or symbolic behaviours) how important and urgent your change initiative is?*

2. Creating the guiding coalition

Change programmes require a designated task force to champion them to successful completion. Naturally, not every employee can be on this coalition but a combination of leadership (to drive the change) and management (to control the process) appears to be the optimal mix. Furthermore, Kotter

(1996) advocates that the coalition is well represented in terms of *position power*, *expertise*, *credibility* and *leadership*:

- *Position power* or *legitimate power* (French and Raven, 1959) is 'a person's ability to influence others by being in a more powerful position' (Gibson, Ivancevich and Donnelly, 1997, p.250). Individuals with position power are key stakeholders (see 2.4 'Align Stakeholders') and can block or expedite the change process. They can also enforce the change through wielding their legitimate power over their subordinates. This is a generally discouraged approach but where the consequence of non-compliance is severe (e.g. safety), punitive measures may be required. A lack of power slows the process down through the inability to make decisions.

- *Expertise* is another form of power (see 2.4 'Align Stakeholders': 'Five Bases of Power Model'). The exclusion of experts from the change process not only undermines the change as perceived by others but is a poor use of an asset. Furthermore, it runs the risk of the expert being sufficiently displeased to sabotage the change initiative or leave the company.

- *Credibility* includes those already mentioned and informal leaders (sometimes called social architects). Informal leaders are employees who have influence over others but have no formal authority. They can be identified through observation, speaking to effective line managers or asking employees (anonymously if necessary) who they respect most in their team/department and why. Where such individuals disagree with or resist the proposed change, their opinions should be taken seriously as their influence will cause others to disengage from the change.

- *Leadership* with experience in instigating and implementing change is desirable.

Questions regarding building a guiding coalition that the Leader Coach can address to the coachee here might include:

- *Which individuals in your organisation hold the greatest positional/ legitimate sway? How will you co-opt them either directly or indirectly (through representation) on your guiding team?*

- *Who are the real experts in your organisation who have the real tacit knowledge relating to your change initiative? How do you get some of them onside to join your guiding coalition?*

- *Who are the highly respected 'opinion formers' – those who might lack positional power and expertise in this particular initiative but whose judgement and authenticity is highly rated across your organisation? How do you convince them to join the guiding team?*
- *Who are the leaders that have a track record of landing things in your organisation? How are you going to get some of them to commit to being part of the guiding team for this project?*

3. Developing a vision and strategy

This is covered in 3.1 'Clarify Strategy'. Questions that the Leader Coach can ask here include:

- *What is the (long-term) uplifting and noble vision of your change initiative? What is its emotional meaning and appeal to people? Does it pass the 'get out of bed' test?*
- *What is your intended medium-term strategy to get it done (in terms of milestones and resources)?*
- *What are your short-term KPIs and tactics that will articulate the vision and strategy at all levels of the organisation? How will they be monitored?*

4. Communicating the change vision

The ability to articulate the desired change is paramount to its success. A change to employees' current reality means a hitherto-unexperienced workplace. This requires a leap of faith, which is particularly difficult if people can't see what they are being expected to commit to.

Communication as a complicated concept is articulated exceptionally well by Peters' (2012) Square of Communication.

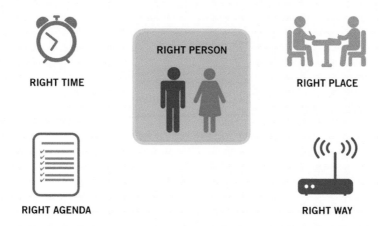

Figure 37: Square of Communication Model

- *Right person/people* includes the employee body and any other stakeholders affected by the change, such as customers, partners and suppliers.

- *Right time* can be as subtle as the time of day, week, month and/ or year in terms of people's receptivity to hearing the message. Timing may be staggered on a need-to-know basis, but this may fall foul of the pervasive rumour mill, so its effectiveness should be carefully considered. The message should be repeated often at the *right time*.

- *Right agenda* draws on the drivers for change in alignment with the business's strategy and should include an articulation of what success/the outcome will look like. Prioritised work lists, assigned roles, resources allocation, work schedules, interim deadlines and preferred completion date for the change come under the *right agenda*.

- *Right way* is less tangible because it involves soft skills. Several communication channels should be used. Delivery should be through multi-channels (individuals, groups, departments, etc.) in multi-media. Content is critical, with the use of simplicity, stories and metaphor encouraged but hyperbole and jargon discouraged. Charismatic speaking skills also prove to be a distinct advantage.

- *Right place* includes delivering the message where it can be heard (e.g. not where large noisy machinery is operating), where employees feel safe to challenge/object and for productive discussion about the initiative.

Questions that the Leader Coach can ask the coachee here might include:

- *Which stakeholders need to be communicated to concerning this change initiative?*
- *When should relevant parties be contacted and informed? How frequently?*
- *What should the content and tone of your communications look like? How can they successfully address the 'what's in it for me' concerns of each stakeholder?*
- *Which channels should we use to convey the communications? Which ones are most appropriate for each stakeholder group?*
- *Where can you deliver the message, making people feel safe enough to challenge your questions or proposals?*

5. Empowering employees for broad-based action

When employees feel blocked or impeded, it is difficult for them to commit to the change and enthusiasm may wane. Providing resources in terms of appropriate tools/materials, physical/emotional support and training is a basic starting point for promoting action. Establishing guidelines and tolerances around budgets and resources can help to de-centralise decision making, giving autonomy to individuals and teams. This empowers employees and motivates through recognition (i.e. the acknowledgement that they are capable and responsible).

A powerful method of empowering employees is to include them in the decision-making process using an approach such as 'participatory decision making'. Why? Empowering employees to 'participate' creates buy-in. ('*Which are you more likely to commit to: a decision made by others that is being imposed upon you or a decision you've had a chance to provide input on?*' – Blanchard, 2007, p.220)

Questions that the Leader Coach can ask here might include:

- *Have you given your employees the resources (tools, time and budget) and delegated authority to make this change happen?*

- *Have you clearly set out their prescribed level of empowerment (i.e. flexibility within a fixed frame)?*
- *Have you removed any fear of failure? Do you trust them to get it wrong as well as trust them to get it right?*

6. Generating short-term wins

Achievement as a lead motivator should be leveraged in the change process. When setting their agenda (see above), leaders should incorporate visible, straightforward, relevant KPIs, performance goals and/or measurable interim deadlines to keep everyone committed to the bigger goal because 'goals begin behaviours; consequences maintain behaviours' (Blanchard and Johnson, 1986, p.169). However, the variety of stakeholders in any change process means a one-size-fits-all short-term win is unlikely to exist. For example, while improved morale may be a measure for employees, hitting budget projections will be of more importance to senior management. Where leaders fail to demonstrate progress on the change journey, stakeholders may become disillusioned and underperformance, bruised confidence, reversion to old habits and poor employee morale will fester.

Probing questions that the Leader Coach can ask here include:

- *How can you quickly demonstrate momentum within this project/ change initiative?*
- *How can you quickly illustrate that its benefits completely compensate for any (personal and organisational) perceived costs?*
- *Have you made sure that your acclaimed quick wins are tangible, credible, laudable and (emotionally) impactful?*

7. Consolidating gains and producing more change

Jim Collins' best-selling book *Good to Great* (2001) is a critical analysis of why comparable organisations on the same trajectory diverge, with the greats achieving stellar results and the remainder staying at good, average or worse. It profiles exceptional change management and its opening gambit 'Good is the enemy of great' encapsulates the threat being confronted in Kotter's seventh step – as does 'complacency'.

Complacency is the scourge of many change programmes that showed promise but failed to deliver. Substantial change programmes such as organisational restructuring or re-engineering can take several years. Maintaining long-term focus is a challenge but it is possible where there is:

- *A firm belief in the change need*
- *Ongoing facilitation including blockage removal to ensure employee commitment*
- *Capitalisation upon the motivation of interim achievement*
- *Proactive emotional support that the short-term disruption will be worth the long-term gain*
- *Continuous review of the process with the courage to change course if necessary.*

Questions that the Leader Coach can ask here include:

- *How do you ensure that this change initiative doesn't fizzle out (like so many do!)?*
- *How can you maintain enthusiasm, drive and momentum to make sure it delivers over the longer term?*
- *How do you guard against complacency that the 'battle has been won' when actually the 'war is far from over'? How do you spark other change initiatives off the back of this one?*

8. Anchoring new approaches in the culture

The paradigm at the centre of Johnson and Scholes' (1993) Culture Web refers to an organisation's culture. It is a unique integrated profile of the six orbiting factors.

Figure 38: Culture Web

'When the new practices made in a transformation effort are not compatible with relevant cultures, they will always be subject to regression' (Kotter, 1996, p.42). Systematically incorporating the change into each of the six factors increases the likelihood of the changes being anchored into the culture.

- **Stories** – All cultures have a rich storytelling tradition and business organisations are no different → *changes need to be woven into the narrative, so they become part of the organisation's paradigm*

- **Rituals and routines** – These are the accepted norms and practices of the organisation → *changes need to be assimilated into the daily work practices until they become normal/habit*

- **Symbols** – These are the physical/visual representations of the organisation → *change initiatives need to be incorporated into these symbols, so they are 'part of the furniture'*

- **Organisational structure** – Such as on an organisational chart (i.e. the power chains and communication channels) → *re-structuring, promotion, recruiting, selection and retention should reflect the new changes*

- **Control systems** – Systems that regulate the daily business of the organisation including output, financial, quality, communication, reward/incentive and bureaucratic controls → *must be updated and aligned with the changes to prevent friction and ensure seamless facilitation of the change*

- **Power structures** – The people with the greatest amount of overall influence; could be an individual, a group, a department, with or without formal authority (informal leaders), etc. → *primary influencers need to be included in the guiding coalition, promoted and supported to uphold the changes.*

Questions that Leader Coaches can pose here – with regards to anchoring the new approaches into the culture – might include:

- *Have you woven the stories of this change initiative's success into the narrative of the organisation (i.e. heroes and legendary feats)?*

- *Have you incorporated the change initiative into 'business as usual' practices?*

- *Are the change initiatives now part of the furniture in your organisation?*

- *Have your policies, processes, structures and systems been adapted to sustain the change?*

- *Have your management control systems (KPIs, incentives, bonuses and budgets) been adjusted to accommodate and facilitate the sustainability of the change initiative?*

- *Have you ensured that the senior leadership tier of the organisation continues to buy into, advocate and drive the promulgated changes?*

ACCELERATING A CHANGE CULTURE WITH COACHEES

Examples of change failure because of follower resistance/lack of engagement are frequently given and Kotter cites many change programmes that failed because management missed out/didn't invest in one of the eight steps in the change process, causing employees to revert to previous methods. A further reason change fails is through a misunderstanding of the impact/disruption of the change on employees.

The Change Curve

As discussed previously (see 1.1 'Raise Self-Awareness') – except for the minority of rational decision makers – everyone judges scenarios based on an emotional response interpreted as a physical reaction, typically termed a 'gut reaction'. Therefore, when a change is introduced the typical initial human response will be 'how do I feel about this?' Where the change is a substantial shift for individuals, a raft of emotional responses will be experienced.

Swiss psychiatrist Elisabeth Kübler-Ross graphed the emotional rollercoaster people experience when bereaved (the Grief Cycle). Although at a less intense and difficult level, all change involves loss or a need to let go of the current reality; thus people experiencing change will go through the emotional states described by Kübler-Ross. For organisations implementing change, this understanding of the human state has proved extremely helpful, leading to Kübler-Ross's Grief Cycle being co-opted into the change-management domain as the Change Curve.

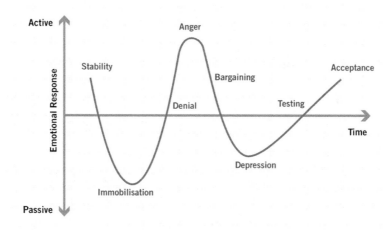

Figure 39: Grief Cycle Model

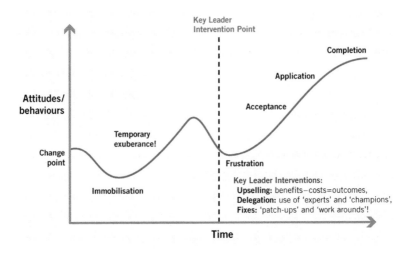

Figure 40: Change Curve Model

The Change Curve typically includes five stages (D.A.B.D.A.), although as many as eight may appear on the Grief Cycle.

STAGE	DESCRIPTION
1. **D**enial	A brief initial refusal to believe the change is happening
2. **A**nger	Denial passes, leading to frustration and anger that the change *is* happening
3. **B**argaining	Hopes to postpone or delay the inevitable by reaching a compromise
4. **D**epression	Forlorn realisation that it is inevitable and the individual is powerless to prevent it
5. **A**cceptance	Conclusion that it's time to accept the change and get on with the new reality

Figure 41: D.A.B.D.A. Grief Stages

The level of an individual's emotional response is dependent on how meaningful (important/unimportant) the change is for him/her. The time taken for the cycle to complete not only depends on the extent of the change but also on the level of support given to the individual to expedite the process. A well-conceived, well-planned and well-executed change process such as that laid out by Kotter will substantially mitigate the level of response and the time taken for cycle completion.

Further people skills such as those outlined in the social competence section of Goleman's (1996, p.27) Emotional Competence Framework will improve leaders' ability to respond appropriately to the needs of employees at the various stages of the change/grief curve. To this end, the Leader Coach can pose specific questions to facilitate coachee Emotional Intelligence development to assist in sparking a Change Culture.

EMPATHY	
Awareness of others' feelings, needs and concerns	
Understanding others	To what degree can you sense others' feelings and perspectives? How do you demonstrate an active interest in their concerns?
Developing others	To what degree do you sense others' development needs? How do you actively bolster their abilities?
Service orientation	On a scale of one to ten, how good are you at anticipating, recognising and meeting customers' needs? How can you improve?
Leveraging diversity	Give me examples when you have cultivated opportunities through different kinds of people? What value did this add?
Political awareness	On a scale of one to ten, how good are you at reading a group's emotional currents and power relationships? How can you improve this?

SOCIAL SKILLS

Adeptness at inducing desirable responses in others

Influence	Tell me about how you persuade others? What are your tactics? When and why have they been successful/failed?
Communication	When and how do you listen openly and send convincing messages?
Conflict management	How do you go about negotiating and resolving disagreements?
Leadership	Give me tangible examples of when you have guided and inspired individuals and groups to achieve something of significance?
Building bonds	Give me examples of how you nurture instrumental relationships?
Collaboration and co-operation	Give me examples of how you have successfully worked with others towards shared goals in the past?
Team capabilities	Tell me about how you have gone about creating group synergies in pursuing collective goals?

QUICK RECAP: LEADER COACHING TO SPARK A CHANGE CULTURE

- **Why?** – The survival of any business is dependent on its agility, adaptability and change readiness.
- **Main Concepts?** – Change management, culture, change difficulty, power, communication
- **How?** Coaching Conversations using:
    - **Kotter's Eight-Step Process for Leading Change**
        - Establishing a sense of urgency
        - Creating a guiding coalition
        - Developing a vision and strategy
        - Communicating the change vision

- Empowering employees for broad-based action
- Generating short-term wins
- Consolidating gains and producing more change
- Anchoring new approaches in the culture

- **Accelerate Change Culture Coaching? Use:**
  - **The Change Curve**
    - Helps with understanding people's emotional response to change
    - Based on Elisabeth Kübler-Ross's Grief Cycle
    - Contains five-to-eight stages but typically based on D.A.B.D.A. (Denial, Anger, Bargaining, Depression and Acceptance)
  - **Social Competence Skills**
    - *Empathy* (understanding others, developing others, service orientation, leveraging diversity, political awareness)
    - *Social skills* (influence, communication, conflict management, leadership, building bonds, collaboration and co-operation, team capabilities)

3.4 COACHING LEADERS TO DRIVE INNOVATION

Thus far in this chapter on accelerating business growth we have outlined how Leader Coaches can facilitate challenging coaching conversations around strategy, operations and cultural change. But this is not enough. For sure business leaders need to shape strategic clarity, gain operational grip and propagate a change culture to propel their organisation/SBU forwards. But they also need to foster a high degree of ingenuity and innovation to ensure that their organisation provides goods and services that are exciting, fresh and *relevant*, addressing real customer needs. This is troublesome – several blocks to innovation exist in most organisations as the previous chapter on change illustrated. But all organisations *must* innovate or face the prospect, sooner or later, of perishing. It is incumbent on the business leader to establish the climate and structures for innovative behaviour to develop – where *idea generation*, precise *evaluation* and rapid *implementation* can flourish. This is where the Leader Coach can help. How? By challenging the business leader's perceptions over the level of innovation that exists in their organisation and helping them to reflect upon how they can *drive innovation* forwards to secure sustainable growth in the future.

CORE CONCEPTS

But how do business leaders spark innovation? Prior to embarking on coaching conversations with them on this topic, the Leader Coach requires a deeper understanding of the core concepts underlying innovation in the corporate/business domain.

- *Innovation Leadership* – Over the past fifteen years a body of work has emerged which has concerned itself with which leadership styles match which types of innovation. To this end researchers have located two specific types of innovation that require totally different stylistic approaches:

  - *Value-added Innovation* – Within this innovation paradigm, business leaders are focused upon modifying and improving ideas that already exist. Researchers postulate that the leadership style required here is one of a *'closed' transactional leadership style*, where minimal risk taking is permitted during the incremental improvement of goods and services.

  - *Exploratory Innovation* – At the opposite end of the spectrum, where leaders are focused upon generating brand new ideas, strategies and solutions, an *'open' transformational leadership style* is required to encourage search, discovery and experimentation behaviours. Flexibility, optimism and adaptability are promoted through charismatic, motivational, inspirational leadership, underpinned by flat, responsive and agile structures, strategies, processes, capabilities and cultures.

- *Innovation Management* – In tandem with this body of work, researchers have analysed innovation from a 'functional' management perspective, focussing upon the range of tools, techniques and methods available to propagate creativity (Burns and Stalker, 1961). Observing that creativity is the result of both *imitation* and *invention*, they conceive of *'pushed innovative processes'* (where profitable applications for existing technologies are found) and *'pulled innovative processes'* (where solutions to unfulfilled customer needs are located and addressed). Tools and techniques that are advanced in this paradigm to enable managers and workers to cooperate on fostering innovation come from a variety of disciplines:

- *Knowledge management tools* (mapping and document management)
- *Market intelligence techniques* (patent analysis and CRM)
- *HRM techniques* (corporate intranet, e-learning, flat organisations)
- *Creativity development techniques* (brainstorming, lateral thinking, TRIZ, SCAMPER, mind-mapping)
- *Process improvement techniques* (benchmarking, business process re-engineering, JIT, Six Sigma, Kaizen, TQM, Deming, EFQM, etc.)
- *Design and product development tools* (computer-aided design, rapid prototyping)
- *Business creation tools* (business simulation, research spin-offs).

- Other concepts within the Innovation Management domain that are of use to Leader Coaches include:

  - *Innovation Cultures* – The notion of 'open', 'flexible' and 'learning cultures' where organisations view innovation as a corporate asset, actively encouraging the transfer of creative knowledge from one unit to another or its external acquisition (Menon and Pfeffer, 2003). Here issues of size and scale can be culturally overcome by a 'continuous learning' philosophy where organisations build non-hierarchical systems, incentivising and facilitating communities of practice where personal development and 'mastery' are seen as major keys to success (Kolb, 1984; Senge, 2005).

  - *Formal Continuous Improvement* – Previous reference has been made to how firms seeking to generate formal continuous process improvement utilise systems and frameworks such as TQM (Total Quality Management), EFQM (European Framework for Quality Management), Deming and Six Sigma; with the first two stressing *content* (what to address), the latter concentrating on *process* (how to address it). These formulaic approaches to fostering creativity certainly bolster organisations' innovative capability, although their 'stop–start', 'here today, gone tomorrow' manifestations within Anglo-American corporate contexts have led to disillusionment (certainly amongst workers) as to their effectiveness.

- *Vertical Middle-Up-Down* – With respect to innovation management, a vital contribution is also made by Nonaka and Takeuchi (1995) through their *'middle-up-down'* management concept. One of their seven pathways for knowledge creation and diffusion within organisations, this construct conceives senior management setting the vision for the organisation whilst employees confront reality. The *gap between both parties is mediated by middle managers* (occupying a key intersection point) who synthesise the tacit knowledge flowing from the bottom, translating it into valuable explicit practice and 'ways of doing business' for senior leaders. But how does this conversion from explicit to tacit knowledge take place? In their SECI model of knowledge conversion, they frame the transformation process of tacit into explicit knowledge as flowing through a dynamic process where it is converted 'spirally' through the four modes of knowledge conversion: *socialisation* (direct experience), *externalisation* (articulation), *combination* (systemising) and *internalisation* (acquiring new knowledge in practice). Furthermore, this tacit knowledge can be subdivided into two categories: technical (know how) and cognitive (values, beliefs and ideals) (Nonaka and Konno, 1998; Nonaka et al., 2000).

- *Horizontal Knowledge Diffusion* – Alongside vertical knowledge interchange, horizontal knowledge transfer is also important within the field of innovation management, the main point of enquiry being how managers can break down silos and 'hoarding' to increase transmission and sharing across organisations. Techniques advanced here include building reciprocity, rewarding 'sharing' behaviours, building 'safe' social spaces where tacit knowledge can be exchanged (during social 'downtime' or over social media groups) and fostering a climate of trust.

- *Open Innovation* – Another concept that the Leader Coach might find useful to reacquaint themselves with is the notion of open innovation systems (as opposed to open cultures, described above). This concept is highly relevant in the digital age, where an 'open door' mentality towards innovation runs counter to the secrecy and silo mentality of traditional corporate entities. Essentially, open innovation is a paradigm that assumes that leaders and firms *can and should* use external and internal ideas and paths to market (whether through knowledge networks, collaborative programmes, purchasing or licensing businesses and patents or developing JVs and spin-offs). To this extent, it departs from the 'corporate centricity' of innovation by conceiving the best innovation as being derived from tapping into insights from communities of innovators and (even) creative consumers. Why is this paradigm important? Because all available research evidence suggests that innovations tend to be produced by outsiders and founder entrepreneurs in start-ups, rather than in 'closed' corporate systems. Allied to this concept is also the notion of 'open innovation ecosystems' where knowledge sharing, co-development and collaboration take place for mutually beneficial purposes, facilitated and aided by advanced digital platforms.

- *Ambidexterity* – Another concept of use to the Leader Coach during their conversations with business leaders – given the difficulty of innovating from the 'core' of organisations (due to resistance, resource constraints and potential loss of focus) – is ambidexterity. Some firms have been exceptionally successful (acting in a so-called ambidextrous manner) at creating a 'disruptive space' in which they permit independent agents and structures to evolve, decoupled from the existing entity:

> some companies have actually been quite successful at both *exploiting the present and exploring the future*, and as we looked more deeply at them we found that they share important characteristics. In particular, they separate their new, exploratory units from their traditional, exploitative ones, allowing for different processes, structures, and cultures; at the same time, they maintain tight links across units at the senior executive level. In other words, they manage organizational separation through a tightly integrated senior team. We call these kinds of companies 'ambidextrous organizations' and we believe they provide a practical and proven model for forward-looking executives seeking to pioneer radical or disruptive innovations while pursuing incremental gains. A business does not have to escape its past, these cases show, to renew itself for the future...

> (O'Reilly and Tushman, 2004, p.75)

Thus, decoupled units are granted the autonomy and resources to develop new norms, processes and values outside the constraints of the dominant space. As long as these are ring fenced against inter-ventions from vested interests and the dominant political coalition within the core, these offshoots can flourish using the resources of the parent. Reverse diffusion might take place, where knowledge, ideas and concepts from this new structure permeate back into the main business. Alternatively, organisations might buy or partner with a firm whose processes, capabilities and values more effectively fit new commercial realities and requirements. Although expensive, this approach can be a fast-track route to achieving more quickly in months what would otherwise have taken years to put into effect.

- *Induced Innovation* – But innovation can be forced rather than emergent, as Hicks (1932) points out in his seminal economic tract: 'a change in the relative factors of production is itself a spur to invention of a particular kind – directed to economising the use of a factor which has become relatively expensive'. For instance, the effect of wage increases encourages labour-saving innovations and new means of generating sales and margin. In recent times increases in energy costs have acted as a motivation for more rapid innovation in alternative energy technologies. Thus, so-called 'Hicks Theory' (a change in factor prices stimulates innovation to reduce factor costs) is a powerful contribution to a Leader Coach's understanding of how innovation occurs.

- *Disruptive Innovation* – Finally, there is the powerful notion of inno-vation being more powerful and sustainable when it *disrupts* rather than *sustains* (Christensen and Overdorf, 2000). *Sustaining* innova-tion – that doesn't significantly affect existing markets – can be *evolutionary* (an innovation that improves a product in an existing market in ways that customers are expecting) or *revolutionary* (an innovation that is unexpected but nevertheless does not affect existing markets). On the other hand, disruptive innovation – an innovation that creates a new market by providing a different set of products/services which ultimately (and unexpectedly) overtakes an existing market – might not be profitable enough in its early stages, might soak up scarce resources, take longer to develop and be high risk, but once fully developed have a much faster degree of penetration and impact on established markets. Why? This is not necessarily due to its technology but because of its advanced busi-ness model (think computer mainframes being disrupted by cloud, music and video CDs and DVDs being disrupted by downloadable digital media and chemical photography being disrupted by digital photography).

KEY INNOVATION MODELS

The previous section should equip Leader Coaches with the vocabulary to conduct coaching conversations with business leaders on the topic of innovation. Being cognisant of the fact that *different innovation paradigms* (value added or exploratory) require *different leadership styles* (transactional or transformational), a plethora of *management innovation tools/techniques* from a variety of disciplines can facilitate creative 'out of the box' thinking and *'open' cultures/systems, induced conditions* (higher wages or costs) and *disruptive business models* can all spark dynamic creativity, will be of use to the Leader Coach. But how should the Leader Coach anchor coaching conversations in this area? It is clear to us – based on extensive experience – that many business leaders overestimate their innovative capabilities. What the Leader Coach needs to do is increase the self-awareness and curiosity of the coachee by using proxy frameworks that can assist challenging conversations. Which ones? We suggest three – the Formal Innovation Process Model, the Knowledge Barriers/Solutions Model and the Upwards Impact and Influencing Model – which provide the Leader Coach with platforms from which they can probe their coachee's innovative capacity and capability.

The Formal Innovation Process Model (FIPM) is a useful framework for the Leader Coach to use with coachees because it provides a ready-made checklist that they can use, sequentially, to establish formal effectiveness. At the very least, the Leader Coach can use the model to help their coachee reflect on multiple dimensions of value-added innovation in their business contexts.

Recognise – Publically reward/recognise

Roll-out – If it works go for it!

Test – 'Kick the tyres' and modify/discard

'Big Rocks' – Pick and prioritise some 'tankbusters'

Brainstorm – Surface value-added growth/savings ideas

Gaps – Assess gaps in product/offer and 'set up'

Trends – Examine micro-market trends and hyper trends

'Buy-In' – Communicate innovate/evolve or die!

Forum – Pick the right context (area meetings?)

Figure 42: Formal Innovation Process Model

Using this model, the Leader Coach can probe the business leader by asking the following questions:

- *Forum – Where do you discuss and brainstorm innovative ideas? Is the environment conducive to creative thinking? (Comfort, space and 'atmosphere')*

- *Buy-in – How do you grab your team's attention on this vital topic? ('Innovate or die' imperative without paralysing discussion!)*

- *Trends – Where do you start in your 'ideas' forums/discussion? How do you surface micro-trends and needs? (Total focus on unfulfilled consumer needs)*

- *Gaps – In light of these trends, how do you surface gaps in your current offer/systems/processes? (Providing avenues for value-added opportunity)*

- *Brainstorm – How do you brainstorm value-added solutions to close these gaps? (Preventing groupthink, social loafing and bystander behaviours; also stimulating both the conscious and unconscious minds of your team members)*

- *Select – How do you prioritise 'big rock' runners? (Low cost but HIGH IMPACT)*

- *Test – How do you generally test initiatives and ideas? (Pilot, trial, measure and review)*

- *Roll Out – How do you ensure successful implementation? (Reduce resistance and accelerate acceptance by communicating benefits to all stakeholders)*

- *Recognise – How do you generally reward and recognise success? (Planned or spontaneous)*

The exercise above will help the coachee reflect upon how effectively they go about formally generating and implementing value-added ideas, propagating a discussion about a fairly top-down, mechanistic innovation process. However, often ideas emerge more informally and organically – especially from the front line where operators are in frequent contact with the customer. The question is, how can business leaders create the climate of *mutuality, reciprocity and interdependence* where these valuable ideas and insights are shared across and up the organisation? The Knowledge Barriers/ Solutions Model provides a framework for the Leader Coach to help the coachee understand and reflect upon how they create the conditions to allow knowledge and creativity transfer to flourish by removing/ameliorating the common barriers to their transmission.

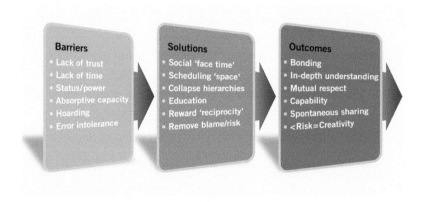

Figure 43: Knowledge Barriers/Solutions Model

How can the Leader Coach use this model? Covering up the solutions and outcomes elements, the Leader Coach can ask:

- *How do you overcome a **lack of trust** (i.e. a belief amongst innovators that their ideas might be diluted or stolen without reciprocation)?*

Solutions include face-to-face communications/interaction (meetings, conferences, visits, etc.); i.e. social 'face time' that will lead to bonding.

- *How do you overcome a **lack of time** (i.e. distance and BAU activities prevent transmission)? Here, business leaders should create time and space for idea exchange. Smarter methods require deployment for instant communication (such as digital) which will facilitate swifter access to knowledge.*

- *How do you reduce **status/power differences** (i.e. time servers and senior operators refuse to share with newbies)? Create a set of values that stresses inclusivity, respect and sharing. Make ideas transcend status.*

- *How do you increase your teams' **absorptive capacity** (i.e. personnel don't have the mental capacity to absorb/understand new ideas)? Educate those that are willing but can't do; exit those that are unwilling and can't do! Use credible experts to expand capability through tailored training (show, not just lecture/tell).*

- *How do you eliminate **knowledge hoarding** (i.e. innovators jealously guard ideas for reasons of internal competitive advantage)? Reward/recognise the sellers or purveyors of knowledge/innovation and encourage reciprocity between parties through social interaction.*

- *How do you reduce the fear of **error intolerance** (i.e. a belief among innovators that if their ideas fail to work elsewhere, they will be punished)? Remove gameplay, blame, sanction and retribution. Make it ok to try and fail. Create an environment in which people seek forgiveness rather than permission!*

So, the Leader Coach can facilitate rich discussions about formal and informal idea generation, but often the business leader will appear frustrated that their ideas cannot gain traction within the organisation. We have often been confronted by coachees, inhabiting the middle of the organisation, who complain that nobody listens to their ideas. This is often because their uncosted pipedreams are unworkable and illogical! Sometimes, however, their lack of impact is a direct consequence of how they have *gone about selling* their ideas. The Upwards Impact and Influencing Model provides a useful device with which the Leader Coach can help the coachee reflect upon how they go about getting their ideas to gain traction within organisations.

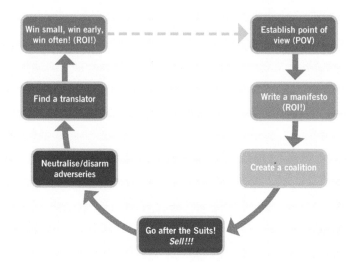

Figure 44: Upwards Impact and Influencing Model

Using this framework, the Leader Coach can ask the following questions:

- *Establish a Point of View (POV) – How do you create a credible, coherent, compelling and commercial POV based on hard data? (Senior people talk a 'financial language' – does your idea stand up commercially?)*
- *Write a Manifesto – How can you infect others (potential advocates) with your ideas? (Capture their imagination by painting a picture of how you can resolve their discomfort!)*
- *Create a Coalition – How can you assemble a group of colleagues who share your vision and passion (in order to present yourselves as a coordinated group speaking in 'one' voice)?*
- *Go after the Suits – Who are your main targets? (Find powerful people who are searching for new ideas and, if necessary, bend your ideals a bit to fit their goals.)*
- *Neutralise – How do you disarm and co-opt adversaries rather than humiliate and demean them? (Reciprocity wins converts; ranting leaves you isolated and powerless.)*
- *Find a Translator – How do you find someone who can build a bridge between you and the people in power? (Ambitious senior staffers*

and new hires are often good translator candidates – they're usually hungry for an agenda they can call their own.)

- *Win Small, Win Early, Win Often! – How can you demonstrate that your ideas work and have a real ROI? (Start small! As your record of wins grows longer, you'll find it easier to make the transition from launching isolated initiatives to making your ideas an integral part of the business.)*

ACCELERATING INNOVATION WITH COACHEES

The frameworks above will help the Leader Coach facilitate conversations with the coachee around formalising value-added innovation processes, creating the right climate for idea/knowledge transfer and successfully feeding their ideas up the chain. But this is not enough. Very often the problem in this area (i.e. driving innovation) lies not in processes, structures and decision-making obstacles but within the business leader's inherent capacity to innovate themselves. Creative leaders have three fundamental characteristics which help them stand apart: a visceral *dissatisfaction* with the way things are, the *desire* to improve things and the *imagination* to create new solutions that make a real difference! Imagination and implementation are the key ingredients. How can the Leader Coach help?

First, the Leader Coach can use the Creativity Grid (which categorises leaders according to their levels of innovation/implementation and creativity/imagination) to establish where their coachee lies in terms of their innovative/creative ability.

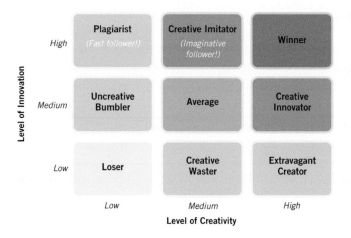

Figure 45: Creativity Grid

The Leader Coach can either get the coachee to indicate where they sit on the grid voluntarily or verify the coachee's typology by talking to their line manager, peers or colleagues prior to the coaching conversation. Establishing whether they are a *winner* (generate impactful ideas and make them happen), *imitator* (fast follower), *plagiarist* (scanners who copy and instigate), *average* (display median levels of creativity/innovation), *creative* (generate great ideas and land some of them), *extravagant* (uncommercial idealists), *waster* (daydreamer), *bumbler* (blaggers and time wasters) or *losers* (useless) will help the Leader Coach determine where the business leader sits with regards to creative *imagination* and/or *implementation*. This allows the Leader Coach to meld the right conversation!

Are business leaders born with creativity or can they learn to be creative? We would argue that it is *both* inherited and learned! Creativity is as much a method and approach as it is an emotional preference. So how can Leader Coaches help their coachee to become more creative if they lack inherent imagination? We would advocate the Egg Timer Model, which was designed and developed for coaching, providing a framework for greater creativity and imagination for those wishing to become more creative leaders. The utility of this framework – as opposed to brainstorming or blue-sky thinking – is its grounding in the realities of the here-and-now, current context of the business leader. So, what is it and how can Leader Coaches deploy it?

The Egg Timer Model (see Figure 46) illustrates the three levels of initiative (could, should and must) that need to be applied when creatively thinking through solutions/ideas to address current problems/opportunities. It is highly effective in opening up the mind to the 'art of the possible', valuably connecting imagination, thought and action.

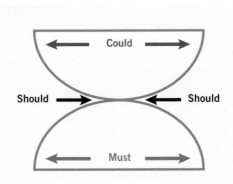

Figure 46: The Egg Timer Model

How can the Leader Coach use it?

- *The Power of 'Could' (e.g. what ideas/solutions could improve the customer experience now!?) – Here the Leader Coach opens the coachee's mind to the possibilities that can be imagined and created. In doing so, the Leader Coach gets the coachee to resist the temptation to envisage what should or must be done. This is a high-volume part of the process, with the Leader Coach encouraging an open flow of ideas/ solutions (ranging from the obvious to the outrageous) for increasing the customer experience now!*

- *The Importance of 'Should' (e.g. what ideas/solutions should be adopted to improve the customer experience now!?) – This 'action and commitment' question now acts as a filter to let only the highest-quality ideas progress to the next stage. Factors to take into consideration here are time, resources, costs and impact. For instance, some ideas will have to be excluded due to the time they would take to implement or their lack of a defensible ROI. During this stage, the Leader Coach must act as a strict taskmaster because it will determine the quality of the outcome of this process!*

- *The Value of 'Must' (e.g. in light of all of this, what must we do now in order to improve the customer experience?) – Finally, the Leader Coach facilitates a challenging discussion with the coachee, to identify the highest-value ideas from all of the filtered solutions. When these are located, the discussion is trained upon implementation.*

QUICK RECAP: LEADER COACHING TO DRIVE INNOVATION

- **Why?** – Businesses that win create trends and keep on trend by relentlessly innovating and trialling new products and services. To this extent, leaders need to demonstrate a healthy paranoia about being at the leading edge – rather than the trailing edge – of their industries.

- **Main Concepts?** – Value-added and exploratory innovation, innovation management, innovation cultures, formal continuous improvement (middle-up-down and horizontal knowledge diffusion), open innovation, induced innovation, disruptive innovation and ambidexterity

- **How?** Coaching Conversations using:

  - **Formal Innovation Process Model**

    - Forum? > 'Buy In'? > Trends? > Gaps? > Brainstorm > 'Big Rocks'? > Test > Roll Out? > Recognise!

  - **Knowledge Barriers/Solutions Model**

    - Barriers: trust, time, status/power, capacity, hoarding, intolerance

    - Solutions: 'face time', 'space', collapse hierarchies, education, reciprocity, remove blame culture

    - Outcomes: bonding, understanding, mutual respect, capability, spontaneous sharing, creativity

  - **Upwards Impact and Influencing Model**

    - Establish a point of view > write a manifesto (ROI) > create a coalition > go after the suits (sell) > neutralise/disarm adversaries > find a translator > win small, win early, win often (ROI)

- **Accelerating Innovative Drive with Coachees? Use:**
  - **Creativity Grid**
    - Categorise leader behaviours according to their levels of innovation/implementation and creativity/imagination
  - **Egg Timer Model** – Establish:
    - The Power of 'Could'
    - The Importance of 'Should'
    - The Value of 'Must'

BRIEF CHAPTER SUMMARY – ADVANCING BUSINESS GROWTH

This chapter has built upon the previous two chapters, which examined advancing coachee *personal and interpersonal growth*, by highlighting a range of tools and techniques that Leader Coaches can use to help advance *business growth*. It is worth reiterating that coaching conversations relating to business growth will amount to nothing unless the Leader Coach has, at least partially, addressed some of the issues raised by these previous two constructs of our Advanced Leader Coaching Model. Why? Because – and again, we cannot stress this too firmly – getting coachees *personally* to think more clearly and feel positive will affect how they behave *interpersonally*, which in turn will greatly determine their overall *business* performance.

However, business performance is where the rubber hits the road for coachees. To that end, in this chapter we have advocated that Leader Coaches should be equipped to coach leaders to:

- **Clarify Strategy** by understanding the key concepts underpinning strategy (*strategic management, competitive advantage, strategic complexity, etc.*) and using key models (*Strategic Process and Strategic Pyramid*) to elevate coachee capability in strategic decision making. Accelerated development in this area, which will help dampen confusion and increase coachee clarity, can be made by using *De Bono's Six Hats Thinking Technique*.
- **Grip Operations** by absorbing key operational control concepts (*simple control, technical/systems control, bureaucratic control, multi-layered, concertive, chimerical, socio-ideological*) and using the

Operational Excellence Model (structural congruence, performance articulation, process control and team alignment) to increase coachee insight into the essential requirements of this activity. Accelerated coachee learning can be facilitated by using the *GAPPAR Model* and/or the *Ishikawa Technique*, which will enable Leader Coaches to assist coachees to identify causality rather than surface symptoms.

- **Spark a Change Culture** by firstly understanding the different types of resistance to change (using the *Change Difficulty Pyramid*) and then using the *Eight Phases of Change Model (urgency, guiding team, vision, communication, action, short-term wins, don't let up and make it stick)* to help coachees understand how they can spark change in rigid cultures. Accelerated insight can be provided by Leader Coaches using both the *Change Curve* and *Grief Models* (including D.A.B.D.A.) to understand how quickly they can transition people through change processes.

- **Drive Innovation** by absorbing key innovation concepts (*value-added and exploratory innovation, innovation management, innovation cultures, continuous improvement, open innovation and ambidexterity*) and using key models (*Formal Innovation Process and Knowledge Barriers/Solutions*) to heighten coachee appreciation of this vital activity. Accelerating coachee insight into this area can be facilitated using the *Creativity Grid* and the *Egg Timer Model (which unpacks the power of 'could', the importance of 'should' and the value of 'must')*.

This extemporisation of the third construct (advancing leader business growth) marks the end of our exploration of the Advanced Leader Coaching Model! But we have two more important things to do in this book. First, we need to advance a robust coaching philosophy and methodology that will help Leader Coaches to hold structured coaching conversations and, second, we need to end by addressing some of the key questions which still remain unanswered – in spite of its wide-ranging analysis of high-performance Leader Coaching. So next, we outline our proposed coaching philosophy (Courageous Coaching) and methodology (BUILD-RAISE) for Leader Coaches.

4 COURAGEOUS COACHING

The previous chapters unpacked our Advanced Leader Coaching Model, highlighting how Leader Coaches can facilitate and accelerate business-leader *personal, interpersonal and business growth*. **But we wish to go further than this**. Although the previous chapters highlighted a myriad of techniques, models, questions and approaches for Advanced Leader Coaching, it is useful if the Leader Coach has a ***specific coaching methodology*** to fall back upon during key coaching conversations. To that end, this chapter includes insights and instruction from from Edger's coaching books (2017, 2019a,b) which – at the time of publication of this book – were listed in 583 university libraries worldwide. Edited and updated for the purposes of this book, we believe they provide Leader Coaches with a *robust method and toolkit* to facilitate successful coaching interventions with leaders in almost any circumstances.

Hence, this chapter will outline our concept of Courageous Leader Coaching, a process through which Leader Coaches – *acting as loving boots* – challenge and stretch business leaders to achieve *extraordinary* things by RAISING their *self-awareness* and BUILDING *accountability* through our BUILD-RAISE model of coaching. Reading this chapter will help you to understand:

- What the Courageous Leader Coaching concept is
- Why it is important (within the context of modern-day leadership, work and organisations)
- What qualities Leader Coaches require to bring it alive
- HOW to Courageously Coach using our BUILD-RAISE model
- What the key REFRAMING and MAGIC questions are during Courageous Coaching
- How our approach works in reality, as seen through a major case study.

4.1 THE COURAGEOUS LEADER COACHING CONCEPT

Great leaders 'move' people within organisations by inspiring them: *mobilising* positivity, *shifting* attitudes and behaviours, *stirring* feelings, *resetting* mindsets and *galvanising* teams into action. But not all leaders can achieve this, for a variety of reasons. This is where the Leader Coach steps in, applying what we term the Courageous Coaching philosophy. So what is this?

Courageous Leader Coaching takes place in a trusting one-to-one learning context where great Leader Coaches help coachees <u>RAISE their SELF-AWARENESS</u> and <u>BUILD CONFIDENCE</u> *by* CHALLENGING self-limiting mindsets, *accelerating* PERSONAL, INTERPERSONAL AND BUSINESS GROWTH…

But what is the significance of each component of this definition?

- *'Courageous Leader Coaching'* – a process in which Leader Coaches drop their 'expert consultant' or 'performance management' persona (a courageous act in itself!) to CHALLENGE and move false preconceptions of coaches
- *'Trusting one-to-one learning'* – a space outside normal 'performance reviews' where – with no hidden agendas – the focus is purely upon personal development and increased effectiveness
- *'Great Leader Coaches help coachees'* – where the Leader Coach facilitates and guides a coaching (and mentoring) process designed to improve and progress coachees' goals
- *'RAISE their self-awareness'* – focusing upon uncovering 'blind self' and false preconceptions which might be holding them back
- *'BUILD confidence'* – in order to generate belief that they can overcome obstacles and devise a plan of action that achieves a clear goal
- *'CHALLENGING self-limiting mindsets'* – reframing and breaking down false conceptions of limitations and barriers
- *'Accelerating PERSONAL, INTERPERSONAL AND BUSINESS GROWTH'* – leading to lasting behavioural change and sustainable personal and commercial progression

Figure 47: Courageous Leader Coaching Concept

Further on, we will outline the core practices that great Leader Coaches use during Courageous Coaching through the BUILD-RAISE method, but first we need to outline why this skill is so important and what Leader Coach qualities are required to underpin its successful delivery.

4.2 THE IMPORTANCE OF COURAGEOUS LEADER COACHING

We believe Courageous Leader Coaching is important for several reasons – some of which relate to individual and others to interpersonal and organisational performance:

- **Enhanced PERSONAL Growth:** From our extensive experience of coaching and mentoring, those that have been exposed to Courageous Leader Coaching (CLC) often comment that they have a greater ability to *solve problems, make better decisions, acquire new skills, think more creatively, manage stress and anxiety more effectively,* and *reach career goals* due to increased:

  - *Clarity*: CLC brings focus and value-added prioritisation (big rocks) as it begins with establishing (credible) aims and goals for coachees.

  - *Meaning and purpose*: As CLC is forward looking, progressive and focused upon advancement (rather than being backward looking and retrospective) it brings a sense of meaning and purpose to coachees.

  - *Learning and 'unlearning'*: CLC also provides a valuable space for coachees to contemplate change and new ways of addressing what might have seemed, previously insurmountable obstacles.

  - *Positive mindsets and behaviours*: This ability to address and overcome both real and imagined constraints enables coachees to abandon previously self-limiting approaches and restrictive behaviour patterns, fostering a sense of positivity and momentum.

  - *Happiness and wellbeing*: Furthermore, this positivity and action orientation creates a sense of greater happiness and wellbeing amongst coachees, engendering feelings of enthusiasm, hope and aspiration.

  - *Self-awareness and reflection*: Overall CLC prompts a sense of perspective and opportunity, born of Accurate Self-Awareness and reflection – a sense of new personal insight and discovery that enables individuals to develop a heightened sense of self-control over their destiny.

- **INTERPERSONAL and BUSINESS Growth:** In addition, we have observed that CLC – when applied within 'coaching cultures' across business units and organisations – results in higher levels of engagement, productivity and discretionary effort due to improved:

  - *Leadership skills:* CLC releases the gift of accountability, enabling organisations to disseminate and manage change more effectively, unlocking higher levels of proactivity and independent action. This is important. Due to 'distance' from subordinates and the minutiae of tasks they perform, senior leaders cannot always supervise and regulate behaviour. CLC fosters a sense of personal ownership and encourages individuals to seek their own solutions independently to issues and problems – a key characteristic of advanced leadership practice.

  - *Communications and relationships:* In addition, due to its emphasis upon heightening levels of personal self-knowledge, CLC improves coachees' awareness and understanding of others, leading to better relationships and communications within organisations, allied to a reduction in petty politicking and conflict.

  - *Climate and culture:* The by-product of these behaviours is a more cohesive entity where people work with rather than against one another to achieve superordinate goals. An environment where collaborative 'teamship' prevails, strengthening the collective capability of the organisation.

  - *Retention and succession planning:* As a result, recipients of this inclusive, learning, 'collaborative coaching climate' are far more engaged and disposed to stay. Research by Aaron Allen in 2016 established that engaged employees had 87% less turnover than disengaged ones (with a 78% recommendation level, three times more knowledge of customer needs and 59% higher creativity level!).

But before we explore the process that Leader Coaches should use to RAISE awareness, BUILD accountability and REFRAME perspectives, what are the skills and characteristics required to underpin their approach?

4.3 KEY LEADER COACH QUALITIES

It is a great benefit if the Leader Coach is blessed with a fair amount of Emotional Intelligence in order to assist them to coach sympathetically and courageously. What do we mean by this? As Goleman pointed out in his masterful books on the subject, 'people who move people' generally have *great levels of self-awareness*, which in itself affords them *superior awareness and understanding of the feelings and motives of others*, resulting in healthy and *productive relationships*. Bearing this in mind, what qualities, skills and attributes should Leader Coaches possess for truly effective Courageous Coaching?

- **Listening and Mirroring:** The first attribute they require is excellent listening and mirroring skills. On a range of five levels (where Level 1 denotes *planning what to say* rather than listening and Level 5, actively listening to *what people mean*) it is critical that Leader Coaches are equipped with Level 5 listening skills! This will also invariably result in them being able (due to concentrated listening) to probe potential hidden meanings behind what people say and interpret momentary silences and hesitations. In addition, they must be adept at mirroring their coachee's demeanour and tone in order to show empathy and respect for their feelings. That is not to say that Leader Coaches abandon their aura of positivity; rather, they should gauge the moment and temperature, acting with empathetic consideration and understanding.

- **Methodology and Questioning:** In addition to this, Leader Coaches should be equipped (either through explicit or tacit knowledge) with a robust methodology and appropriate battery of questions that will allow them to guide conversations effectively, help coachee's resolve their issues and formulate action plans. Those that have been trained will most commonly use the TGROW model (topic, goal, reality, options and will) as their 'compass', although we propose our alternative BUILD-RAISE model outlined below (build rapport, uncover aims, isolate issues, locate solutions and determine execution). The questions they have at their fingertips to underpin their approach should be open and non-judgemental, although effective coaches will have a range of golden *'reframing questions'* that will enable coachees to see themselves and their circumstances in a new perspective (see 4.5 below).

- **Clarification and Summarising:** One method by which Leader Coaches can check their understanding of what the coachee has said and give them time to formulate the next pertinent question is through clarifying and summarising what has been said. Also, playing back what has been said or asking the simple question 'what do you mean by that?' are powerful means of reducing long-winded answers to their core! Additionally, such interventions also give the coachee time to contemplate and expand upon what they have just said.

- **Intuition and Agility:** Whilst we strongly urge Leader Coaches to use a systematic method such as TGROW or BUILD-RAISE to advance the coachee's levels of self-awareness and accountability, effective Leader Coaches (having listened deeply to what has been said) should allow their intuition to guide their questioning and probing (the first three chapters in this book provide deep instruction on this!). There will be certain 'windows of opportunity' during the coaching interaction when the Leader Coach can seize the moment to interpret hidden meanings and uncover self-justifying agendas. They should also be adept at reading *non-verbal communication* (such as body language; facial expression and posture) to assist their interpretation of the essence of what is *really* being said and meant.

- **Mentoring:** Great Leader Coaches will also have another formidable weapon at their disposal, namely: the ability to pass on their reflective experience to their coachees. Often the *internal* Leader Coach (unlike a third-party external coach) will have the benefit of insight into the coachee's world (being familiar with context, pressures, demands and personalities, etc.). It is therefore a waste if Leader Coaches miss the opportunity to pass on some of their wisdom and advice to help out coachees. However, we would make two points here. First, the whole point of the coaching process is that coachees are encouraged to solve their own issues and attain their own goals with the minimum assistance possible, in order to foster feelings of accomplishment and self-determination. Second, Leader Coaches who frequently lapse into 'expert managerialism', constantly saying 'when I did' or 'in my experience', are likely to seem patronising and egotistical – a real turn-off to the coachee. The coachee hasn't gone to the Leader Coach for an extensive 'how I did it in my day' lecture; (s)he expects assistance in clarifying goals, strategies in eliminating interference and credible options to move things forward!

4.4 THE BUILD-RAISE COACHING PROCESS

Great Leader Coaches either develop their own tried-and-tested method of coaching which they have trialled and honed over a number of years coaching peers and subordinates, or they use a proxy process which they rely on as a 'route map' to help individuals resolve *career, development* or *performance* issues. In the previous sections we have outlined the broad skills, attributes and characteristics they require to be effective coaches, but which method do we advocate? Most coaching models are very similar; they start with a focus upon establishing a *purpose*, moving onto assessing *context* and the *options* available to the coachee to realise their goal, wrapping up with an agreed *plan* of action to move things forward. Over the years we have used a number of tools and techniques to coach subordinates and colleagues which – based on our experiences and observations – we have rolled into our BUILD-RAISE model of coaching (see Figure 48). This outlines a clear process for Leader Coaches to follow in order to achieve the principles underlying the model which are signposted by the pneumonic, namely: to *raise self awareness and build accountability* – the essential cornerstones of succesful coaching!

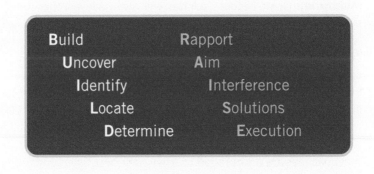

Figure 48: BUILD-RAISE Coaching Model

What this coaching model does is enshrine the *principle* of what the Leader Coach is attempting to do (*build* and *raise* leader capability through increased accountability and self-awareness) with memorable sequential steps that assist them in achieving positive outcomes. The sections below will go into the five elements of this model, highlighting *what* each component is seeking to achieve, *why* it is important and how Leader Coaches go about using it (including vital tools and questions).

STEP 1 – **B**uild **R**apport

What is the Leader Coach trying to achieve in STEP 1?

- *Create a trusting relationship* – The Leader Coach might or might not know the coachee but, whatever the previous relationship, a *climate* of trust must be established
- *Establish readiness* – The Leader Coach needs to find out whether the coachee is a willing, receptive volunteer or a reluctant, press-ganged 'victim'
- *Generate chemistry* – The Leader Coach and coachee must be able to 'rub along' not 'rub one another up the wrong way'
- *Frame realistic expectations* – At this initial stage, the Leader Coach needs to set expectations by outlining where the boundaries of the relationship lie, what the responsibilities of each party are and what the coachee can expect from the sessions (i.e. *challenge with support*).

Why?

- *Honest and open exchange* – Coachees will open up and be transparent if both 'cognition-based trust' and 'affect-based trust' are evident. What are these two essential dimensions?
    - *Cognition-based trust* is established according to how competent, reliable and dependable the coachee feels the Leader Coach is (generating feelings of confidence and respect)
    - *Affect-based trust* is the emotional bond that develops between the coachee and Leader Coach according to how much *genuine* care for their welfare the coachee thinks exists (generating feelings of attachment and gratitude).
- *Generate a topic* – The coachee might approach the first meeting with the Leader Coach firmly believing that they know what issues they wish to discuss. The process of building a rapport (which can take up the entire first session) enables the coachee to relax and think more clearly about what it is they wish to achieve and/or resolve.

How do Leader Coaches HELP 'build rapport'?

- *Contracting* – First, the Leader Coach and coachee need to agree parameters and boundaries:

- Confidentiality: stress the confidentiality of the discussion (or agree what can and cannot be shared with the line manager)
- Definition of coaching: explain what coaching is (challenge with support; a coachee-led process where ownership firmly lies with coachee, etc.) and isn't (Leader Coach owns problems, has all the answers and drives the action plan!)
- Scope: agree what is 'in scope' and 'out of scope'
- Coaching agreement: draw up a (formal or informal) coaching agreement detailing:
    - Values and principles by which each session will be conducted (honesty, realism, maturity, positivity, forward-looking, etc.)
    - Responsibilities, process and timings ('roles', time-keeping, attendance, action notes, etc.)
    - Expectations and outcomes (Leader Coach challenge and support in exchange for coachee honesty and progression).
- *Personal interests* – Take a genuine interest in the whole person, generating 'problem-free' discussion (possibly using the Coaching Wheel of Life Model – see Chapter 1):
    - *What do you do outside of work?*
    - *What is your passion?*
    - *Tell me about your family.*
- *Career* – Understand the coachee's career journey to date:
    - *What are you most proud about in your career?*
    - *What motivates you?*
    - *Tell me about three people you most admire?*
    - *What do you admire about them? (This will tell the Leader Coach a lot about the preferences and motivations of the coachee!)*
    - *What is your purpose in life/career? (i.e. establish discomfort with the present and a willingness to change.)*
- *Current role* – Understand the coachee's current context, asking:
    - *Draw a picture of yourself in your current job (a useful icebreaker that enables the Leader Coach to 'see' how their coachee perceives themselves 'in context')*
    - *Tell me about current stresses, strains, opportunities*

- *What would be the most valuable topic to focus upon?*
- *Review and discuss pre-coaching data (where available)* such as psychometric test results (including Mental Toughness variables), business performance results, pre-coaching questionnaire responses, 360-degree questionnaire results (see sections 1.1, 1.2, 1.4 and 2.2), asking:
    - *What do these results tell us about you?*
    - *What do they say about your strengths and weaknesses?*
    - *What would be the most valuable topic to focus upon?*

STEP 2 – **U**ncover **A**im

What is the Leader Coach trying to facilitate in STEP 2?

- Unearth an *aim* that is:
    - *Aspirational* (i.e. stretching – will be satisfying once it is achieved)
    - *Meaningful* (i.e. matters either to the coachee or organisation)
    - *Inspirational* (i.e. passes the get 'out of bed' test)
    - *Realistic* (i.e. achievable rather than fanciful)
    - *Clear* (i.e. simply and easily expressed)
    - *Impactful* (i.e. makes a quantifiable and visible difference)
    - *Tangible* (i.e. can be measured and verified).
- *Uncover* 'the roots' not just 'the tree'! Very often, objectives, aims and goals are agreed by coaches and coachees which address *symptoms rather than root causes*. Plenty of time must be taken to set an aim which will *really* advance and progress the coachee. Sometimes the Leader Coach must be courageous enough, having moved through the BUILD-RAISE process stages, to revisit this element and (given exploration of circumstances and resources) get the coachee to redefine their aim!

Why?

- *'Essence of human spirit'* – Having achieved a fair degree of rapport, the process of establishing the coachee's aim runs right to the existential heart of being (i.e. what are we here for and what are we trying to achieve in our lives?). Clarifying and carving out a meaningful purpose and goal is the most critical function of the Leader Coach.

- *Compass and focus for discussion* – Coaching sessions aren't a cosy chat. They focus on tangible issues and outcomes that are of high perceived value to the coachee. Establishing a core aim provides a reference point for subsequent discussions further on in the BUILD-RAISE process.

How do Leader Coaches HELP 'uncover aim'?

The following questions will assist Leader Coaches in helping coachees to uncover their main aim:

- *What do you want to achieve from this coaching session? When this session is over what outcome would be most valuable for you? What is the most valuable thing you could take away?*
- *What aim do you want to achieve?*
- *What would you like to happen with X?*
- *What do you really want?*
- *What would you like to accomplish?*
- *What result are you trying to achieve?*
- *What outcome would be ideal?*
- *What do you want to change?*
- *Why are you hoping to achieve this aim?*
- *What would the benefits be if you achieved this aim?*
- *If our coaching sessions are successful, what would be different for you?*
- *How would other people be able to tell our coaching sessions had been successful?*
- *What do you really want to take away from this session?*
- *What would you really like to do?*
- *Is it X or Y we need to focus upon?*

STEP 3 – Identify Interference

What is the Leader Coach trying to facilitate in STEP 3?

- *Isolate main barriers* – Having established a viable, uplifting and measurable aim, the Leader Coach needs to get the coachee to list real (and imagined) impediments and derailers (that have prevented them achieving it in the past or might hold them back in the future)

- *Establish their scale* – Leader Coaches should get coachees to 'rank-order' barriers in terms of their significance, to determine the magnitude of the task of overcoming them

- *Challenge false assumptions* – By challenging and/or checking what these impediments are, the Leader Coach can begin the process of challenging false assumptions and perceptions. This is particularly the case with many coachees' perception of the way others perceive what their strengths and weaknesses are. Using pre-coaching data (see above) or the Johari Window (Figure 49), Leader Coaches can begin the process of uncovering the real issue: faulty assumptions about ourselves and others!

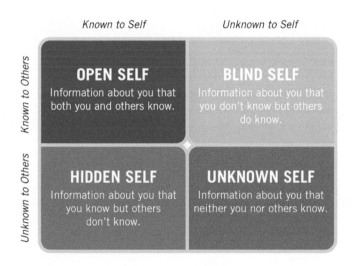

Figure 49: Johari Window of the 'Self'

Why?

- *'Performance = potential – interference'* – The major reason why Leader Coaches need to identify the nature and extent of interference is because – as this equation from Tim Gallwey's masterful book *The Inner Game of Tennis* highlights – the isolation and elimination of interference releases people's potential, resulting in more positive outcomes.

- *Self-limiting attitudes and behaviours* – Very often we are our own worst enemies in preventing ourselves from reaching our aims, objectives and goals. Using the Johari window (see Figure 49) increases coachee awareness of their 'blind self'; but if we were to caricature what really holds coachees back (as we've found over years of coaching and observation) we would highlight:

    - *Excessive ego within men* – A need to be *perceived* as outperforming their peer group and having a position of 'high social standing' within 'the pack' which bolsters their sense of *identity* and self-worth... which in itself causes stress, anxiety and sub-optimal behaviours!

    - *Lack of Self-Confidence within women* – A sense that (in spite of past achievements) what they have done – or plan to do – is *never* good enough... which in itself causes stress, anxiety and sub-optimal behaviours!

- *Create sense of perspective and new insights* – In addition, coachees might be labouring under false misconceptions as to the real barriers facing them at the workplace. Great Leader Coaches help cast new light on the *real* sources and true extent of the obstacles coachees face in attempting to realise their principal aim.

How do Leader Coaches HELP 'identify interference'?

This stage of the process needs to be taken very slowly. Why? Because interference needs to be described in rich detail. The coachee needs time to think and reflect on what might be hindering them. The Leader Coach must make sure at this stage that the coachee does not jump to ill-founded solutions (which is the next stage of the model). Questions that will aid the process at this stage include:

- *What is happening now (what, who, when and how often)? What is the effect or result of this?*
- *Have you already taken any steps towards your aim?*
- *How would you describe what you did?*
- *Where are you now in relation to your aim?*
- *On a scale of one to ten, where are you?*

- *What has contributed to your success so far?*
- *What progress have you made so far?*
- *What is working well right now?*
- *What is required of you?*
- *What factors have prevented you from reaching that aim already (issues)?*
- *What do you think is stopping you?*
- *What do you think is really happening?*
- *Do you know other people who have achieved that aim?*
- *What did you learn from X?*
- *What have you already tried?*
- *How could you turn this around this time?*
- *What could you do better this time?*
- *If you asked X, what would they say about you or advise you to do?*
- *On a scale of one to ten, how severe/serious/urgent is the situation?*
- *If someone said/did that to you, what would you think/feel/do?*
- *What is the present situation in more detail?*
- *What and how great is your concern about it?*
- *Who is affected by this issue other than you?*
- *How much control do you personally have over the outcome?*
- *Who else has some control over it and how much?*
- *What action steps have you taken on it so far?*
- *What has stopped you from doing more?*
- *What obstacles will need to be overcome on the way?*
- *What resources do you already have? (Skill, time, enthusiasm, money, support, etc.)*
- *What is really the issue here, the nub of the issue or the bottom line?*

STEP 4 – Locate Solutions

What is the Leader Coach trying to facilitate in STEP 4?

- *Surface remedies* – Having established the main sources of interference that are hindering progress towards the coachee's aim, the Leader Coach will help them surface a range of viable and *plausible* options that will neutralise them. Often these remedies will not be earth-shatteringly innovative, but having spent a great deal of time considering what the real barriers are, they are more likely to be solutions that fit these obstacles.

- *Highlight enablers* – In addition, the Leader Coach will help the coachee identify a range of core resources that the coachee will require to eliminate interference, namely: developing better skills and capabilities, creating wider networks, drawing upon existing contacts, feeding off past experiences, identifying and utilising key strengths, etc.

Why?

- *Move things forward* – Often coachees have been completely immobilised by what, to them, had seemed to be insurmountable blockages preventing them from realising core goals. What the Leader Coach is doing is helping the coachee to *envision* a credible way of moving things forward. This is not to say that, following the session, the coachee will be fully equipped to eradicate all interference in one go. Often, what the Leader Coach is doing is providing 'the spark' – encouraging the first of a series of small steps in a journey that will ultimately help the coachee achieve their ambition.

- *Provide hope, confidence and unlock energy* – Having been paralysed by a sense of helplessness, the discovery of a range of solutions to seemingly overwhelming odds will, in all likelihood, re-energise the coachee, provoking renewed feelings of hope and confidence that they can reach their desired destination. However, the Leader Coach must caution the coachee that any solution is unlikely to be a complete panacea to (sometimes) complex and ambiguous issues. (S)he must ensure that the coachee understands the scale of their task, which can be broken down into bite-sized chunks by the action plan that they will draw up and agree at the end of the session (see 'Step 5 – Determine Execution' below).

How does the Leader Coach HELP 'locate solutions'?

Fundamentally, what the Leader Coach is attempting to do in this stage is to reframe the coachee's perspective, opening them up to new ways of seeing, viewing and tackling the obstacles they face using:

- *Pictorials* – Using models and frameworks which help coachees discover new ways of tackling problems (see the preceding three chapters)

- *Mentoring* – Intervening with mentoring advice and expertise on how certain issues (based on the Leader Coach's prior experience) can be tackled

- *Reframing questions* – Locating solutions and resources through the use of compliments, exceptions to the problem, prioritisation ('do more of what works', 'do less of what doesn't work'), encouraging small steps through scaling and the use of possibility language. Many of these types of questions are outlined below and are addressed in more detail in the 'reframing perspectives' section, which is elucidated in 4.5.

  - *What are your potential solutions? What could you do? If you could do anything, what would you do? If you could only apply one solution that would add the most value, what would it be? What would be the results of this action?*
  - *What do you think you need to do next?*
  - *What could be your first step?*
  - *What do you think you need to do to get a better result (or closer to your aim)?*
  - *What else could you do?*
  - *Who else might be able to help?*
  - *What would happen if you did nothing?*
  - *What has worked for you already? How could you do more of that?*
  - *What would happen if you did that?*
  - *What is the hardest/most challenging part of that for you?*
  - *What advice would you give to a friend about that?*
  - *What would you gain/lose by doing/saying that?*
  - *If someone did/said that to you, what do you think would happen?*
  - *What's the best/worst thing about that particular solution?*
  - *Which solution do you feel ready to act on?*
  - *How have you tackled this/a similar situation before?*
  - *What could you do differently?*
  - *Who do you know who has encountered a similar situation?*
  - *If anything were possible, what would you do?*
  - *What personal strengths do you bring to this?*

- *How confident are you on a scale of one to ten that you can do this?*
- *What else?*

STEP 5 – Determine Execution

What is the Leader Coach trying to facilitate in STEP 5?

- *Clear action plan* – Having uncovered a clear aim, identified potential interference and located viable solutions, the Leader Coach must now get the coachee to commit to a clear plan of action with timescales and deliverables. During the coaching session (at least in formal circumstances) the Leader Coach will have made notes or sketched a fishbone diagram detailing how the coachee has arrived at this point. It is now beholden upon the coachee, with prompting and probing from the Leader Coach, to commit to a minimum of (in our experience) at least *three* measurable and quantifiable action points.

- *Support and resources* – In addition to 'what' the coachee commits to do, they need to specify 'how' – including the enabling resources they require for success (i.e. time, money, line-manager or stakeholder support, etc.). At this juncture, the Leader Coach can also offer support, offering to draw upon their own resources and contacts to help the coachee fulfil their overarching aim (without the coachee losing accountability for its ultimate achievement).

- *Follow-up and evaluation* – Having agreed a written plan of action, dates for follow-up and analysis of its progress are necessary so that the coachee has clear milestones in place. This follow-up can take place during the next coaching session or 'down the wire'. The important point is that the coachee knows that they will be held to account and judged accordingly at some point in the near future. This motivates them to act swiftly – in spite of the myriad of other things they have to do in their day jobs!

Why?

- *Progress* – At its heart, coaching is all about making progress. The Leader Coach's role is to provide courageous challenge with support, raising the coachee's level of self-awareness and building their accountability to move things forwards. Coachees can experience elation and exuberance in the coaching session.

However, where a coachee is insufficiently mentally, physically and practically prepared, these feelings can immediately dissipate outside the coaching bubble, 'when the rubber hits the road'. The Leader Coach must guard against this. Feel-good coaching sessions have been a waste of time unless they are translated into tangible progress.

- *Momentum* – The Leader Coach has enough to do themselves without signing up to a mountain of post-session support. The Leader Coach must guard against 'carrying' or getting too close to the coachee at this stage. But in order to ensure the plan gathers momentum, a few catch-up calls or emails from the Leader Coach to check on progress in-between coaching sessions can help 'animate' the process.

How does the Leader Coach HELP 'determine execution'?

To mobilise positive, proactive and productive behaviour, the Leader Coach clearly needs to get the coachee to map out a number of clear steps and to check for *absolute commitment* to an agreed plan of action. The questions below are designed to help this process:

- *How are you going to go about executing it? What will you do and when?*
- *What do you think you need to do right now?*
- *Tell me how you're going to do that.*
- *How will you know when you have done it?*
- *Is there anything else you can do?*
- *On a scale of one to ten, what is the likelihood of your plan succeeding?*
- *What would it take to make it a ten?*
- *What obstacles are getting in the way of success?*
- *What roadblocks do you expect or require planning?*
- *What resources can help you?*
- *Is there anything missing?*
- *What one small step will you take now?*
- *When are you going to start?*
- *How will you know you have been successful?*
- *What support do you need to get that done?*
- *What will happen (or what is the cost) of you NOT doing this?*

- *What do you need from me/others to help you achieve this?*
- *What are three actions you can take that would make sense this week?*
- *On a scale of one to ten, how committed are you to doing it?*
- *What would it take to make it a ten?*
- *Is this an efficient use of your time?*
- *How committed are you to actually doing this?*
- *How can you keep track of your success?*
- *What are all the different ways in which you could approach this issue?*
- *Make a list of all the alternatives, large or small, complete and partial solutions.*
- *What else could you do?*
- *What would you do if you could start again with a clean sheet, with a new team?*
- *What are the advantages and disadvantages?*
- *Which would give the best result?*
- *Which of these solutions appeals to you most or feels best to you?*
- *Which would give you the most satisfaction?*

4.5 REFRAMING AND MAGIC QUESTIONS

We referred to the use of reframing questions in Stage 4 'Locate Solutions', but a number of these questions are scattered among the ones we outlined in all stages of the BUILD-RAISE coaching process. However, given their importance – their capacity to 'jolt' and change coachees by generating revelatory perspectives and new ways of thinking and seeing things – further consideration of the specific types and genres of these questions is useful here. A more precise definition of *what* they are and illustration of *how* they can be used is of assistance to Leader Coaches who really wish to shift feelings, attitudes, perceptions and behaviours.

Reframing Perspectives by using and leveraging...

- **Compliment-based questions** (flattering concerns to move forwards) e.g.
  Coachee: 'It's far <u>too costly</u> to implement.'
  Leader Coach: 'I'm <u>impressed that you are cost conscious</u>! How can you make the solution less expensive?'

- **_Exception_-based questions** (highlighting previous successes to advance) e.g.

  Coachee: 'I find that <u>person really difficult</u> to work with.'

  Leader Coach: 'It sounds difficult... Tell about the <u>times or a situation you have worked well</u> together.'

- **_Possibility_-based questions** (envisioning options to nudge things on) e.g.

  Coachee: 'I really <u>can't relate to that individual</u>.'

  Leader Coach: 'So, to date you really haven't been able to communicate in order to develop a relationship... I wonder <u>what might assist in forging good communications</u>?'

- **_Resistance_ statements** ('reducing the problem' to get started!) e.g.

  Coachee: 'There is <u>no way I could get all of that done</u> given the pressure I am under!'

  Leader Coach: 'That's understandable! <u>What elements could you do</u>?'

- **_Relationally_ based questions** (third-party perspective to stimulate) e.g.

  Coachee: '<u>I can't do it</u>!'

  Leader Coach: 'Tell me <u>who would be surprised</u> to hear you say that?' ('What else would your boss see?', 'Who else would notice a difference?', 'If you had a friend in a similar situation, what would you advise?')

- **_Miracle_-based questions** (envisioning a positive future to change mindset) e.g.

  Leader Coach: 'If you awoke tomorrow to find <u>this problem gone</u>, how would you feel? What would your life be like?' ('Imagine you were performing more effectively – what are you actually doing differently?')

- **_Scaling_ questions** (a point of reference for measuring change over time) e.g.

  Leader Coach: 'Rank the <u>importance of this aim on a scale from one to ten</u>. Now rate your actual performance against this objective. Where do you want it to be?'

- **_Comparison_-based questions** (uses context to generate proper perspective) e.g.

  *Leader Coach***;** 'when you say this is a major issue can you be more specific; <u>is it *more/less* than *who/what*</u>?!'

- **_Coping_-based questions** (surfaces coachee resilience to generate hope) e.g.

  Leader Coach: '<u>What do you do</u> to keep going?!' ('Tell me about the reserves you currently draw upon to cope with your situation.')

- **_Mindfulness_-based questions** (promotes self-awareness leading to more solution-focused options for improvement) e.g.

  Leader Coach: '<u>What else </u>did you see/feel/do?'

- **_Metaphor_-based questions** (helps coachee to think differently/ creatively) e.g.

  Leader Coach: 'Paint a picture for me – what are you actually trying to achieve?'

  'If you were to write a book on this, what would it say?! What character would you play?'

- **_Problem-free_ talk**

  This is where the Leader Coach creates a judgement-free zone and conversations about (seemingly) irrelevant life experiences help illuminate coachee strengths and resources to move things forward!

4.6 LEADER COACHING CASE STUDY (USING REFRAMING AND MAGIC QUESTIONS)

Here, in a scenario based on true events, the HR Director ('the LEADER COACH') of a major multi-branded leisure corporation holds a coaching session with the Chief Operating Officer ('the BUSINESS LEADER') utilising the BUILD-RAISE process, interspersed with reframing questions.

(Stage 1 – Build Rapport)

LEADER COACH: 'Great to see you. How's the family? How are the kids?'

BUSINESS LEADER: 'Growing up fast...' [_Discussion on family ensues_]

LEADER COACH: 'In our last session we set a clear goal – for you to _strengthen your team_ by appointing Claire to run Brand _X_ and move John – the incumbent – to a Central Support role. This was to be achieved within six weeks and we discussed strategies as to how you might achieve this. Can you update me on progress?'

BUSINESS LEADER: 'Since that meeting I've met with both John and then Claire. John has agreed to move to Central for career-development purposes. I think he was relieved really – he's been heading the brand for four years – and accepts that he has taken it as far as he can. I've agreed with Simon (CEO) and Alison (Marketing Director) that he takes up the vacant Marketing Services Director position – he'll add a lot there. Claire is really excited about taking over the brand and we've organised handover dates etcetera.'

LEADER COACH: 'So everybody's happy and, overall, you've strengthened your organisation. Your worries about how John might react were unfounded! Well handled! *I think our session helped you last time! Would you agree that these discussions are useful*? [BUSINESS LEADER nods] Now – what topic would you like to discuss this time? Anything causing you concern or slowing you down? What would you like to achieve in this session?'

[NOTE – After some PROBLEM-FREE talk to put the BUSINESS LEADER at ease and check on their state of mind (asking about family etc.) the LEADER COACH uses his expert *summarising and clarifying* skills to check on progress and (most importantly) establish levels of satisfaction regarding the efficacy of their previous coaching session. *READINESS* and buy in to a further coaching conversation is established by getting the BUSINESS LEADER to agree – non-verbally (a powerful cue in any coaching conversation) – that a further Courageous Coaching conversation would add manifest value. The LEADER COACH has clearly established a high level of CREDIBILITY and TRUST with this BUSINESS LEADER, due to the effectiveness of their previous conversations.]

(Step 2 – Uncover Aim)

BUSINESS LEADER: 'Obviously, growing the business – I don't think we're going fast enough! But I always feel that way! …

LEADER COACH: 'Is that it? It's something that drives you all the time! What is concerning you at present? *What problem have you got that – if it disappeared tomorrow – would make it a lot easier for you to focus on growth*?'

BUSINESS LEADER: 'Something specific that's really causing me concern at the moment is my relationship with the new Chairman. I don't think he rates me! And that's not great for my career or the business – the Chairman thinking I'm an idiot!'

LEADER COACH: 'So what do you want to accomplish?'

BUSINESS LEADER: 'I suppose I want to change his perception of me.'

LEADER COACH: *'If our coaching session on this issue were successful, what would be different for you?'*

BUSINESS LEADER: 'I would have a plan going forwards, whereby I could get the new Chairman to have confidence in me and forge a good relationship'

LEADER COACH – 'So – if I understand rightly – your main aim is to shift your Chairman's perception of you from negative to positive territory. In addition, you want a clear plan of how you might achieve this. Am I right?'

BUSINESS LEADER – 'That's spot on.'

[NOTE – At this stage, the LEADER COACH uses *probing techniques* to establish what the BUSINESS LEADER's real aim is, *by unearthing his 'root goal'*: in this case, improving the BUSINESS LEADER's relationship with the Chairman. The use of 'MIRACLE' and 'PROBLEM GONE' REFRAMING QUESTIONS helps focus the BUSINESS LEADER upon what he would *really* value resolving. As previously discussed in this book, relationships and conflict often lie at the heart of business-leader issues. Their *HIDDEN* sense of paranoia (stemming from a fear of being found out), false self-confidence, raging self-doubt and mild self-loathing make them feel highly vulnerable and susceptible to *perceived* attack; especially from higher authorities. *These NEGATIVE DRIVERS, which they believe drive them on to ever-higher levels of performance, can often end badly through wilfully self-destructive behaviour*! The experienced LEADER COACH – sensitised to these types of generic problems amongst business leaders – has helped the BUSINESS LEADER (due to their high level of mutual trust and understanding) to disclose an issue which threatens to derail their advancement and progress.]

(Step 3 – Identify Interference)

LEADER COACH: *'If you had to rate your relationship with your Chairman on a scale of 1–10,* where is it now and where would you like it to be?'

BUSINESS LEADER: 'Currently I'd rate it at a 2/10. It would be great if it were 8/10! Obviously we're never going to be bosom buddies.'

LEADER COACH: 'OK. Describe the present situation in more detail... What really is the issue here, the nub of the issue or the bottom-line?'

BUSINESS LEADER: 'Got off on the wrong foot... First time out in the business, he started asking silly questions and then making naïve comments about how we could do things better... He suggested we rename one of our implant concepts... So I started questioning him on his view about upcoming legislation (he clearly didn't have a clue about it!) and I think that offended him... I have no chemistry with him... He doesn't understand the business... Since then he's sort of dismissed or ignored me when he's been in meetings!'

LEADER COACH: 'Describe to me what you felt when you'd heard he'd been appointed? *How did you rate his appointment on a scale of 1–10?*'

BUSINESS LEADER: 'I thought, "Who is this guy? Is this the best we can do?" I rated him no better than a two!'

LEADER COACH: 'So, just to clarify – you rated his appointment as a two and you think he rates you as a two! *If somebody you knew was listening to this conversation, what would they say to you?*'

BUSINESS LEADER: 'They'd say, "Typical! You don't rate this guy – even though he's more powerful than you – and you've let it show! He's sensed your attitude. And now you're paying the price!"'

LEADER COACH: 'You clearly don't rate him; that's what you feel. *But tell me three things about him that you have a sneaking admiration for...*'

BUSINESS LEADER: 'One, he has built some good businesses in other sectors. Two, he is energetic. Three, he does have very good manners towards our colleagues.'

LEADER COACH: 'So, he does have some redeeming features. Tell me, if you woke up tomorrow and this problem was gone, how would you feel?'

BUSINESS LEADER: 'Relieved. I really don't need this stress at the moment.'

[NOTE – Here the LEADER COACH uses 'SCALING', 'RELATIONAL' AND 'EXCEPTION'-BASED REFRAMING QUESTIONS to help the BUSINESS LEADER place this interference (his relationship with the Chairman) into context. After scaling the issue and measurably establishing where

the **BUSINESS LEADER** would ideally like relations to be, the **LEADER COACH** subtly guides the **BUSINESS LEADER** towards the realisation that *he personally (through his self-destructive FEELINGS and attitude) is the main barrier to good relations*. How? First, the **LEADER COACH** forces the **BUSINESS LEADER** to confront his 'BLIND' self (i.e. immature behaviour that others can see but the **BUSINESS LEADER** can't see themselves) by asking him how others would comment if they were 'listening in' on the conversation. Second, the **LEADER COACH** starts to REFRAME the **BUSINESS LEADER**'s attitude and FEELINGS towards the Chairman by asking him to list three redeeming features about him that he has a 'sneaking admiration for'.]

(Stage 4 – Locate Solutions)

LEADER COACH: 'So, what are your potential solutions? *If you were advising someone else who was in exactly the same position*, what would you say?'

BUSINESS LEADER: 'Perhaps – now I think about it – I need to change *my* attitude towards him. Perhaps I have been a little immature. He has picked up on the fact that I don't rate him and he has responded in kind. This situation isn't going to benefit either of us – certainly not me! So I really need to get closer to him.'

LEADER COACH: '*In the past when you've had a rocky relationship with somebody who matters, how have you mended fences?*'

BUSINESS LEADER: 'I've learnt to take more time understanding their anxieties and viewpoint.'

LEADER COACH: '*So what anxieties and concerns does your new Chairman have, do you think? If you were in his shoes what would you feel?*'

BUSINESS LEADER: 'I suppose he feels his reputation is on the line by taking this job. He wants to show some progress quickly; he wants to grow the business…'

[NOTE – Having RAISED the BUSINESS LEADER's level of SELF-AWARENESS (over the 'self-inflicted' cause of the problem, namely his own poor attitude and behaviour) the LEADER COACH now has to BUILD the BUSINESS LEADER's level of ACCOUNTABILITY for solving the issue *himself*. Here, the LEADER COACH uses 'RELATIONAL' and

'COMPARISON'-based REFRAMING techniques to prompt the BUSINESS LEADER to come up WITH THEIR OWN SOLUTION to their pressing issue, namely: changing his FEELING and attitude to the Chairman. Knowing that business leaders often lack EMOTIONAL INTELLIGENCE (for the predicament of others), the LEADER COACH builds the EMPATHY of the BUSINESS LEADER by asking him to place himself in his Chairman's shoes. NEGATIVISM is thus replaced with POSITIVITY.]

(Step 5 – Determine Execution)

LEADER COACH: 'If I understand you right, that's what you said *your* overarching goal was at the top of this discussion! So you are both aligned in that. So tell me what you are going to do next to mend relations. What one small step can you take NOW?'

BUSINESS LEADER: 'Funnily enough, I am out with him next week for the day. So I can use my time with him to forge a better relationship.'

LEADER COACH: *'How do you move your relationship towards an 8/10 during that day out?'*

BUSINESS LEADER: 'First – as I've said – change my attitude towards him. Second, ask him about his concerns, anxieties and objectives – try to understand where he is coming from. Three, try and allay some of those fears by showing him what we are doing to grow the business. Set things up on the day so that he goes away with more knowledge and confidence about me and the business.'

LEADER COACH: 'So to clarify: your plan is to a) change your attitude towards him, b) listen and understand where he is coming from and c) demonstrate alignment and competence. Is there anything I can do to help?'

BUSINESS LEADER: 'Not at the moment, thanks. But, I've written those three things down in my log. Do you mind if I reflect on them and give you a quick ring before I go out into the business with him next week?'

LEADER COACH: 'Not at all! I've also made notes. *Report back to me on how you believe you have fared in moving his perception of you from a 2/10!* Next time we will reflect on what happened and consider further actions you can take to strengthen your relationship with him.'

[Step 5 – The LEADER COACH has BUILT READINESS (by getting the BUSI-NESS LEADER to accept the efficacy of their coaching conversations – based on previous outcomes), UNDERSTOOD AIM (by clarifying that the BUSINESS LEADER's main goal is to improve his relationship with his Chairman), IDENTIFIED INTERFERENCE (locating the main 'HIDDEN' and 'BLIND' sources of interference as the BUSINESS LEADER's negative attitude and feelings towards the Chairman) and LOCATED SOLUTIONS (by getting the BUSINESS LEADER to take accountability and owner-ship for changing his attitude and behaviour towards the Chairman). In this final step (DETERMINE EXECUTION), the LEADER COACH uses a 'SCALING' REFRAMING question to get the BUSINESS LEADER to put forward a definitive plan of action, which the LEADER COACH repeats and summarises for complete buy-in and clarity. The LEADER COACH also makes himself available for a further 'support' discussion before the BUSINESS LEADER goes out into the business with the Chairman, in order to both strengthen the resolve of the BUSINESS LEADER and increase the bond between them. A further meeting to totally eliminate this issue is also implied in the coach's last comment.]

5 FURTHER INSIGHTS AND FINAL WORDS

Whether as a prospective or a practising Leader Coach, we hope that you have found this book to be full of stimulating ideas, insights, tools, models, questions and methods that will help you facilitate high-class coaching conversations with business leaders, helping them grow *personally, interpersonally and commercially*. But there are some questions that – until this point – we have purposefully left unattended because we did not wish to delay readers, at the front end of the book, from *firstly* accessing and digesting our Advanced Leader Coaching Model and then *secondly* absorbing our Courageous Coaching BUILD-RAISE coaching methodology.

The three crucial questions that we have not sufficiently addressed up to this point are:

Q1 What sort of leaders are Leader Coaches advised to *avoid*?

Q2 Which *business lifecycle 'leader typologies'* pose particular coaching challenges?

Q3 What practical problems will Leader Coaches face coaching *Star Performers*?

Q1 – What sort of leaders are Leader Coaches advised to avoid?

Leader Coaches would be wise to abandon the preconception that all leaders are coachable. There are still too many managers who prefer to 'speak in poetry whilst governing in prose', peddling a rhetoric of transformation ('our greatest asset is our staff') whilst meting out a reality of harsh transactional practice. Why? Here are some of the reasons why leaders reject or ignore the concept of *emotionally connecting* with their people and teams:

- *It is too difficult!* – Spending time and energy tapping into and harnessing people's positive emotions requires a high degree of time and effort. Some leaders have risen to the top due to their IQ but lack EI skills (failing to surround themselves with peers who might compensate for this blind spot). Others cannot be bothered to make the effort, falling back instead on command-and-control practices to 'get things done'.

- *Emotion is taboo!* – Furthermore, in the atmosphere of 'macho' boardrooms, where discussion of hard financial outputs rather than of soft people inputs is preferred, the notion that board members should discuss the feelings of employees (other than giving a cursory glance at the annual employee survey) would be regarded as laughable – a sign of weakness on the part of any individual that tried to push this agenda. This sets the cultural dynamic within which many companies operate, creating a trickledown effect of greater focus upon the numbers rather than the people. Rationalism is the order of the day in many companies. This is an approach that flies in the face of the fact that humans respond more readily to inspiring imagery than to dry fact.

- *They don't get the service–profit connection!* – In addition, many leaders fail to accept (or understand) the well-established linkage between a motivated workforce, satisfied customers and positive sales outcomes. They fail to understand that, particularly in service businesses, where staff members are required to requite customers' desires for *speed, quality and warmth*, employees need to feel *cared* for before they show the same level of appreciation and concern for customers. They reject this equation, misguidedly believing staff to be expendable cogs in a machine that – because of the way 'they' have designed it – will continue to perform well, with or without staff that care.

- *Race to the bottom!* – Within the prevailing business environment where technological innovation is overturning outmoded business models, leaders turn to reducing costs on the labour line as a means of sustaining short-term profit. In service businesses, employment costs can account for anything up to 35 per cent of overall operating costs in some operations, so it stands to reason that reducing costs in this area will have the largest (and quickest) payback in terms of reducing overhead. Whilst such approaches might be needed from time to time to 'rebase' the business, the fact remains that leaders often embark on wave after wave of staff overhead reductions that spread disillusion, fear and uncertainty amongst their teams, which has a knock-on effect on customer perceptions of service. They fail to communicate their reasons for making these reductions, when they will end and how such actions will ultimately contribute to growing the business. In short, they fail to engender feelings of *hope* that things will ultimately get better!

Whilst Leader Coaches can move some leaders out of this paradigm, the reality is that many are too far gone and are best avoided! But what, in our view, are the typologies of some of the most truly execrable leaders we have come across?

- **Clueless** – This type of leader is completely unsuited to running any type of business, lacking the tacit skills to manage it during its transitional phase of development. With regards to lack of tacit expertise, it is not uncommon for business owners – in order to seek 'new perspectives' – to go outside the sector to hire new leaders, in spite of all the evidence (both practitioner and academic) that promoting talent from within or across their sector from similar concepts is the most fool-proof way of safe-guarding a business's future. For instance, sometimes new hires in leisure have been made from food retail, but these new recruits – steeped in knowledge of 'functional retail' – lack a recognition of the centrality of 'service performance', 'on-site production' and 'emotional connectivity' within a leisure context. Tangible factors such as range, availability, quality and price are the main drivers of customer satisfaction in food retail. Intangible attributes such as service, sociability and environment are just as important within food service. Also, leaders from a food-retailing background – where brands are highly systemised and 'homogenised' – often cannot cope with the heterogeneous nature of food service; they are insufficiently attuned to the fact that 'one size cannot fit all' within this context (see 'Introduction'). Lacking these insights, the clueless leader wrecks the emotional dynamic of the business by searching for solutions based more upon efficiency (cost) than effectiveness (customer and employee).

- **Reckless** – This category of leader jeopardises the future of the enterprise by making high-risk decisions to achieve preposterous stellar growth and/or generate dubious shareholder 'value crea-tion'. Unsuitable assets are acquired for the sake of the appearance of scale (the notion of expansion being conflated with growth) or complicated exercises in 'value engineering' are conducted. The reputation of the business is diminished rapidly by vainglorious 'financial' rather than 'industrial' strategies that end in unmitigated disaster. It is not that the leader in this instance is clueless; rather they possess a dangerous combination of a lack of self-control and a low boredom threshold. They seek immortality by 'putting all their chips on red' and – in some instances – they get away with it on the first or second occasion. Inevitably, however, they get found out. To the reckless, taking risks is a stimulant that they crave in order to feel energised, excited and alive! But why are these chancers in a position of authority in the first place? Likely explanations include business-owner greed (the fact that they buy into a 'wrecker's' vision for their own self-serving financial purposes), the fact that executives can dangerously morph into this category through boredom (they have been in position too long) and/or they are subject to a complete lack of corporate governance (checks and balances that thoroughly review key strategic decisions). Whatever the reasons, this type of leader comes with a strong health warning: they should either not be appointed in the first place or stopped in their tracks before they do irreparable damage!

- **Egoist** – The egoist is probably one of the most common of the leader typologies that we deem uncoachable. This individual has an almost improbable and delusional sense of infallibility. Their lack of self-awareness, coupled with a misguided belief in 'divine superiority', drives them to make decisions without consulting others whose views and opinions they regard as derisory or unworthy. Soon the egoist has created an organisation which relies upon them for all the answers; decisions are deferred or delayed for fear of retribution or being cast out of the circle of patronage. The all-powerful monarch with a sense of unbridled self-destiny has surrounded him- or herself with compliant followers who have learnt to flatter and preen the leader's sensitive ego rather than draw their attention to unpalatable truths. But because the egoist is in it for themselves rather for the long-term prosperity of the business (the project is about them rather than the common good), the enterprise is usually doomed to failure. Following conception, no successful business can be the entire preserve of one man or woman. Engagement and innovation can only be sustained through a feeling of common purpose and public recognition of the contribution of others. The egoist cannot see or recognise this. Eventually, even though they are surrounded by sycophants, they are left isolated and become detached from the truth. At some point a regime change will occur and all those that the egoist believed were close colleagues and confidents will spurn and ignore them!

- **Toxics** – Our final category of business-leader typologies (although not totally mutually exclusive to the types outlined above) best avoided by Leader Coaches incorporates the consciously venal. These individuals have managed their careers successfully because they have been outstanding at 'managing upwards'. They are nasty users who plot, scheme and dissemble deliberately to get their own way, whatever the human consequences. Lacking any empathy for the feelings of others, they actively seek to divide and rule – deliberately setting business colleagues against one another through gossip and misinformation. They do this because they believe that it augments and strengthens their position; they become indispensable puppet masters, the only people who can lay claim to being able to control the unruly rabble – which they created! Toxics are hard to catch and despatch because they are sly and mendacious. As they are used to preying on the insecurities and fears of others to control them, they are artful in seeing off any challengers by deploying equally ruthless tactics (i.e. whispering campaigns challenging their moral probity and good character). But in the end, their game play 'hoists them with their own petard'. Toxics run out of people, the business runs out of energy and they run out of track! At some point, their tactic of blaming everybody else for poor performance loses credibility and they become the victim, along with the business, which is probably too far gone for redemption.

So, these are the some of the reasons why some leaders are uncoachable: they are too far gone (being hideously committed to focussing on *financial outputs* at the expense of *emotional inputs*) and/or they display characteristics portrayed by our *clueless, reckless, egoist* and *toxic* typologies. Our advice to Leader Coaches? Avoid them at all costs!

Q2 – Which *business lifecycle 'leader typologies'* pose particular coaching challenges?

The structure and narrative underlying our Advanced Leader Coaching Model are based on the presupposition that Leader Coaches should aim to facilitate an *interconnected leadership coaching approach* that, *firstly*, promotes high levels of insight into coachee personal mindsets, styles and contexts enabling, *secondly*, a high degree of empathy to the needs of their customers, teams and stakeholders which, *thirdly*, converts directly into superior business-performance outcomes (facilitated by strategic clarity, operational grip and an agile, innovative culture). Whilst this book has dealt with which leadership styles should be facilitated by Leader Coaches in particular situations (see 1.4 'Adjust Style'), a consideration of which approaches should be adopted according to differing business lifecycle requirements has been neglected thus far (apart from a brief reference in 1.5 'Transition Roles/Careers'). An elucidation of five lifecycle leadership typologies (caveated with distinctive Leader Coach challenges) offers a more in-depth insight.

- **Originators** – Through their creative spark and drive, the founder–entrepreneur has brought their business proposition to life, creating a vibrant culture which bears the heavy imprint of their personality. Their leadership style during this phase of start-up is 'charismatic and values-led'.

Challenge posed to the Leader Coach: Self-made founder–entrepreneurs are by their very nature hard to coach! Obsessive, highly driven and (usually) indifferent to the views and advice of outsiders – because they believe they have got to where they are by exploiting their own inner resources (see 1.3 'Increase Capacity') – they are loath to let anyone else in. Certainly not somebody like a Leader Coach who (obviously!) falls short both in terms of parallel achievement or insight into what they have sacrificed to get into their position. Unless the Leader Coach can bolster their credibility by demonstrating instant added value with founder–entrepreneurs, they will fail to find any traction with this leader typology.

- **Escalators** – As the business scales up and its level of complexity increases, professional management is required to systemise processes, policies and procedures so that it continues its momentum. The leadership style required here is what we would term 'energetic managerialism' (whilst preserving the original DNA of the founder's vision).

  Challenge posed to the Leader Coach: Escalators are very busy people. Charged with scaling up the business/SBU, they lack the time or resources for (what they might regard as) 'diversionary' conversations. Of course, experienced, seasoned Leader Coaches can add a lot of value to Escalators, challenging their plans and aspirations, helping expose dangerous misconceptions that could prove costly further on down the track. How does the Leader Coach gain traction with this typology? By getting under the skin of their business plans in order to formulate some pointed questions that will get the Escalator to stop, step back and carefully consider the pitfalls of their intended plans, ensuring that they scale up a business that will be truly sustainable.

- **Evolvers** – Having experienced its growth spurt with its original proposition, the brand now requires evolution and refreshment. The leadership style required here is 'agile incrementalism'.

  Challenge posed to the Leader Coach: Evolvers must grapple with some seemingly intractable problems. How do they sustain earnings and growth from assets that (in some instances) are running out of growth potential? This group should be most receptive to coaching because they have more time to contemplate and plan. The problem for Leader Coaches is that Evolvers are often riven with indecision as to how they should move things forward. How does the Leader Coach gain traction with this typology? By being uncompromisingly challenging and provocative to disrupt their coachee's pattern of thinking and way of viewing things. Evolvers will only believe that value has been added if they emerge from coaching conversations with new angles and perspectives that will help them drive their businesses upwards, avoiding the cul-de-sac of bureaucratic ossification.

- **Revivers** – However, due to excessive bureaucracy, competitive pressure and consumer trends, the business might at some stage experience severe difficulty, requiring revival. The leadership style here is 'transformational turnaround'.

Challenge posed to the Leader Coach: Like Escalators, Revivers are extremely time poor. The clock is ticking as (s)he tries to save the business from obsolescence. What they don't think they need at this point is coaching – but they do! Why? The stresses and challenges they face need to be put in perspective by somebody who sits outside their bubble. They need to be reminded: what is the worst that can possibly happen? But how does the Leader Coach gain traction with this typology? By proving to be an excellent listener and sounding board, empathising with the Reviver's extreme circumstances. But at the same time, they must help the Reviver focus on their controllables and maintain a positive mindset, whatever (personal or business) forms of jeopardy might lie ahead.

Q3 – What practical problems will Leader Coaches face when coaching Star Performers?

If there are uncoachable *types of leaders* that should be avoided by Leader Coaches and business-lifecycle leadership typologies that throw up all sorts of challenges for Leader Coaches, what about the final elephant in the room? Namely, how can Leader Coaches engage with and coach 'star performer' leaders who – by their very nature – display excessive behavioural traits and characteristics? Some are successful and widely regarded by their peer mavericks – abnormally driven and obsessive! Who are they, what generic behaviours do they display and how should the Leader Coach handle them?

First, who are highly driven, star-performer leaders? Broadly speaking, we believe managers and leaders can split into five segments on the performance–potential spectrum:

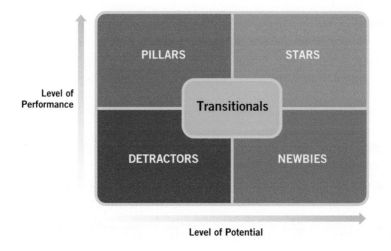

Figure 50: Performance–Potential Model

Within Figure 50 above, Star Performers lie within the top right-hand box; by their very definition, they are *high-performance, high-potential* individuals who are recognised as having huge present and future value to the organisation. In essence, we would define them as:

> *valuable high-potential, high-performance employees who consistently deliver outstanding results who have the potential – based on this performance – for further progression.*

Why are Star Performers so important to organisations? First, they commonly constitute a relatively small proportion of the overall organisational population, but make a disproportionate contribution to the firm's performance. Second, their careful and patient nurturing gives organisations an important source of *competitive advantage*. Their vital importance, however, can be summarised as follows:

- *Talent* – Star Performers improve the 'gene pool' of the organisation, improving its intellectual DNA. They provide a talent pipeline and improve the 'bench strength' of the organisation.
- *Energy and Pace* – Star Performers are exemplars, improving the dynamic capability of organisations with their agile, 'can

do' mentality, infecting those around them, upping levels of productivity and effort. In short, Star Performers improve the organisation's 'installed capacity' to get things done faster.

- *Creativity and Innovation* – Star Performers, who often display more curiosity than their peer group, are constantly pushing the boundaries, seeking solutions to get things done more elegantly and smarter. They are willing to trial new methods and participate in projects and initiatives to improve the 'way things are done around here'.

- *Impact and Performance* – Ultimately, though, it is their consistently high performance that sets the benchmark within organisations and marks out Star Performers from their peer group. They set the gold standard of achievement to which others in the organisation aspire.

This caricatured account of their dominant characteristics mainly concentrates on their *positive* rather than their *negative traits*. In itself, it does not provide Leader Coaches with a sufficiently robust set of insights to coach Star Performers effectively.

Based on extensive research from the MTQ48 Mental Toughness survey and ILM 72 leadership questionnaire (see 1.2 'Build Mental Toughness' and 1.4 'Adjust Style') that we have used as an accompaniment to our coaching of Star Performers over the last decade, we would argue that there are a *number of potentially self-destructive attitudinal and behavioural issues* that require resolving by the Leader Coach. Using the Johari Window (see Figure 49), Leader Coaches can help with issues arising from their 'OPEN' selves.

- *CAREER/DEVELOPMENTAL CONCERNS* – The primary issue that Star Performers are most likely to wish to focus upon during coaching conversations – due to their ambitious and highly aspirational nature – is career progression or accessing value-added personal development. Here the Leader Coach can help facilitate discussions around different career route maps, milestones and the skills development required to achieve desired outcomes. In addition, however, the Leader Coach's job involves instilling a degree of PATIENCE and REALISM, helping the Star Performer to understand that reaching their ultimate career destination might take longer and involve far greater *transitional planning and preparation* than they had previously thought, involving some left-field assignments in order to secure the Star Performer's optimal career outcomes (without extinguishing hope and aspiration).

- *RAPID GOAL ACHIEVEMENT* – The second issue most likely to be raised by Star Performers is rapid goal achievement. This is unsurprising: Star Performers are highly driven and want to quickly dispatch stretch targets and tasks. Here the Leader Coach can help by facilitating discussions around resources, prioritisation, time management and so forth. What the Coach can also help with is placing Star Performers' goals within CONTEXT and PERSPECTIVE, reducing the pressure that Star Performers constantly feel under to consistently outperform their competitive set.

- *LACK OF FREEDOM/EMPOWERMENT* – A common issue raised by Star Performers – given their preference for unfettered freedom, autonomy and flexibility – is the stifling constraints imposed by them by their organisations and/or line managers. Given their need to push the envelope through creative and innovative initiatives, to get things done better and faster, any perceived constraints are regarded as impertinent restraints of their trade! Here the Leader Coach can probe to establish whether these restrictions are real or imagined. In addition, (s)he can facilitate a debate on how the Star Performer can extend their 'freedom within a fixed frame' through NETWORKING, INFLUENCING AND NEGOTIATION, rather than acting in unnecessarily deviant, disruptive and provocative ways that could destabilise the wider organisation.

Of course, the Leader Coach can deal with these *common* star-performer issues in a fairly systematic manner, but progress will only be made if (s)he deals with the *root cause* of any issues that lie within the Star Performer's 'BLIND' and 'HIDDEN' selves. *Dealing with and resolving these (potentially self-destructive) negative, feelings, behaviours and drivers is absolutely fundamental to making any real LONGER TERM progress for Star Performers.* Thus, some common BLIND issues and Leader Coach solutions would (in our view) include:

- *LACK OF EMOTIONAL CONTROL* – One of the most common problems exhibited by Star Performers that can be seen by others but is either mislabelled (as passion or desire to win) or not acknowledged by them is a lack of Emotional Control. This is expressed through outbursts of frustration, anger, anxiety and disgust. These fierce outpourings (directed at 'faceless' bureaucracy, 'incompetent' peers/stakeholders and 'useless' senior managers) diminishes the standing and reputation of Star Performers. These behaviours bring into question whether they have the TEMPERAMENT and SELF-CONTROL to assume more senior responsibilities. Time and again during our commercial and academic careers we have observed that the Star Performers most likely to make it all the way have learned to manage their emotions, displaying extreme coolness and grace under pressure. They rarely get flustered over barriers and impediments to progress, instead focusing their energies upon how they can navigate an elegant course around them to secure their desired outcomes.

So, what does the Leader Coach do here? (S)he must, *first*, get the Star Performer who lacks Emotional Control to build up their awareness of the issue, accepting that it is a destructive feature of their behaviour (see 1.2 'Build Mental Toughness'); *second*, help Star Performers to recognise the 'trigger signs' when they begin to lose Emotional Control; *third*, help them work out strategies and coping mechanisms to either hide, suppress or extinguish these energy-zapping behaviours, focusing instead upon 'controlling the controllables'.

- *LACK OF EMPATHY FOR OTHERS* – Given their obsessional drive and (typically) large egos – forged through a belief that they contribute, produce and deliver more than the rest – Star Performers struggle to cope with what they perceive to be poor outputs by 'inferior' colleagues and stakeholders. They are unable or unwilling to take a rounded view of context or understand the world from the perspective of others (*their* problems, issues, barriers, struggles). This behaviour will give rise to conflict, jealousy and resistance at the workplace and will be extremely problematic for Star Performers later on in their careers when – in far more senior roles – they will have to lead and co-ordinate cross-functional teams that do not report in to them directly. Unless they develop a collaborative style, respecting the contribution and acknowledging the problems faced by others, they will be derailed by 'indirect' stakeholders who – because they have been (in extreme cases) humiliated, mocked and traduced – *subtly* withdraw any effort or support.

What the Leader Coach has to do here is raise the awareness of Star Performers of their level of co-dependency at the workplace; of their need to foster strong coalitions, alliances and supportive networks through TRUSTING MUTUAL EXCHANGE (of effort, support, ideas, knowledge, etc.). How do they do this? By asking Star Performers how they think others perceive them and then producing the unexpurgated results of 360-degree feedback instruments (which include not just data from direct reports and bosses but also *peers* and wider *service/support function providers*).

Unless Star Performers understand that you should treat all others as they would wish to be treated themselves, they are in serious danger of hampering their progress and career advancement.

Also, taking what we have found to be frequent hidden issues secretly playing out in the HIDDEN minds of Star Performers, how should Leader Coaches reposition and reframe these negative drivers into positive motivators?

- *FEAR/PARANOIA* – In spite of all outward appearances, Star Performers are often driven by a paranoid fear of failure (and how this will reflect upon them amongst peers, family and friends). What the Leader Coach must do here is replace this sense of fear with feelings of DETERMINED OPTIMISM – that even if things do not go to plan, the Star Performer's bloody-minded determination will get them there in the end.

- *SELF-DOUBT* – These feelings of fear and paranoia that drive them forwards are caused – in some cases – by a crippling sense of self-doubt and low self-esteem. This is their dirty little secret. Despite how they act, what they say and how they appear *externally*, *internally* they are wracked with a lack of Self-Confidence. Their internal 'voice' tells them that they aren't good enough – failure is an inevitable by-product of their shallow talents! Of course, this leads to over-compensatory behaviour that hides this psychological vulnerability. But again, a failure to resolve this 'conversation' stores up problems for the Star Performer. At some point it will become a self-fulfilling prophecy. What the Leader Coach must do here is instil PERSONAL SELF-CONFIDENCE, getting the Star Performer to identify and celebrate THEIR INTERNAL PERMANENT QUALITIES THAT WILL ALWAYS OVERCOME TEMPORARY EXTERNAL INTERFERENCE.

- *SELF-LOATHING* – But ultimately, the root cause of Star Performers' negative motivators has a simple explanation: they simply don't really like or love themselves. For the time being, their obsessional and addictive behaviour – resulting in preposterous levels of over-achievement – bolsters their sense of self-worth and self-efficacy. But these feelings soon disappear once the rush of acclamation is over and the Star Performer is drawn back into their own personal vortex of self-loathing. How can the Leader Coach assist here? This is complex territory, better travelled by qualified therapists and psychologists. In mild cases of self-loathing, the Leader Coach can help Star Performers to LEARN TO LOVE THEMSELVES by getting them to understand and appreciate the good works they have done in the past and how they are loved by others. In extreme cases, however, where this self-loathing has started to manifest itself in destructive behaviours (i.e. alcoholism, self-harming, gambling addictions, etc.) the Leader Coach has to cease all coaching conversations and strongly suggest that the Star Performer obtains professional medical advice/treatment.

- *INSECURITY* – All of these negative motivators – fear, self-doubt and self-loathing – drive the Star Performer on to levels of performance that they believe will ameliorate or extinguish these feelings. But they don't. As a result, the Star Performer feels a sense of permanent insecurity. They will be found out. It will all come to calamitous conclusion. What the Leader Coach has to do here is help place their work in PERSPECTIVE, help them to see that their work and their obsession to succeed at all times are not the be-all and end-all (see 1.5 'Transition Roles/Careers').

Final Words

If you have stayed with us this far, we salute you! It is a little-known fact that only 20 per cent of business books are actually read end-to-end by their readers. However, maybe you cheated and jumped to this conclusion, having dipped in and out of the book, merely reading the sections that interested you. Nevertheless, we are still grateful for your company at this stage!

This book has been a modest attempt to present to you our integrated model of Advanced Leader Coaching, which exhorts aspirant and existing leader coaching to take a holistic approach to coaching leaders, accounting for their interconnected needs for personal, interpersonal and business growth. Why? Because **how leaders *think and feel* determines how they *behave*, which in turn affects how they *perform*.** Coaches who adopt a one-dimensional approach to business-leader coaching – focusing either on personal/life issues or business matters – will only provide partial solutions to business-leader growth. In addition, through its Courageous Coaching BUILD-RAISE methodology, we hope that this book has given you a robust structure and reframing methodology to help you get the best out of your leader coachees. Our final insights chapter will also give you some food for thought on *who* you don't want to coach, *what* coaching challenges pertain to which business-lifecycle leader typologies, and *how* to handle the delicate task of coaching highly driven Star Performers.

But in the end, we will say this. Up to this point, there has been no reference text (other than Passmore's excellent *Leadership Coaching*) that has explicitly tackled how Leader Coaches should coach business leaders. This has been a grave omission in the business literature because business is ultimately about people, and people need inspiring leaders who can instil a sense of meaning, purpose and belief into their enterprise. Otherwise, they are likely to feel that their endeavours count for nothing – and in the end, their enterprise will, almost certainly, amount to nothing! So Leader Coaches, believe in what you are doing. Help grow the best, to do their best, so that their organisations can be the best! We wish you all the best in your future coaching conversations.

SOURCES AND FURTHER READING

Aaron Allen & Associates (2016) 'The Cost of Pissed Off Employees Quantified'. https://aaronallen.com/blog/associate-engagement-cost-of-pissed-off-employees-quantified

Albrecht, K. (1992) *At America's Service*. NY: Warner Books.

Albrecht, K., and Zemke, R. (1995) *Service America! Doing Business in the New Economy*. NY: Warner Books.

Alvesson, M., and Karreman, D. (2004) 'Interfaces of control: Technocratic and socio-ideological control in a global management consultancy firm'. *Accounting, Organizations and Society* 29: 423–4.

Anderson, L., and Krathwohl, D. (2001) *A Taxonomy for Learning, Teaching and Assessing: A Revision of Bloom's Taxonomy of Educational Objectives*. New York: Longman.

Ansoff, I. (1968) *Corporate Strategy*. London: Penguin Publishing.

Arnold, J. (2009) *Coaching Skills for Leaders in the Workplace – How to Develop, Motivate and Get the Best from your Staff*. Oxford: How to Books.

Association for Coaching. 'Code of Ethics and Good Practice'. associationforcoaching.com [accessed 04/03/16].

Bandura, A. (1986) *Social foundations of thought and action: a social cognitive theory*. NJ: Prentice Hall.

Barker, J.R. (2005) 'Toward a philosophical orientation on control'. *Organization* 12(5), 787–91.

Bass, B.M. (1985) *Leadership and Performance Beyond Expectation*. New York: Free Press.

Bass, B.M., and Avolio, B.J. (1991) *The Multifactor Leadership Questionnaire*. Palo Alto: Consulting Psychologists Press.

Bass, B.M., and Bass, R. (2008) *The Bass handbook of leadership: Theory, research, and managerial applications* (4th ed.). NY: Free Press.

Beaufre, A. (1963) *Introduction à la Strategie*. Paris: Fayard.

Beck, A.P. (1981) 'A study of group phase development and emergent leadership'. *Group Dynamics: Theory, Research and Practice*. 5, 48–54.

Belbin, R.M. (1981) *Management Teams – Why They Succeed or Fail*. Oxford: Butterworth-Heinemann.

Belbin, R.M. (2000a) *Team Roles at Work*. NY: Butterworth-Heinemann.

Belbin, R.M. (2000b) *Beyond the Team*. NY: Butterworth-Heinemann.

Berry, L. (2000) 'Cultivating Service Brand Equity'. *Academy of Marketing Science*. 28 (1), 128–37.

Bird, J., and Gornall, S. (2014) *The Art of Coaching: A Handbook of Tips and Tools*. Abingdon: Routledge.

Blanchard, K. (2007) *Leading at a Higher Level*. London: Prentice Hall.

Blanchard, K., Carew, D., and Parisi Carew, E. (2004) *The One Minute Manager Builds High Performing Teams*. London: Harper Collins.

Blanchard, K., and Johnson, S. (1986) *The One Minute Manager*. New York: Harper Collins.

Bluckert, P. (2006) *Psychological Dimensions of Executive Coaching*. NY: McGraw Hill.

Browne, M.N.M. (2008) *An Integrated Model of Leadership*. PHD Thesis, University of Hull, UK.

Burns, T., and Stalker, G.M. (1961) *The Management of Innovation*. London: Tavistock.

Byford, M., Watkins, M., and Triantogiannis, L. (2017) 'Onboarding isn't Enough'. *Harvard Business Review*, 1 May.

Chandler, A.D. (1962) *Strategy and Structure*. Boston MA: MIT Press.

Christensen, C.M., and Overdorf, M. (2000) 'Meeting the Challenge of Disruptive Change'. *Harvard Business Review*, 78 (2), March–April, 67–76.

Clough, P.J., Earle, K., and Sewell, D. (2002) 'Mental Toughness: the concept and its measurement'. In I. Cockerill (ed.), *Solutions in Sport Psychology* (pp.32–43). London: Thomson.

Clough, P.J., and Strycharczyk, D. (2008) 'Developing resilience through coaching – MTQ48'. In J. Passmore (ed.), *Psychometrics in Coaching: Using Psychological and Psychometric Tools for Development*. London: Kogan.

Clough, P.J., and Strycharczyk, D. (2015) *Developing Mental Toughness: Coaching Strategies to Improve Performance, Resilience and Wellbeing* (2nd ed.). London: Kogan Page.

Clutterbuck, D. (2014) *Everyone Needs a Mentor*. London: CIPD.

Clutterbuck, D., and Megginson, D. (2015) *Making Coaching Work – Creating a Coaching Culture*. London: CIPD.

Cohen, A.R., and Bradford, D.L. (1989) *Influence without Authority*. NY: John Wiley.

Collins, J. (2001) *Good to Great: Why Some Companies Make the Leap... and Others Don't*. London: Random House.

Collins, J., and Porras, J. (1994) *Built to Last: Successful Habits of Visionary Companies*. London: Random House.

Covey, S.R. (1989) *The 7 Habits of Highly Effective People*. London: Simon & Schuster.

Crabtree, S. (2017) 'Weak Workplace Cultures Help Explain UK's Productivity Woes'. *Gallup Blog*, October 6. Retrieved 11/10/19.

Csikszentmihalyi, M. (1990) *Flow*. New York: Harper Collins.

CURE (2020) 'National Framework for Mentoring and Coaching'. www.curee.co.uk/mentoring

Dale, E. (1969) *Audio-Visual Methods in Teaching* (3rd ed.). NY: Holt, Rinehart and Winston.

Dansereau, F., Graen, G., and Haga, W.J. (1975) 'A vertical dyad linkage approach to leadership within formal organisations: A longitudinal investigation of the role making process'. *Organizational Behavior & Human Performance* 13(1), 46–78.

De Bono, E. (1985) *Six Thinking Hats: An Essential Approach to Business Management*. Boston: Little Brown and Company.

de Chernatony, L. (2001) 'A Model for Strategically Building Brands'. *Brand Management* 9(1), 32–44.

de Chernatony, L., and McDonald, M. (1992) *Creating Powerful Brands*. London: Butterworth-Heinemann.

de Chernatony, L., and Segal-Horn, S. (2003) 'The Criteria for Successful Service Brands'. *European Journal of Marketing* 37(7/8), 1,095–118.

de Vries, M.F., Korotov, K.R., and Florent-Treacy, E. (2007) *Coach or Couch: The Psychology of Making Better Leaders*. Paris: INSEAD Business Press.

Deci, E. (1972) 'Intrinsic Motivation, Extrinsic Reinforcement and Inequity'. *Journal of Personality and Social Psychology* 22(1), 113–20.

Dobelli, R. (2013) *The Art of Thinking Clearly*. London: Sceptre.

Doran, G. (1981) 'There's a S.M.A.R.T. way to write management's goals and objectives'. *Management Review* 70(11): 35–6.

Dotlich, D., et al. (2006) *Leadership Passages: The Personal and Professional Transitions That Make or Break a Leader*. London: CIPD.

Downey, M. (2003) *Effective Coaching: Lessons from the Coach's Coach*. London: Texere Publishing.

Drucker, P.F. (1955) *The Practice of Management*. London: Pan Books.

Drucker, P.F. (1989) *The Practice of Management* (9th ed.). London: Heinemann Professional.

Dweck, C. (2017) *Mindset: Changing the Way You Think to Fulfil Your Potential*. New York: Ballantine Books.

Dyer, J.G., and McGuinness, T.M. (1996) 'Resilience: analysis of the concept'. *Archives of Psychiatric Nursing* 10, 276–82.

Edger, C. (2012) *Effective Multi-Unit Leadership – Local Leadership in Multi-Site Situations*. Farnham: Gower Business Publishing.

Edger, C. (2013) *International Multi-Unit Leadership – Developing Local Leaders in Multi-Site Operations*. Farnham: Gower Business Publishing.

Edger, C. (2014) *Professional Area Management – Leading at a Distance in Multi-Unit Enterprises* (1st ed.). Oxford: Libri.

Edger, C. (2015) *Professional Area Management – Leading at a Distance in Multi-Unit Enterprises* (2nd revised ed.). Oxford: Libri.

Edger, C. (2016) *Area Management – Strategic and Local Models for Growth*. Oxford: Libri.

Edger, C. (2018) *Courageous Coaching – Using the BUILD-RAISE Model (A Practical Guide for Leader Coaches)*. Oxford: Libri.

Edger, C. (2019a) *Coaching Senior Hires – Transitioning Performance into Potential*. Oxford: Libri.

Edger, C. (2019b) *Coaching Star Performers – Reframing Negative Drivers and Feelings*. Oxford: Libri.

Edger, C., and Emmerson, A. (2015) *Franchising – How Both Sides Can Win*. Oxford: Libri.

Edger, C., and Hughes, T. (2016) *Effective Brand Leadership – Be Different. Stay Different. Or Perish*. Oxford: Libri.

Edger, C., and Hughes, T. (2017) *Inspirational Leadership – Mobilising Super-performance Through eMOTION*. Oxford: Libri.

Edger, C., and Oddy, R.E. (2018) *Events Management – 87 Models for Event, Venue and Experience Managers*. Oxford: Libri.

Egon Zehnder (2017) in 'Onboarding Isn't Enough'. *Harvard Business Review*. May–June 2017.

Elsner, R., and Farrands, B. (2012) *Leadership Transitions: How Business Leaders Take Charge in New Roles*. London: Kogan Page.

Ely, K., Boyse, L., Nelson, J., Zaccaro, S., Hernez-Broome, G., and Whyman, W. (2010) 'Evaluating Leadership Coaching: A Review and Integrated Framework'. *Leadership Quarterly* 21(4), 585–99.

European Mentoring and Coaching Council (EMCC) 'Global Code of Ethics for Coaches and Mentors'. emccouncil.org [accessed 04/03/16].

Fiedler, F. (1967) *A Theory of Leadership Effectiveness*. New York: McGraw Hill.

French, J., and Raven, B. (1959) 'The Bases of Social Power' in D. Cartwight, *Studies in Social Power*. Ann Arbor, MI: Institute for Social Research, pp.150–67.

Gallwey, T. (1986) *The Inner Game of Tennis: The Ultimate Guide to the Mental Side of Peak Performance*. London: Pan.

Garvin, D.A., and Levesque, L.C. (2008) 'The Multi-Unit Enterprise'. *Harvard Business Review*, June, 1–11.

George, B., Sims, P., McLean, A.N., and Meyer, D. (2007) 'Discovering Your Authentic Leadership'. *Harvard Business Review*. February, 129–38.

George, J., and Jones, G. (2008) 'Understanding and Managing Organisational Behaviour' (5th ed.). Upper Saddle River: Pearson.

Gibb, C.A. (1954) 'Leadership', in G. Lindzey (ed.), *Handbook of Social Psychology Volume 2*. MA: Addison-Wesley.

Gibson, J., Ivancevich, J., and Donnelly, J. (1997) *Fundamentals of Management*. New York: Irwin.

Gladwell, M. (2008) *Outliers: The Story of Success*. NY: Little, Brown and Co.

Goffee, R., and Jones, G. (2006) *Why Should Anyone Be Led By You? What It Takes To Be An Authentic Leader*. Boston MA: Harvard Business School Press.

Goleman, D. (1996) *Emotional Intelligence*. NY: Bloomsbury.

Goleman, D. (1998) *Working with Emotional Intelligence*. NY: Bantam Books.

Haeckel, S.H., and Nolan, R.L. (1993) 'Managing by Wire'. *Harvard Business Review* 71, September–October, 122–32.

Hall, L. (2013) *Mindful Coaching: How Mindfulness can Transform Coaching Practice*. London: Kogan Page.

Hamel, G. (2000) 'Waking Up IBM: How a gang of Unlikely Rebels Transformed Big Blue'. *Harvard Business Review*, July–August, 137–44.

Hamel, G., and Prahalad, C. (1990) *The Core Competence of the Corporation*. London: Macat.

Hase, S., Davies, A., and Dick, B. (1999) *The Johari Window and the Dark Side of Organisations*. SCU: USA.

Hawkins, P., and Smith, N. (2007) *Coaching, Mentoring and Organizational Consultancy: Supervision and Development*. NY: McGraw Hill.

Henderson, B. (1972) *Perspectives in Experience*. Mass: Boston Consulting.

Hersey, P., and Blanchard, K. (1969) 'Life cycle theory of leadership'. *Training and Development Journal* 23, 26–35.

Hersey, P., and Blanchard, K.H. (1993) *Management of Organizational Behavior: Utilizing Human Resources* (6th ed.). NY: Prentice-Hall.

Herzberg, F. (1959) *The Motivation to Work*. New York: Wiley.

Herzberg, F. (1987) 'One More Time: How Do You Motivate Employees?' *Harvard Business Review*, September–October.

Heskett, J., Jones, T., Loveman, G., Sasser, W., and Schlesinger, L. (1994) 'Putting the Service Profit Chain to Work'. *Harvard Business Review*, March–April, 164–74.

Heskett, J.L., Sasser, W.E., and Schlesinger, L.A. (2003) *The Value Profit Chain*. NY: The Free Press.

Hicks, J. (1932) *The Theory of Wages*. London: Macmillan.

House, R.J. (1971) 'A Path-Goal Theory of Leadership Effectiveness'. *Administrative Science Quarterly* 16, 321–38.

Illeris, K. (ed.) (2008) *Contemporary Theories of Learning*. Oxford: Routledge.

Janis, I. (1972) *Victims of Groupthink*. Boston: Houghton Mifflin.

Johnson, G., and Scholes, K. (1993) *Exploring Corporate Strategy*. London: Prentice Hall.

Johnston, R. (2001) *Service Excellence = Reputation = Profit*. Institute of Customer Service.

Johnston, R., and Clark, G. (2008) *Services Operations Management – Improving Service Delivery*. London: Pearson.

Kahneman, D. (2012) *Thinking, Fast and Slow*. London: Penguin.

Kellerman, B. (2008) *Followership: How Followers are Creating Change and Changing Leaders*. London: Penguin.

Kobasa, S.C. (1979) 'Stressful life events, personality and health: An enquiry into hardiness'. *Journal of Personality and Social Psychology* 37, 1–11.

Kolb, D. (1984) *Experiential Learning: Experience as the Source of Learning and Development*. Upper Saddle River, NJ: Pearson.

Korn Ferry (2020) *Accelerating through the turn – shaping the future workforce*. Global Survey Paper, 20 April.

Kotter, J.P. (1982) 'What Effective General Managers Really Do'. *Harvard Business Review* 60(6), 156–62.

Kotter, J.P. (1996) *Leading Change*. Boston: Harvard Business Press.

Kramer, M. (1974) *Reality Shock – Why Nurses Leave Nursing*. St Louis: Mosby.

Kübler-Ross, E. (1997) *On Death and Dying*. New York: Simon & Shuster.

Levitin, D. (2014) *The Organized Mind*. London: Penguin.

Levitt, T. (1980) 'Marketing Success through Differentiation – of Anything'. *Harvard Business Review*, January–February.

Lewin, K. (1951) *Field Theory in Social Science*. New York: Harper and Row.

Lindblom, C. (1959) 'The Science of Muddling Through'. *Public Administration Review* 19, 79–88.

Locke, E. (1968) 'Toward a Theory of Task Motivation and Incentives'. *Organisational Behaviour and Human Performance* 3, 157–89.

Loehr, J.E. (1982) *Athletic Excellence: Mental Toughness Training for Sport*. Lexington: Forum.

McGee, P. (2015) *S.U.M.O. (Shut Up, Move On): The straight talking guide to succeeding in life*. Chichester: John Wiley.

McKinsey (2006) 'The "Moment of Truth" in Customer Service'. *McKinsey Quarterly*, February.

McKinsey (2008) 'Maintaining the Customer Experience'. *McKinsey Quarterly*, December.

Mann, C. (2016) *The 6th Ridler Report – Strategic Trends in Coaching*. London: Ridler.

Martin, J. (2014) 'For Senior Leaders, Fit Matters More Than Skill'. *Harvard Business Review*, 17 January.

Maslow, A. (1943) *Motivation and Personality* (republished 1987 ed.). Hong Kong: Longman Asia Ltd.

Mayer, J.D., Salovey, P., Caruso, D.R., and Sitarenios, G. (2001) 'Emotional Intelligence as Standard Intelligence'. *Emotion* 1, 232–42.

Mayer, J.D., Salovey, P., Caruso, D.R., and Sitarenios, G. (2003) 'Measuring Emotional Intelligence with the MSCEIT V2.0 Edition'. *Emotion* 3, 97–105.

Menon, T., and Pfeffer, J. (2003) 'Valuing Internal versus External Knowledge'. *Management Science* 49(4), 497–513.

Mintzberg, H. (1973) *The Nature of Managerial Work*. NY: Harper Row.

Mintzberg, H. (1979) *The Structuring of Organisations*. NY: Prentice Hall.

Mintzberg, H. (1987) 'Crafting Strategy'. *Harvard Business Review* 65, 66–75.

Mintzberg, H. (2009) *Managing*. London: Pearson.

Mintzberg, H., Ahlstrand, B., and Lampel, J. (1998) *Strategy Safari*. NY: Free Press.

Mischel, W. (2014) *The Marshmallow Test*. NY: Little, Brown and Company.

Morris, J., Brotheridge, C., and Urbanski, J. (2005) 'Bringing humility to leadership: Antecedents and consequences of leader humility'. *Human Relations* 58, 1,323–49.

Naude, J., and Plessier, F. (2014) *Becoming a Leader Coach: A Step-by-Step Guide to Developing Your People*. CCL: USA.

Nayar, V. (2010) *Employees First, Customers Second*. Boston: Harvard Business School Press.

Neisser, U. (1997) 'The roots of self-knowledge: Perceiving self, it, and thou'. In J.G. Snodgrass and R.L. Thompson (eds), *The Self Across Psychology: Self-Recognition, Self-Awareness, and the Self-Concept* (pp.18–33). New York: New York Academy of Sciences.

Nonaka, I., and Konno, N. (1998) 'The Concept of Ba: Building a foundation for knowledge creation'. *California Management Review* 40(3), 40–54.

Nonaka, I., and Takeuchi, H. (1995) *The Knowledge Creating Company*. New York: Oxford University Press.

Nonaka, I., and Takeuchi, H. (2011) 'The Wise Leader'. *Harvard Business Review*, May, 58–67.

Nonaka, I., Toyama, R., and Konno, N. (2000) 'SECI, Ba and Leadership: A Unifying Model of Dynamic Knowledge Creation'. In D. Teece and I. Nonaka, *New Perspectives on Knowledge-Based Firm and Organization.*

O'Reilly, C., and Tushman, M. (2004) *The Ambidextrous Organisation.* Harvard Business Review, April, 74–81.

Passmore, J. (2011a) ed. *Supervision, Ethics and Continuous Professional Development.* London: Kogan Page.

Passmore, J. (ed.) (2011b) *Diversity in Coaching – Working with Gender, Culture, Race and Age.* London: Kogan Page.

Passmore, J. (2015) *Leadership Coaching: Working with Leaders to Develop Elite Performance.* London: Kogan Page.

Peters, S. (2012) *The Chimp Paradox: The Mind Management Programme to Help You Achieve Success, Confidence and Happiness.* London: Vermilion.

Pfeffer, J. (1994) *Competitive Advantage through People.* Boston MA: Harvard Business School Press.

Pfeffer, J. (1998) *The Human Equation: Building Profits by Putting People First.* Boston MA: Harvard Business School Press.

Piaget, J. (1970) *Genetic Epistemology.* NY: Norton.

Pink, D. (2009) *Drive – The Surprising Truth About What Motivates Us.* London: Canongate Books.

Porter, M. (1985) *Competitive Advantage: Creating and Sustaining Superior Performance.* NY: Free Press.

Porter, M.E. (1987) 'Corporate Strategy: The State of Strategic Thinking'. *Economist*, May 23, 17–22.

Potts, H. (2015) *The Executive Transition Playbook.* US: CreateSpace.

Reichheld, F. (2003) 'The One Number You Need To Grow'. *Harvard Business Review*, December.

Riddle, D. (2017) 'Equipping Transitioning Leaders for Success'. *Center for Creative Leadership Report.*

Rock, D. (2008) 'SCARF: a brain-based model for collaborating with and influencing others'. *NeuroLeadership Journal*, 1–21.

Ryan, B., and Gross, N. (1943) 'The diffusion of hybrid seed corn in two Iowa Communities'. *Rural Sociology* 8(1), pp.15–24.

Schein, E. (1985) *Organizational Culture and Leadership: A Dynamic Review.* San Francisco: Jossey-Bass.

Schein, E. (2013) *Humble Enquiry – The Gentle Art of Asking Instead of Telling.* CA: Berrett-Koehler.

Scoular, A., and Linley, P. (2006) 'Coaching, Goal Setting and Personality Type: What Matters?' *Coaching Psychologist* 2(1), 9–11.

Seligman, M. (2011) *Flourish.* Australia: William Heinemann.

Selznick, P. (1957) *Leadership in Administration. A Sociological Interpretation.* Evanston, IL: Peterson.

Senge, P. (2005) *The Fifth Discipline: The Art and Practice of the Learning Organisation.* London: Random House.

Sewell, G. (1998) 'The discipline of teams: The control of team-based industrial work through electronic and peer surveillance'. *Administrative Science Quarterly* 43(2), 397.

Sills, C. (2016) 'Towards the Coaching Relationship'. Ashridge Business School. http://www.ashridge.org.uk [accessed 26/02/2016].

Sinek, S. (2011) *Start with Why: How Leaders Inspire Everyone to Take Action.* London: Penguin.

Sinek, S (2017) *Leaders Eat Last: Why Some Teams Pull Together and Others Don't.* London: Penguin.

Sinek, S. (2019) *The Infinite Game: How Businesses Achieve Long-Lasting Success.* London: Penguin.

Skinner, B.F. (1965) *Science and Human Behaviour.* NY: Free Press.

Skinner, B.F. (1976) *About Behaviorism.* NY: Vintage Bodis.

Starr, J. (2016) *The Coaching Manual: The Definitive Guide to the Process, Principles and Skills of Personal Coaching* (4th ed.). Harlow: Pearson.

Steele, C. (1988) 'The psychology of self-affirmation: sustaining the integrity of the self'. *Advances in Experimental Psychology* 21, 261–302.

Syed, M. (2016) *Black Box Thinking: Marginal Gains and the Secrets of High Performance.* London: John Murray.

Terman, L.M. (1904) 'A preliminary study in the psychology and pedagogy of leadership'. *Pedagogical Seminary* 11(4), 413–83.

Tuckman, B. (1965) 'Developmental sequence in small groups'. *Psychological Bulletin* 63, 384–99.

Tuckman, B., and Jensen, M.A. (1977) 'Stages of small-group development revisited'. *Group & Organisation Studies* 2(4), 419–27.

Turner, P., and Kalman, D. (2014) *Make Your People Before You Make Your Products*. London: John Wiley & Sons.

Vroom, V.H., and Yetton, P.W. (1973) *Leadership and Decision-Making*. Pittsburgh: University of Pittsburgh Press.

Walker, M. (2017) *Why We Sleep*. London: Penguin.

Watkins, M. (2013) *The First 90 Days*. Mass: HBR Press.

Welch, J. (2001) *Jack: Straight from the Gut*. London: Headline.

Whitmore, J. (2009) *Coaching for Performance: The Principles and Practices of Coaching and Leadership*. London: Nicholas Brealey.

Wilkinson, M. (2013) *The Ten Principles Behind Great Customer Experiences*. Harlow: FT Publishing.

Young, P. (2004) *Understanding NLP: Principles and Practice* (2nd ed.). Carmarthen: Crown.

Zaleznik, A. (1977) 'Managers and Leaders: Are They Different?' *Harvard Business Review*, May–June, 67–78.

ADVANCED LEADER COACHING